THE WAY OF THE MYSTICS

THE WAY OF THE MYSTICS

The Early Christian Mystics and the Rise of the Ṣūfīs

MARGARET SMITH

Original title:
Studies in Early Mysticism
in the Near and Middle East

New York
OXFORD UNIVERSITY PRESS
1978

First published in 1931 as
Studies in Early Mysticism in the Near and Middle East

This paperback reissue first published by
Oxford University Press, New York, 1978

Library of Congress Catalogue Card Number: 77-93663
Printed in the United States of America

TO THE MEMORY OF

THOMAS WALKER ARNOLD

In grateful recollection of his teaching and his friendship

CONTENTS

CONTENTS

FOREWORD

Nowhere are religions closer than in mysticism, where experience takes over from formal statement and communal organization. Islam and Christianity are two of the world's greatest religions, but they have fought each other in Holy Wars and Crusades and have misunderstood or misrepresented each other's doctrines. Yet on the mystical level they often co-operated in the early days and the Qur'ān itself speaks of Christians as 'nearest in love' to Muslims because among them are priests and monks. The doctrine of the Trinity was criticized or misinterpreted but Jesus has constantly been honoured in mystical works, and while Muḥammad was 'the Seal of the Prophets' a Ṣūfī writer declared that Jesus was 'the Seal of the Saints'. In their first centuries devout Muslims lodged in Christian monasteries, read their books and admired their devotions, 'where neither trade nor bargaining divert man from the remembrance of God'. The very name Ṣūfī for an Islamic mystic probably came from the woollen dress (*Ṣūf*) which he wore like a Christian monk in the simplicity and severity of the desert and quiet places.

The early relations of Ṣūfī and Christian mystics are not well known and Margaret Smith's book is unique in describing them. It is one of my favourite books but it has long been out of print and this new edition is very welcome. It is that rare thing, a scholarly book inspired by a devotional spirit. One great virtue of this book is the way in which the development of Christian mysticism is traced, especially in the east, leading on to its contacts with Islam in eastern countries. The rise of Ṣūfism is seen as natural within Islam, not an intruder or a different religion as some have thought, yet related to Christian devotion. The discipline and prayerfulness of early Islam led to an asceticism which was partly a reaction against too much worldliness following the astounding success of the Arab armies in rapidly conquering much of the Near and Middle East. Dr Smith looks at the lives and teaching of some early Ṣūfīs, notably the woman Rābi'a of Baṣra who was called 'a second spotless Mary', and elsewhere she has written her full biography.

Definitions of mysticism are many but if there is a key word it is Unity; as Margaret Smith says, 'To the mystic, Ultimate Reality, true Being, is one'. Unity of God and man might seem to be impossible in religions like Islam and Judaism, which teach the omnipotence and transcendence of God in relation to his creature and slave. But if only God can annihilate the distance between God and man, then he does it by his infinite will. Some Ṣūfīs declared that the Islamic confession of faith, 'there is no god but God', means that there is no reality except God, no being but his. This might seem to change a deistic religion into something dangerously near to panthesim, and undoubtedly some mystics went to extremes in declaring their unity with God: 'we are two spirits in one body', or 'how great is my majesty!' Some writers have traced Indian influence in this near-pantheism, and others have pointed out that it is more prevalent in monotheistic Islam than in Trinitarian Christianity. Dr Smith herself emphasizes that 'the human soul is in very truth one in essence with the Divine', and notes that some eastern Orthodox Christians spoke of the 'divinization' of the soul. Yet there is a union which is different from identity, and it distinguishes this mysticism from philosophical pantheism or monism. For a constant stress among Christian and Ṣūfī mystics is on the love of God, and love requires both unity and distinction. So Margaret Smith affirms that 'the mystics, throughout the ages, have conceived the Object of their search as the Beloved, and it is as lovers that they seek for the consummation of their love in union with the One'.

GEOFFREY PARRINDER

Professor of the Comparative Study of Religions
University of London
1976

PREFACE

THESE Studies represent an attempt to show the relationship between the rise and development of a mystical element in Islām—that which we know as Ṣūfism—and the mysticism which was already to be found within the Christian Church of the Near and Middle East at the time when the Arab power established itself as a political force of far-reaching extent, and at a period when the faith of Islām was in the process of development and formulation.

The book deals only with the earliest period of Islamic Mysticism, partly because the contacts between Christianity and Islām were naturally at their closest at the beginning of the Islamic era, and partly because Islamic Mysticism after the end of the ninth century A.D. has been more fully dealt with by other writers.

The mystics, whether Christian or Muslim, can be studied only in their own writings, and I have therefore given their own teaching and allowed it to speak for them, as far as possible, and I trust that these Studies may at least serve the purpose of leading my readers to investigate the writings of the Ṣūfīs and their predecessors among the Christian mystics, for themselves, and to discover the many treasures of mystical thought and teaching to be found there.

My thanks are due to Professor Burkitt of Cambridge, for valuable suggestions given with regard to asceticism and mysticism in the Syriac-speaking Church of the Middle East, to Professor A. Guillaume of Culham, for advice and help, and, in full measure, to Professor R. A. Nicholson of Cambridge, whose wealth of knowledge in respect of the teachings and literature of Ṣūfism is always placed most generously at the disposal of those who have the good fortune to be his pupils or his friends. My indebtedness to Professor Wensinck of Leyden, in my references to Syriac mystical literature, and to Professor Massignon of Paris, in regard to early Ṣūfī sources, will be obvious to my readers.

I would here pay a tribute to the memory of one whose teaching and whose friendship meant so much to those who were privileged to know him, Sir Thomas Arnold, to whose wise counsels and unfailing kindness I myself owe much. He was greatly interested in the subject of these Studies, and I am indebted to him for valuable advice and suggestions, given with his usual generosity, for, busy though his life was, he spared neither time nor trouble, when others claimed his help.

I wish to take this opportunity of thanking Miss Murray Browne, of the School of Oriental Studies Library, for the help and advice which she is always ready to give on request, and her assistant staff for the invariable courtesy and efficient service which are at the disposal of those who make use of this most valuable Library, making it one of the pleasantest in which to work of all the libraries with which I am acquainted.

MARGARET SMITH.

LONDON

PART I

CHAPTER I

THE MEANING AND NATURE OF MYSTICISM

THE name Mysticism is historically connected with the mystery-cults of the Greeks.[1] The mystic was one who had been initiated into the secret knowledge of Divine things, and was under the obligation to keep silence concerning the knowledge which had been imparted to him. The term " mystical " could be applied to any esoteric doctrine which was revealed only to the initiated, and in the early history of Mysticism, as we know it, we find that the mystics were regarded as an inner circle of devotees, possessed of a knowledge revealed rather than acquired, and revealed to them because they were fitted to receive it by an innate capacity not found in mankind at large. So, to St. Clement of Alexandria, the higher mysteries of the Christian faith represent a Gnosis, to be imparted to those qualified to receive it. The mystic is the true Gnostic, who by this higher knowledge can rise above that which is of the earth, earthy, and attain to the goal of the Christian endeavour, the contemplation of God. But this knowledge and this achievement are not for believers in general. In the teaching of the Ṣūfīs also we find that the name given to the mystic is that of *'Ārif*, the gnostic or adept. The mystics are the " elect of the elect," the " friends of God," a chosen circle to whom He grants *ma'rifa*, the mystic knowledge which is the result

[1] For the connection between the Greek " mysteries " and early Christian mysticism *cf.* J. B. Mayor, *Clement of Alexandria. Seventh Book of the Stromateis*, chap. iii., and W. R. Inge, *Christian Mysticism*, Appendix B.

of intuition, not of acquired learning. So, in the early development of Mysticism, we find this idea of an esoteric knowledge destined for, and imparted to, the chosen few who were found fit to receive it.

Yet Mysticism itself represents something much wider than its derivation : it represents a spiritual tendency which is universal, for we find it in all religions worthy of the name and in all true faiths, and it is often the most vital element in such faiths. It represents, too, a craving of the human soul which is eternal, for it has appeared at all periods of the world's history, far back in the religious teachings of India and China, in the civilisations of Greece and Rome, among Buddhists and Jews, as well as among Muslims and Christians.

All religious consciousness is based on a realisation, however dim, of a something beyond our finite ken, a realisation which distinguishes the human being from all lower forms of existence. In Mysticism this consciousness is deepened to a sense of that Beyond as a unity, from which all has come, to which all things tend, and in which all things are contained —that is to say, to the mystic, Ultimate Reality, true Being, is One. " Mysticism consists in the spiritual realisation of a grander and a boundless Unity, that humbles all self-assertion by dissolving it in a wider glory."[1] This Unity, the One Reality, is represented under varying aspects by the mystics, as the Ultimate Source, Perfect Goodness, the Eternal Wisdom, Unclouded Light, Beauty Supreme, Divine Love, God.

Mysticism, then, permeated through and through with this consciousness of the Divine, represents an attitude of mind in which all other relationships are as nothing compared with the relation of the soul to God. Mysticism has been described as a " religious experience in which the feeling of God is at its maximum of intensity. . . . To it God seems to be at once nothing and all things, nothing because He transcends every definite form of reality, and all things, because nothing can be apart from Him."[2] In the view of the mystic, God contains yet transcends every-

[1] J. A. Picton, *The Mystery of Matter*, p. 356.

[2] E. Caird, *The Evolution of Theology in the Greek Philosophers*, ii. 286.

thing; He appears as the One in Whom all is lost and also the One in Whom all is found.

Mysticism, therefore, involves an intense and continuous awareness of the all-pervading Presence of God, but it goes beyond this in aiming at a knowledge of Ultimate reality, and finally at the establishment of a conscious relation with the Absolute, in which the soul shall attain to union with God. So the one supreme desire of the mystic comes to be, to merge the consciousness both of the world and of himself in the consciousness of God, or rather in God Himself.[1] The mystic, therefore, claims that it is possible to have direct intercourse with God, an immediate apprehension of the Divine, when God is no longer regarded as objective to the soul, but becomes a subjective experience.

To the mystics God is no mere abstract Being, but is conceived of as the personal object of their love; they desire to know Him better that they may love Him the more. That union which they seek is "the supernatural union of likeness, begotten of love, which is the union of the human will with the Divine. They seek to realise the unfelt natural presence of God in creation—by entering into a personal relationship with the concealed Presence which is the Source of being."[2] Religion normally draws a clear distinction between the Divine and the human, and emphasises the separation between the two; Mysticism goes beyond religion, and while still making a distinction, refuses to recognise the separation, and aspires to intimate union with the Divine, to a penetration of the Divine within the soul, and ultimately to the disappearance of the individuality, with all its modes of acting, thinking and feeling, in the Divine substance.[3] "Where this Light is, the man's end and aim is not this or that, Me or Thee, or the like, but only the One, Who is neither I nor Thou, this or that, but is above all I and Thou, this and that; and in Him all goodness is loved as one Good."[4] The mystic, therefore, seeks to pass from what is finite to what is infinite, from that which seems to

[1] E. Caird, *op. cit.*, ii. 214.
[2] A. B. Sharpe, *Mysticism: its True Nature and Value*, p. 140.
[3] H. Delacroix, *Etudes d'histoire et de psychologie du mysticisme*, p. vii.
[4] *Theologia Germanica*, p. 153.

that which is, out of all lower forms of reality to that which is Supremely Real, and, in the end, to become Being itself.

Mysticism claims that the soul can undertake this tremendous journey and pass from that which is temporal to that which is Eternal, and it bases its claim on certain postulates.

Firstly, it maintains that the soul can see and perceive by a spiritual sense, " a unique mode of perception, corresponding to the unicity of that which is perceived."[1] All Mysticism affirms that Reality, in its highest form, cannot be understood by intelligence, but only by something above it, that inner sense which is called intuition, by which a man can receive direct knowledge and revelation of God, and perceive things hidden from reason. " It is a spiritual sense opening inwardly, as the physical senses open outwardly, and because it has the capacity to perceive, grasp and know the truth at first hand, independent of all external sources of information, we call it intuition."[2] St. Augustine speaks of the " eye " of the soul, the " ear " of the mind: " I entered with Thy guidance into my inmost self, and I was enabled to do so, for Thou wert my Helper. And I entered and beheld with the eye of my soul (such as it was), above the same eye of my soul, above my mind, the Light Unchangeable."[3] Mysticism, then, asserts in the first place that knowledge is not attained only by the senses or the intellect or the normal processes of consciousness, but that the highest knowledge is attained, and can only be attained, by this spiritual sense of intuition.

Secondly, Mysticism maintains that the soul, in order to know God, must itself be a partaker of the Divine nature. Only if there is something real in the nature of the self can it hope to know Reality, and so Mysticism has always assumed that there is within the soul an " inward light," a Divine spark, that which seeks reunion with the Eternal Flame. God Himself is " the ground of the soul," which was made in His image and " in the first shaping was wonderfully bright and fair, full of burning love and spiri-

[1] A. B. Sharpe, *op. cit.*, p. 88.
[2] R. W. Trine, *In Tune with the Infinite*, p. 40.
[3] *Confessions*, vii. 10.

tual light."[1] All men, therefore, however much the image may have been defaced, in the depths of their being have some share in that Divine life which is at the heart of the Universe. If the soul is essentially related to God, then God is essentially related to the soul.[2] By the mystic, "God is realised as the foundation of the soul's being, and the soul's perception of its own essence is, in fact, the perception of its unity with the essential Divine nature."[3]

Thirdly, Mysticism assumes that none can attain to a direct knowledge of God except by purification from self. The soul must be stripped of the veils of selfishness and sensuality if it is to see clearly the Divine Vision. "Except a man be born again, he cannot see the kingdom of God";[4] and the Persian Ṣūfī al-Hujwīrī writes, "Purity is the characteristic of the lovers of God, who are like suns without shade—for the lover is dead as regards his own qualities and abiding in the qualities of his Beloved."[5] Only when the tumult of the senses is stilled, and the images of earth are hushed, and the soul, by ceasing to think of self, has passed beyond itself, can the Eternal Wisdom be revealed to the one who seeks that mystic communion with the Unseen.[6] "Behold, in such a man must all thought of Self, all self-seeking, self-will and what cometh thereof, be utterly lost and surrendered and given over to God."[7]

Fourthly, Mysticism assumes that the guide and inspiration of the soul in its ascent to God is Love. The life of communion with God must be rooted and grounded in love. "He that loveth not knoweth not God; for God is Love."[8] The mystics, throughout the ages, have conceived of the Object of their search as the Beloved, and it is as lovers that they seek for the consummation of their love in union with the One. The Oriental mystic, seeking to get

[1] Walter Hilton, *The Scale of Perfection*, i. 3.
[2] *Cf.* E. Caird, *op. cit.*, ii. 315, 316.
[3] A. B. Sharpe, *op. cit.*, p. 143. For a full discussion of this doctrine of the "divine Spark," *cf.* W. R. Inge, *op. cit.*, Appendix C, pp. 359 *ff.*
[4] St. John iii. 3.
[5] *Kashf al-Mahjūb*, p. 37.
[6] St. Augustine, *Confessions*, ix. 10.
[7] *Theologia Germanica*, p. 154.
[8] 1 John iv. 8.

rid of that element of not-being, which is opposed to true Being, the Divine Reality, finds that self, the great hindrance, can be overcome by Love alone. Love, said one of the Ṣufīs,[1] means to give all that thou hast to Him Whom thou lovest, so that nothing remains to thee of thine own; and another mystic teacher, al-Shiblī, says: "Love is a fire in the heart consuming all save the Will of the Beloved."[2] A later mystic gives the same description of the work of Love: "Love has set the soul on fire and transmuted it into love, has annihilated and destroyed it to all that is not love. The soul on fire with love to God longs for the perfection and consummation of its love that it may be completely refreshed."[3] Love alone can perfectly purify the soul and set it free from the bonds of self-seeking and the fetters of the flesh, and so enable it to pass on its upward way, to look upon God as He is in truth, and to realise that it is itself one with the Divine Goodness, one with that Reality which is also Everlasting Love.

Mysticism, starting from these assumptions, has developed a philosophic doctrine concerning the nature of the Godhead, the relation of God and the soul, the possibility of the soul's ascent to God, and of its abiding union with Him, but it is also practical, representing a life to be lived by a rule, the mystic Way, which must be trodden by all who seek to attain to that blessed communion with the Divine. The stages of the Way vary to some extent in the mystical teachings of the West and East, but in nearly all forms of Mysticism, repentance or conversion is recognised as the starting-point, when the soul awakes to a consciousness of the Divine Reality and turns its back on the world of unreality. Three stages of the Way have been accepted in the West, and these three stages will be found to cover the stages of the Way as set forth in the religious systems of the East. The first stage is known as the Purgative life, the stage of purification from the fetters of sin, represented by sensuality and self-will. "It is one and the same thing to be 'Holy' and to be 'free,' and the mystics are right when

[1] Abū 'Abd Allah al-Qurashī.

[2] al-Qushayrī, *Risāla*, pp. 189, 190.

[3] St. John of the Cross, *Spiritual Canticle*, ix. 7, xxvi. 18.

they say that there is no other evil than sin, and sin is everything which entails a loss of Freedom."[1] Purification is secured only by self-discipline, and to the majority of mystics, both in East and West, a life of strict asceticism has seemed the only way by which the carnal self could be purged of the sins which defile it. Contrition, fasting, prayer and vigils have proved to be the means of purifying the soul and ridding it of the desires of self. But this stage has not meant simply a negation of the vices, it has also meant a positive assumption of the virtues and especially of the social virtues, so that the mystics, in most cases, have occupied themselves with the humble and self-sacrificing service of their fellow-men, as well as with the struggle to become pure in the sight of God.

When the soul has been cleansed from sensuality and stripped of all that is opposed to the One Perfect Good, when it has become " pure from Self as flame from smoke," it is ready to pass on to the next stage, known as the Illuminative Life. The mystic, purified from the grosser hindrances to perfection and enabled to conform in his outward life to what is required of the servant of God, has now the harder task of purifying the inner self, bringing all the faculties, thought, feeling and will, into conformity with that which he now knows to be the Divine Will. Now he is walking in the Light and must seek to be transformed wholly into the likeness of That in which no darkness dwells. It means that the soul has no desires or wishes of its own; having renounced all that was unlawful, and then all that was lawful, it has at last renounced all save God Himself. All that was its own is merged in the sole desire to serve Him in adoring love. " The soul now seeks not and possesses not, any other will but that of doing our Lord's Will, and so it prays Him to let it be so; it gives to Him the keys of its own will—from henceforth the soul will have nothing of its own—all it seeks is to do everything for His glory and according to His Will."[2]

The mystic who has passed through the stages of the Purgative and the Illuminative life now enters upon the last

[1] Récéjac, *Bases of the Mystic Knowledge*, p. 262.
[2] St. Teresa, *Life*, p. 154.

stage of the Way, which is also the goal of the quest, the Unitive life, when the soul passes from that which is imperfect to that which is perfect, when it ceases to see through a glass darkly, and beholds the Supreme Reality face to face in the Beatific Vision, and is joined thereunto in conscious union, so that the mystic can now say in truth, " I live, yet not I, but God in me." In the first stage of the Way, that of the Purgative life, the soul had felt the Divine to be in opposition to the human ego ; then, as it passed through the stage of the Illuminative life, the opposition had decreased and the soul had been conscious of its own greatness as the image of the Divine. Finally, in the Unitive life, the soul is conscious of a Being Who surpasses the ego and yet at the same time is identified with it, " great enough to be God, intimate enough to be me."[1]

Now knowledge becomes vision and with unveiled face the mystic looks upon the Eternal Beauty, and in the moment of that Vision is made one with that which he beholds. Of that experience the poet writes,

" . . . there is in God
Which being seen would end us with a shock
Of pleasure. It may be that we should die
As men have died of joy, all mortal powers
Summed up and finished in a single taste
Of superhuman bliss : or, it may be
That our great latent love, leaping at once
A thousand years in stature—like a stone
Dropped to the central fires, and at a touch
Loosed into vapour—should break up the terms
Of separate being, and as a swift rack
Dissolving into heaven, we should go back
To God."[2]

The soul of the mystic feels itself identified in union with the Divine ; it has passed from consciousness of self and is absorbed in the consciousness of God ; it has become deified. " This deification and elevation of the spirit in God," says St. John of the Cross, " whereby the soul is, as it were, rapt and absorbed in love, one with God, suffer it not to dwell

[1] Récéjac, *op. cit.*, p. 45.

[2] Sydney Dobell.

upon any worldly matter. The soul is now detached, not only from all outward things, but even from itself; it is, as it were, undone, assumed by and dissolved in love—that is, it passes out of itself into the Beloved."[1] The spiritual marriage has been consummated, the soul has become one with its divine Bridegroom. In that Presence, says the Ṣufī mystic, "I" and "thou" have ceased to exist, they have become one: the Quest and the Way and the Seeker are one.[2] So, too, the Christian mystic finds that in that act of union "the sole Unity, which is God, answers truly to the oneness of the soul, for then is there nothing in the soul beside God."[3]

These, then, in brief, represent the assumptions and the aim of Mysticism, and its teaching as to the means by which the end can be attained. In the following chapters we shall endeavour to show how Mysticism—which we have seen to be a practically universal tendency, an attitude of mind which has shown itself in all religions which have life within themselves, and in itself to be a spontaneous growth which has appeared at all ages in the world's history, in environments apparently unpromising as well as in circumstances favourable to its nature—developed and established itself in the Near and Middle East, and how among Christians and Muslims alike it was accepted, on the one hand, as a way of life to be practised as a means to an end, and on the other, as a religious philosophy which satisfied the soul's innate craving to understand its relationship to God, and justified its adoption of the Way which should lead it onward and upward till the Goal should be attained, and the soul, long parted from its Source, once more find its home in the One Reality—God.

[1] *A Spiritual Canticle*, xxvi. 14.
[2] Shabistarī, *Gulshan-i rāz*, i. 448.
[3] J. Tauler, *Sermon for the Twenty-third Sunday after Trinity.*

CHAPTER II

EARLY CHRISTIAN ASCETICISM

BETWEEN Mysticism and the ascetic spirit which led to the development of the monastic life there is a close connection. The mystic is one who seeks for an ever closer and more direct relationship with Reality, that is, God, and he seeks this by the life of self-discipline, by which he may be cleansed from the sins that have their root in self-indulgence and self-will, a discipline which applies to both the body and the will, and when by this self-stripping he has brought himself into harmony with the Eternal Will, he seeks by contemplation to attain to the direct knowledge of God which is his goal. It is small wonder, then, that we find the earliest mystics of the Christian Church among those who practised the ascetic ideal, and at a later stage, among those who lived, or who had lived, a regular monastic life. Solitude and a period of retreat, whether short or long, have always been found necessary for the development of the mystic ideal, and for the realisation of that ideal in the practical affairs of human life. " All great undertakings are matured in solitude," says a writer on the monastic life. " It is not in the hurry and confusion and excitement which accompany execution, but in the stillness and calm silence of preparation, that the strength which does great deeds is accumulated and concentred."[1] This is true enough of merely human undertakings : it is still more true of great spiritual enterprises. It is therefore side by side with the development of the ascetic ideal and the growth of monasticism that we shall find the beginnings of Christian mysticism.

The tendency to asceticism did not begin with Christianity, it had been found to a limited extent among the Jews. John the Baptist lived an ascetic life in the wilderness, and the Essenes and the Therapeutæ were Jewish ascetics,

[1] Montalembert, *The Monks of the West*, introduction by F. A. Gasquet, p. x*iii*.

though probably influenced by Hellenism. In Egypt we hear of a community of ascetics in the Fayoum as early as 340 B.C., pursuing an ideal opposed to all the thought and feeling of the Mediterranean world at that time. Among the pagan cults of Egypt, in connection with the worship of Isis and Serapis, asceticism was practised, and there were recluses of the Serapaion at Memphis about 170 B.C., and the same type appeared in A.D. 211.[1] This pagan asceticism included the custom of seclusion in cells, and the practice of celibacy by both sexes. The Greek schools of Alexandria had distinguished between the natural and the supernatural life, and taught a perfection which might be attained by the adept who had conquered his lower self. In addition to these precedents, Christians found an example for the ascetic life in the life of Christ upon earth and an incentive thereto in His teachings on otherworldliness. Moreover, the circumstances of the time urged them to the acceptance of this ideal. The corruption and the excesses of the pagan world around them represented the enemy they were called upon to fight, and it was only by withdrawal from the world and the things which belonged to the world, by opposing virtue to vice, continence to licence, purity to lewdness, that the Christians could hope to maintain their own position and to overcome their enemy. It has been said, indeed, that all Christianity in the first centuries was really ascetic, in the original sense of the word (ἄσκησις = exercise), for these early ascetics were athletes, fighting against the world, the flesh, and the devil, subjecting themselves to severe self-discipline for religious ends. At first these Christian ascetics did not withdraw from the world altogether, but followed the ascetic life within their own homes, renouncing marriage and property, and practising solitude, silence, fasting and other austerities. This earthly life was regarded as a trial and discipline for the life of the next world, as it might well be, in an age when the life of every Christian was liable to be cut short by the fury of persecution, and through tortures, and in the face of death by the sword and by fire and the arena, each Christian must be prepared to stand firm in the faith, and so to win the coveted crown of martyrdom.

[1] *Cf.* Flinders Petrie, *Egypt and Israel*, pp. 133, 134.

Even after the persecutions had spent their force and Christianity had become the official religion of the Empire, the corruption of the Church and the lowering of its ideals which resulted from its close association with the State, led devout Christians to develop a still more rigid asceticism, in order to maintain the old standard of purity and renunciation, and to express their refusal to make that compromise with the world to which the Church had now consented. Asceticism meant a discipline of the will and soul as well as the body, and it came to stand definitely for the great renunciations involved in poverty, obedience to a spiritual leader, and chastity, and also various forms of bodily austerities, and since it became increasingly difficult to practise the ascetic life while in the world, albeit a nominally Christian world, the tendency developed to seek in solitude and seclusion an opportunity to live the unworldly life completely apart from the world. So the monastic ideal was evolved, representing originally the solitary life (*μόνος* = alone). At first monastic life was individualistic : we find the hermits and anchorites living each one apart in the desert. Then, about the fourth century, monasticism began to assume a corporate character, and there were formed the " laura " or group of monks each living in a separate cell or hut and forming one community, and the " cœnobium," in which the monks lived under one roof and under the rule of a common superior, and which became the type to which the name of monastery was definitely attached.

The monastic life was intended, firstly, to bring to perfection the individual soul, but secondly to enable that soul, when brought to perfection, to be of service to its fellowmen, whether by prayer or by active good works. It was in no case a life of idleness, for to occupy oneself with God, says St. Bernard, is not idleness, but the occupation of occupations.[1] It is in the monastic life that we see " the permanent strife of moral freedom against the bondage of the flesh, the constant effort of a consecrated will in the pursuit and conquest of Christian virtue : the victorious flight of the soul into those supreme regions where she finds again her

[1] "Otiosum non est vacare Deo, negotium negotiorum omnium."

true, her immortal grandeur."[1] The monk withdrew from other men out of love to God and to his neighbour, in order that when he had purified and disciplined his own soul, he might the better serve his fellow-men.

(*a*) Asceticism in Egypt

Egypt, as might have been expected, was the first home of that development of asceticism which produced Christian monasticism, as it also played the chief rôle in the Christian world from the beginning of the fourth to the middle of the fifth century. The trials and tribulations of the Christians in Egypt from the second century onward, including the Decian persecution of A.D. 250, no doubt drove many to take refuge in the desert and the mountains, in order to escape persecution and dishonour, and by the year A.D. 300 there were many Christian monks and ascetics leading a solitary life. Origen (born at Alexandria in A.D. 185) had advocated asceticism to his followers, and encouraged the Christians of Alexandria to desire the contemplative life and to seek after flight from the world to God; and at the same time the appreciation of virginity as the highest type of life was increasing, and Hieracas, one of Origen's disciples, who flourished *c.* A.D. 300, collected round him a body of learned ascetics of both sexes.

But it is to Paul of Thebes and St. Anthony that the foundation of the eremitic type of monasticism in Egypt has always been ascribed. Of Paul of Thebes, said to be the first of the Egyptian anchorites, living in the desert from the age of twenty-three to his death at one hundred and thirteen, we know little that is historical, but St. Anthony is said to have visited him and received teaching from him. There is a delightful legend which relates how St. Anthony went to the cave of Paul after the old man's death to bury his body, and forgot to take a spade with him. While he stood in perplexity, for his abode was far away, two lions appeared " and stood near the body of the blessed Paul and they wagged their tails at the blessed Anthony and they crouched down before him in perfect tameness, and they rubbed their teeth

[1] Montalembert, *op. cit.*, p. 9.

together and purred so loudly that the blessed man knew that they wished to be blessed." Then the two lions dug the grave with their paws, and when St. Anthony had blessed them they departed.[1] As regards St. Anthony, we have a full account of his life, ascribed to St. Athanasius, which can be accepted as historical. Born about A.D. 250, an Egyptian of noble birth, at the age of twenty he adopted the ascetic life, living at first near human habitations and then for twenty years in solitude in the desert. After this he came out of his seclusion, gathered disciples round him, and instructed them in the principles of the ascetic life. He is related by his biographer to have said, "It is right that we should at all times follow after the food of the soul, for the soul worketh together with our spirit in the striving which is against the adversary, but it is meet for the body to be in subjection and tribulation."[2] And again he said, "As fish die if a man lift them out of the water, so, if we monks prolong our stay with men, do our minds become perverted and troubled: therefore it is meet that as fish pass their life beneath the waters, we also should let our lives and works be buried in the wilderness."[3] St. Anthony reduced monastic life to a system, but it was as yet a system of solitaries. Yet from the Athanasian *Life*, we see that the Antonine asceticism, while it aimed at the purification of the individual soul, also found time for good works. Prayer and contemplation were combined with manual labour and service to others. We read that in the days of the blessed Anthony "the habitations of the monks were accepted as tabernacles of praises, and Psalms and hymns and spiritual songs were heard therein: and love and righteousness rejoiced therein, and therein was found the rest of prayer coupled with fasting. And the monks toiled in the labour of their hands that they might not be a burden upon any man, and of the sweat of their faces, the poor and the needy were relieved."[4] St. Anthony's type of monachism prevailed in Lower Egypt and along the Nile as far as Asyūt, and later reached its greatest development in Nitria and Scete.

Contemporary with St. Anthony was Pachomius, a native

[1] *The Paradise of the Fathers*, i. 202, 203.
[2] *Paradise*, i. 38. [3] *Ibid.*, p. 69. [4] *Ibid.*, p. 37.

of the Thebaïd, born about A.D. 292, who became a convert to Christianity, and who originated the cœnobitic system in Egypt, and was the founder of the first Christian monastery in the modern sense of the word. This monastery was established at Tabennisi, near Denderah, in A.D. 320. Before his death in A.D. 346, he had founded nine monasteries containing some three thousand monks. Under the Pachomian system the monks lived in cells under absolute obedience to their superior, and they had a common church where they met for prayer. The monks engaged in agriculture and in handicrafts, the surplus output being available for the women's convents[1] and for the needy. Pachomius instituted a Rule for his monks, according to which no pressure was to be exerted in the matter of eating or drinking or fasting: the monks were to live three in a cell, and to eat together. They were to sleep sitting, not lying down, and were to wear a linen under-garment at night, and by day an outer robe of sheep-skin, with a girdle and hood. They were to pray constantly and to partake of the Eucharist on Saturdays and Sundays. Novices were to undergo a three years' probation. This system of monachism became dominant in Upper Egypt, and by the beginning of the fifth century the number of monks was said to be fifty thousand.

Shenoudi of Atripé, a fellah born in A.D. 333, continued the work of Pachomius and developed a stricter rule. He is said to have introduced vows, and by him the community life of the monastery was looked upon as a possible preparation for the solitary life for those who were fitted to endure it. His own monastery contained thousands of monks, who were well organised, and who were encouraged to give the day to labour and to divide the evening between study and sleep. There was to be complete obedience to the superior "perinde ac cadaver."[2]

While Pachomius had organised the cœnobitic type of monasticism, Macarius of Egypt and Ammon were the chief instruments in the organisation of the eremitic type. Macarius (born *c.* A.D. 300) at the age of thirty retired into the

[1] See Chapter III.

[2] For the life and work of Shenoudi *cf.* E. Amélineau, *Les Moines Égyptiens*.

desert of Scete, the southern part of the Nitrian valley, in the Libyan desert, north-west of Cairo, and there he remained for sixty years until his death. Many disciples gathered round him and he taught them the way of salvation by utter renunciation.

Ammon was another great ascetic. He had been married in his youth: he lived with his wife as with a sister for eighteen years, and then they separated and he went to Nitria and there established a semi-eremitical type of monachism between A.D. 320 and 330. Of the ascetics of Scete and Nitria we have full accounts from contemporary writers and travellers, who visited them in their desert solitudes, and wrote of what they had seen. The author of the *History of the Monks* ascribed to Hieronymus of Dalmatia, who flourished about A.D. 386, writes of the monks of Nitria, and says that he saw among them "many great disciples who had departed from the world, and some were natives of the country and some were strangers—and they were emulating each other in the beautiful deeds of strenuousness, and were striving to outstrip each other in their noble and glorious lives and works. Now some of them possessed divine vision and others works of ascetic excellence. . . . Some called us to the doctrine of glory and others to the vision of divine knowledge. . . . They dwell in a waste place and their dwellings are remote, and the men live apart from each other so that one man may not be known to his fellows . . . and they live in the strictest silence and each one of them is secluded in his cell."[1]

John Cassian, born about A.D. 360, who was probably of Western origin, was another who went to Egypt and visited the anchorites there and remained with them for seven years. Later he went to Scete and Nitria, which he found to be full of cells and monasteries, and from him we get much information as to the organisation of the Egyptian monks. Palladius, born probably in Galatia about A.D. 364, who was a friend of Macarius, went to Nitria in 391 and lived there for nine years. His *Paradise of the Fathers*, also called the *Lausiac History*, because it was written at the request of a court official named Lausus, was written in A.D. 420, and gives a

[1] *Paradise*, i. 376.

very full account of Egyptian monasticism. In Nitria he found some five thousand men living separately, but with a great church and guest-house in common. All, by way of handicraft, were engaged in producing linen.[1] Rufinus, a presbyter of Aquileia, who spent six years in Egypt between 372 and 378, wrote of the ascetics there, " Quanti populi habentur in urbibus, tanta pæne habentur in desertis."

From these writers we can get an idea of the methods and ideals of Egyptian monasticism. The monks were first and foremost ascetics practising extreme austerities, in respect of fasting, vigils, exposure to heat and cold, excessive labour, and war against the flesh, believing that the subjugation of the body meant the growth of the spiritual nature and faculties, and the power to see visions and receive revelations. Their food usually consisted of nothing but bread, eaten sometimes with salt or bitter herbs and oil, and water was their only drink. Their clothing was simple and scanty. Their hours of sleep were strictly limited, and if they lay down at all to sleep, it was on mats of plaited papyrus, or on the bare ground, with a stone for a pillow. Some never slept during the night, but prayed, either standing or sitting, until morning. Silence was the general rule, and the monk spent most of his time in the seclusion of his cell, except in the cases where his work required him to be out of doors. The renunciation of property and a state of poverty were expected of all who embraced the monastic life: constant mourning and weeping were considered to be a sign of grace and true repentance for sin. One of the fathers, in answer to the inquiries of a younger monk, said to him, " Fasting is the subjugation of the body, prayer is converse with God, vigil is a war against Satan, abstinence is the being weaned from meats, humility is the state of the first man, kneeling is the inclining of the body before the Judge, tears are the remembrance of sins, nakedness is our captivity which is caused by the transgression of the command, and service is constant supplication to and praise of God."[2]

Chastity was the first thing required of the monk, and apparently the hardest of the virtues to acquire and retain, from what we read of the temptations which assailed these

[1] Cf. *Hist. Laus.*, vii. 2, 5.

[2] *Paradise*, ii. 263.

recluses in their desert homes, and chastity to them meant not only a body undefiled, but also sincerity in speech and a pure heart. Among the reputed sayings of Abbā Paphnutius is one to the effect that " A monk is bound to keep not only his body pure, but his soul free from unclean thoughts. . . . As wicked slaves fly from their lords, even so do lusts fly from the exhaustion of ascetic labours."[1] The prayer-life was the monk's great source of strength, and we are told of an ascetic named Paul who prayed three hundred prayers a day and collected three hundred pebbles, which he placed in his girdle and threw out one for each prayer, which appears to be the first instance of the Christian use of a rosary.[2] Absolute obedience to the abbot or superior was required of all monks : the novice was trained by obedience, even to the most unreasonable of commands, to mortify his own wishes, and the very thoughts of the monk were to be laid bare to the superior. The Egyptian monk was taught from the first that " obedience is the food of all the saints. By her they are nourished. Through her they come to perfection."

It was inevitable that the power to work miracles should be ascribed to the greatest of the Egyptian saints. We are told how the wild beasts were their friends and came to them for help, and how light was granted to them in the darkness. There was an old man of whom it was said that as he was in the light during the day, so also was he in his cell by night, and that he was able to work with his hands and read in the night-time, by this miraculous light, just as he did during the day.[3] Of Abbā Bessarion it was related that he made the waters of the sea sweet, that he crossed over the water of the river without means of transport, that he prevented the sun from setting, and that he healed a paralytic and cast out a devil of sleepiness from a young man.[4]

Such, then, was the life of the Egyptian ascetic, the end of whose profession was the kingdom of God, says Cassian, quoting Abbā Moses, but the immediate aim was purity of heart, without which no one could gain that end. " Whatever then can help to guide us to this, we must follow with all our might, but whatever hinders us from it, we must

[1] *Paradise*, ii. 86.
[2] *Hist. Laus.*, xvii. (1).
[3] *Paradise*, ii. 144.
[4] *Ibid.*, ii. 146.

shun as a dangerous and hurtful thing. For, for this we do and endure all things, for this we make light of our kinsfolk, our country, honours, riches, the delights of this world and all kinds of pleasures, in order that we may retain a lasting purity of heart. . . . This, then, should be our main effort, and this steadfast purpose of heart we should constantly aspire after—viz., that the soul may ever cleave to God and to heavenly things."[1]

Monasticism spread from Egypt into North Africa, but made less progress there than elsewhere, and was not really established on a firm footing until St. Augustine gave it his support in A.D. 388, when he founded a community of clerics living together according to rule. Though the monastic life was not as popular at first in Africa as elsewhere, and the monks were constantly the objects of persecution, yet we find that many monasteries were established there, and that the union of the clerical and monastic lives was much more common there than in other spheres of monasticism, where for the most part the monks sought to avoid taking orders and tried to dissociate themselves from any close connection with the Church. By the fifth century monachism seems to have been strong and flourishing in Africa.

(*b*) Asceticism in Syria and Asia Minor

We find asceticism in Syria and Palestine at an early date. During the latter part of the second century, Narcissus, Bishop of Jerusalem, gave up his see and retired into the wilderness; and in documents of the third century relating to South Syria are found exhortations addressed to certain wandering ascetics, urging them to asceticism and the celibate life. Eusebius, born in Palestine about A.D. 260, speaks of the Syrian ascetics of his time.

The monastic system was early extended from Egypt to Palestine and Syria, where the Antonine form prevailed, and where extreme austerities and asceticism were practised, especially on the physical side, to a greater extent than in Egypt, where the primary aim, as we have seen, was purity

[1] Cassian, *Conf.*, i. 5, 8.

of life and heart. Hilarion, born about A.D. 290, is considered to be the founder of the monastic life and institutions in Palestine. He had been converted by St. Anthony from paganism, and on his return to his native land in A.D. 306, lived in a tiny cell near Gaza and made that his abode for fifty years, for twenty-two of which he lived in solitude; but as time went on, he gathered round him between two and three thousand monks. Within a few years of his death, monasteries and lauræ were to be found in all parts of Palestine, and some of the monasteries of Jerusalem and Bethlehem were the result of his labours.[1] Into Syria the monastic life was introduced by Aones or Eugenius, early in the fourth century, and his followers lived a life of extreme asceticism.[2]

St. Jerome, born about A.D. 331, though himself of Western origin, had a considerable influence on Palestinian monasticism. On attaining manhood, he felt himself called to the religious life and retired in A.D. 374 to the desert of Chalcis, east of Syria, and after returning to Rome, came back again in A.D. 385 to the East, and built a monastery at Bethlehem. We are told by the historian Evagrius that on one of her visits to Jerusalem (the first was made in A.D. 438, the date of the second is uncertain), the empress Eudocia erected holy monasteries and "lauræ," already explained as being enclosures, each including many cells far from each other, in which the monks lived separately as hermits or anchorites. The historian says that these men were not under the influence of any earthly ties, and they had even their clothing in common. They had a common table, and lived on herbs and pulse, taking only sufficient to maintain life. They were occupied in prayer both day and night, and fasted often for two or three days together. Some lived in cells so small that they could neither stand upright nor lie down at ease.[3] On the site of one of these early "lauræ" still stands a monastery bearing the name of the founder, St. Sabha, a Cappadocian who was made chief of all the monks in the lauræ of Palestine, by Sallust the Patriarch of

[1] *Cf.* Montalembert, *op. cit.*, p. 249.
[2] Thomas of Margā, *Book of the Governors*, I. cxxiv.
[3] Evagrius, I., c. 21.

Jerusalem, about A.D. 490, and his Order of prayer for the whole year, which was used in the Jerusalem monasteries, is still extant.[1]

As we have noted, in Syria the ascetics carried their austerity of life to an extreme, inventing hardships of an altogether artificial character, such as the carrying of great stones or iron weights on their backs, and living the life of the wild beasts. Such extremists were the "grazers" (βοσκοί), who ate only grass, herbs and roots, and exposed themselves almost naked to bitter frost in winter and scorching heat in summer.[2] It was in Syria that the pillar hermits or stylites made their appearance at the end of the fourth century. Simeon, probably the earliest, and certainly the most famous, of them, lived on the border of Syria and Cilicia, and gave himself up with great zeal to asceticism, and while still young gained a reputation for the power to work miracles. In his youth he became a monk in the monastery of Eusebonas near Antioch, and was conspicuous for his mortifications. He left the monastery in order to devote himself to the solitary life and lived for ten years in a narrow pen, and finally took to living on the top of a pillar.[3] Pilgrims from many countries, including Persians, Arabs and Armenians, came to see him: he had great authority and frequently exhorted the multitudes who thronged about the foot of his pillar. He is said to have converted thousands from among the Arabs and other nomads. The historian Theodoret (A.D. 387 to *c.* 458), in his *Philotheus*, states that St. Simeon healed the sick, performed the functions of a judge, and had much influence in public affairs, in addition to regulating the affairs of the Church, and combating heresies. Evagrius says of him, "This man, endeavouring to realise in the flesh the existence of the heavenly hosts, lifts himself above the concerns of earth, and, overpowering the downward tendency of man's nature, is intent upon things above: placed between earth and heaven, he holds communion with God, and unites with the angels in praising Him; from earth, offering his

[1] *Cf.* R. Curzon, *Visits to Monasteries in the Levant*, p. 219.
[2] Evagrius, I., c. 21.
[3] Cf. Nöldeke, *Orientalische Skizzen*, chap. vii.

intercessions on behalf of men, and from heaven, drawing down upon them the Divine favour."[1] He died in A.D. 459 and had several successors as pillar-saints.

We find that well-known hermits were regarded with great reverence even in their lifetime, and their advice and counsel were frequently sought in matters secular as well as religious, and with this fact is closely connected the cult of the saints, which developed in the early centuries of Christianity. There was a need felt for intercessors; the discussions concerning Our Lord's divinity made men think less of His humanity, and made them desire someone near to themselves to act as mediator between themselves and God, and we find an increasing reverence paid to the relics and shrines of the saints, whose intercession was sought for temporal and spiritual benefits.[2]

In considering the place of the Syrian ascetics in the history of monasticism and asceticism, we can see that in spite of some misguided eccentricities, they did much to turn men's minds to the consideration of spiritual things and to lead them to value the eternal above the temporal. The aim of their asceticism was, by the subjugation of the body, to give life to the soul. Of Isidore of Pelusium, living in the early part of the fifth century, we read: "To such a degree did he waste his flesh by severe discipline, and feed his soul by elevating doctrine, as to pursue upon earth the life of angels and be ever a living monument of monastic life and contemplation of God."[3] And what these ascetics had gained for their own souls by the life of Purgation, they sought, in many cases, to use for the service of others, as true saints. Some, says Evagrius, "when by virtue they have attained to a condition exempt from passion, return to the world . . . and trample underfoot vain-glory, . . . by a life thus all excellent and divine, virtue exercises a sovereignty in opposition to Nature. . . . Life and death dwell together in them . . . for where passion enters they must be dead and entombed, where prayer to God is required, they must display vigour of body and energy of spirit . . .

[1] Evagrius, I., c. 13.

[2] *Cf.* J. C. Robertson, *History of the Christian Church*, ii. 58 *ff.*

[3] Evagrius, I., c. 15.

being, as it were, fleshless athletes, bloodless wrestlers . . . foes of their own desires and of nature, but devoted to the wills of those around them, in order that fleshly enjoyment may be constantly expelled, and the soul, diligently maintaining whatever is most seemly and pleasing to God, may alone bear sway: happy in their mode of existence here, happier in their departure hence, on which they are ever intent, impatient to behold Him Whom they desire."[1]

Ascetic tendencies were no less strong in Asia Minor, where, as elsewhere, asceticism was no doubt adopted in part as a substitute for martyrdom, when the cessation of persecution made it no longer possible to win that crown, or to wash out sins committed after baptism, as was generally believed to be possible, by a martyr's death. St. Ignatius, the second bishop of Antioch, in the second century, had said: "Nothing either visible or invisible, stirs me to desire, so long as I can gain Christ. Whether it be by fire or the cross, by struggles with wild beasts, the cutting or tearing asunder of my bones, the mangling of my limbs, the bruising of my whole body, let all the tortures of the devil come upon me, so only that I attain to Jesus Christ."[2] He also it was who said: "I am the wheat of God and am ground by the teeth of wild beasts, that I may be found pure bread."[3] Succeeding generations manifested the same spirit in the ascetic life. It was in Asia Minor that Montanism had its rise about A.D. 157. Montanus, its founder, taught extreme asceticism, discouraged marriage, and laid down rigorous rules for fasting. Several of the leaders of the Christian Church, including Apollonius and Serapion, bishop of Antioch, wrote against this heretical sect,[4] but it continued to flourish and to spread, and it must have had an influence on the growth of the ascetic spirit in Asia Minor.

The first appearance of organised asceticism, that is, of the monastic life, in Armenia, was in connection with Eustathius of Sebaste between A.D. 330 and 340. It was of a very austere character; Eustathius condemned marriage, especially of the priesthood, and fasted even on Sundays. He taught that family ties were to be ignored,

[1] Evagrius, I., c. 21.
[2] Eusebius, *H.E.*, iii. 36.
[3] *Ibid.*
[4] *Ibid.*, v. 16-19.

husbands and wives were to separate, and the distinction of sex be done away as far as possible. He had many followers, and societies of Eustathian monks, living under a rigid discipline, were to be found not only in Armenia but also in Pontus and Paphlagonia. The asceticism of Eustathius was not approved by the authority of the Church, and a synod, held at Ganga in Paphlagonia about A.D. 340, condemned this excessive austerity, while upholding the "beauty and holiness of virginity."[1]

St. Basil the Great, who was the founder of the Greek type of monasticism, was for years a close friend of Eustathius of Sebaste, and when he began his work of religious revival, he found the life of asceticism already in existence in Asia Minor, both the solitary type and the type lived in the world by ascetics of both sexes. St. Basil was born *c.* A.D. 329 at Cappadocia, and to his mother Emmelia, mother of three bishops, a nun and a monk, of whom three were canonised, was due the fact that his life from the first was under strong religious influences. To women, indeed, he owed a deep debt of gratitude, for his grandmother Macrina gave him his first teaching in religion, and his sister, a younger Macrina, was responsible for his conversion. He was educated at Cæsarea, Constantinople and Athens, and there formed a friendship with Gregory of Nazianzus; later he went to visit the monks of Egypt, Palestine, Syria and Mesopotamia. About A.D. 358 Basil went into retreat on one side of the river Iris, opposite the home of his mother and sister, and there he gave himself up to the life of Purgation, until he was called to attend the Council of Constantinople in A.D. 360. In 370 he was made Archbishop of Cæsarea, but in the meantime he had been doing his work in gathering monks into monasteries. He chose the cœnobitic type of monastic life as preferable to the eremitic, which had hitherto prevailed in Asia Minor, and it was therefore the Pachomian system that he established, with a common table and a common prayer, under a common roof. He was also responsible for the foundation of double monasteries for men and women, ruled over by an abbot and abbess respectively. St. Basil sought to unite

[1] *Cf.* L. Pullan, *The Church of the Fathers*, p. 319.

the active with the contemplative life, and he limited the austerities to be practised, because work, to him, was more important than fasting. He drew up a Rule for his monks which required withdrawal from the world—for both spiritual and bodily retirement were necessary, in his view, to the truly religious life, and he also required the renunciation of possessions. His monks were to have two meals a day, consisting of bread and water, vegetables and fruit. There were fixed hours for prayers, and sleep was to be light and limited, " especially at midnight is the ascetic's soul alone with God, and wrapt in earnest prayer."[1] The monk's clothing was to be simple but adequate, and was to include robe, girdle and shoes, and he was to engage in labour, which was chiefly agricultural. For the more educated, there was study and the work of instructing the boys and girls who were received into the monastic orphanages. The superior of the monastery had great authority, but he was controlled and assisted by a council of senior brothers. Frequent confession on the part of the monks was advocated. St. Basil speaks of his ascetics as " not regarding the body, nor willing to spend any thought upon it, but living as if in flesh not their own : and showing in deed what it is to sojourn in this world and what it is to have one's conversation in heaven."[2]

Side by side with St. Basil worked his friend Gregory of Nazianzus, who had shared Basil's early retirement, and like him was raised to the episcopate and became a great writer. He speaks of monks as " those men who are on the earth, yet above the earth . . . at once bound and free . . . who have two lives, one which they despise, another which alone fills all their thoughts ; become immortal by mortification ; strangers to all desire and full of the calm of divine love ; who drink at the fountain of its light and already reflect its rays : chastising all voluptuousness, but plunged in ineffable delights : whose tears drown sin and purify the world."[3]

St. Basil's system of monasticism was a considerable advance on the primitive monachism of Egypt and elsewhere ; he brought into it Greek culture and modes of

[1] *Ep.* II. [2] *Ep.* CCXXIII.
[3] *Cf.* Montalembert, *op. cit.*, p. 264.

thought; moreover, he found it a place within the circle of the Church's organisation, and in A.D. 451 the Council of Chalcedon passed a measure which secured the connection of monasteries with the organisation of the Church by directing that no monastery be built henceforth without the consent of the bishop of the diocese, but, on the other hand, no monastery built with the bishop's approval should be abolished or its property diminished. In the sixth century Basilian monasticism spread among the anchorites of Palestine and Syria and became the prevailing rule of the East.[1] There is today evidence of the prevalence of monasticism on the Anatolian plateau, in the monasteries still existing, but going back to the fifth century, in the 'Alī Summassi Dāgh, in the Karadja Dāgh and Ḥassan Dāgh. The remains of small hill-top monasteries are to be found evidently established for the service of monks watching over remote shrines in the mountains. The Council of Chalcedon made special mention of the "memoria" occupied by monks living under an archimandrite, and these were probably connected with the "martyria" or memorial churches so common in Asia Minor.[2] As we have seen above, the cult of the saints, and the reverence paid to their relics and shrines, was a result of the honour with which the ascetic life, which was held to be synonymous with the saintly life, was regarded.

(c) Asceticism and the Monastic Life in Mesopotamia and Persia

From Syria and Egypt monasticism spread rapidly to Mesopotamia and Persia. Edessa (the modern Urfa) stood on a great trade route between the Syrian desert and the mountains of Armenia; Christianity was established there in the second century, and it had been a centre of culture before it was Christian. In Ctesiphon the heresy of the Manichees had been promulgated, and this was always

[1] For a full account of St. Basil's life and writings *cf.* W. K. Lowther Clarke's *St. Basil the Great.*

[2] G. Lowthian Bell, *Monasteries and Monasticism in Central Asia Minor*, International Congress of Religions, Oxford, 1908.

ascetic in its tendencies. Mani, its founder, taught that the way for man from darkness to light was by keeping the soul from all bodily defilement, and by the practice of chastity and renunciation, and the Manichees were divided into monks, who were the Elect, and laymen, who were Hearers only ; the former abstained from marriage and the possession of property, and observed frequent prayer and fasting.[1] The example of the Manichees most probably had an effect on the growth of asceticism among the orthodox Christians of the country and especially on the custom which prevailed in the Syriac-speaking Church, by which the baptised laity, called the Sons and Daughters of the Covenant, lived a life of asceticism in their own homes, while the majority of the adherents of the Church were unbaptised, hearers only. The former were pledged to a life of celibacy and renunciation, living under a definite rule, and later, when infant baptism became the rule and Christianity was established as the state religion, these B'nai Q'yāmā continued as a monastic community. There were also cœnobites, hermits and anchorites to be found living the ascetic life.[2]

Among these was Aphraates, a monk who was writing in A.D. 337. He was by nationality a Persian, and appears to have been converted from heathenism. He wrote in Syriac and shows a profound knowledge of the Scriptures and of Christian theology. He was not only a monk, but a bishop, and is said to have been the head of the convent of Mār Mattai, near Mosul. He was an ascetic of the sternest type himself, and laid great stress on celibacy. In a discourse addressed to penitents, he says : " He whose heart is set on the state of matrimony, let him marry before baptism, lest he fall in the spiritual contest and be slain. He also that loveth his possessions, let him turn back from the army, lest when the battle shall wax too fierce for him, he remembereth his property and turn back, and he that turneth back then is covered with disgrace."[3] On this subject he says also, " Woman ought to dwell with woman, and man with man.

[1] *Cf.* F. C. Burkitt, *Religion of the Manichees*, p. 23.

[2] *Cf.* F. C. Burkitt, *History of Eastern Christianity*, pp. 127, 128. *Cf.* also *Cam. Med. Hist.*, i. 526.

[3] *Hist. of Eastern Christianity*, p. 126.

And also whatever man desires to continue in holiness, let not his spouse dwell with him. Therefore this counsel is becoming and right and good, that I give to myself and to you, my beloved solitaries, and to virgins who do not marry and to those who have loved holiness. It is just and right and becoming that, even if a man should be distressed (thereby), he should continue alone."[1] Aphraates holds that in marriage a man leaves God his Father and the Holy Spirit his Mother,[2] and so his mind is united with this world.[3] Virginity, on the other hand, is the heavenly portion, the fellowship of the Watchers of heaven, with which nothing else is comparable.[4] He urges those who seek to be "the children of the Good," that is, of God, to watch and pray and keep vigil by night. The "children of the Good" forestall Satan's attempts to ensnare them during sleep by being wakeful and vigilant, occupying themselves with the singing of psalms and prayer. If he tries to tempt them by bestowing on them worldly possessions, they foil him by giving these away to the poor.[5] Aphraates teaches also the transience of this world and of this life, and bids all to remember the approach of death. "The upright and righteous and good and wise," he writes, "fear not nor tremble at death, because of the great hope that is before them. And they at every time are mindful of death, their exodus, and of the last day in which the children of Adam shall be judged.

"O Kings, crowned with the diadem, remember Death, which will take away the diadems that are set upon your heads, and he shall be king over you till the time when ye shall rise again for judgment. O ye rich, remember Death; for when the time shall come, and ye shall draw nigh to him there, ye shall not use your wealth and possessions. O ye that trust in this world, let this world be despised in your eyes; for ye are sojourners and aliens in the midst of it, and ye know not the day that ye shall be taken out of it. The

[1] Demonstration VI. *Of Monks*, par. 4.

[2] The Spirit, denoted by a feminine word, was regarded as feminine in the Syriac-speaking Church.

[3] *Hist. of Eastern Christianity*, pp. 88 *ff*.

[4] *Of Monks*, par. 19.

[5] *Ibid.*, par. 2.

sons of peace remember Death; and they forsake and remove from them wrath and enmity. As sojourners they dwell in this world, and prepare for themselves a provision for the journey before them. On that which is above they set their thoughts, and on that which is above they meditate; and those things which are beneath their eyes they despise. They abide in the world as aliens, sons of a far land; and look forward to be sent out of this world and to come to the city, the place of the righteous. They afflict themselves in the place of their sojourning, and they are not entangled or occupied in the house of their exile. Ever day by day their faces are set upwards, to go to the repose of their fathers. As prisoners are they in this world, nor is their hope in it that it will continue for ever. . . . O man without sense, whosoever he be whose trust is in this world!"[1]

The object of asceticism, to Aphraates, was that man should become fit to be the dwelling-place of the Holy Spirit, and to that end he must pursue fasting, prayer, love, virginity, chastity and sadness.

The real founder of Christian monasticism in Mesopotamia seems to have been Mār Awgīn, an Egyptian pearl-fisher who had worked at Suez, and had one day seen the vision of a fiery star which shone like the disk of the sun, and ran along before him on the water. He finally forsook his calling and went to live in the monastery of Pachomius. He chose a number of Egyptian monks to go with him to Mesopotamia, and built a monastery near Nisibis. He died about A.D. 363, and by the end of the fourth century monasticism was well established in Mesopotamia.[2] The type of monastic life which prevailed there tended to be definitely eremitical and individualist. Ephraim the Syrian, who lived in Mesopotamia during the first three-quarters of the fourth century, was a disciple of Jacob of Nisibis, whom we hear of as living the ascetic life as early as 325 A.D. Ephraim himself lived as an anchorite in a cell outside the city. Throughout his life as a monk he ate only barley bread, with the addition of pulse and vegetables. His clothes were patched and drab, and his flesh was dried up on his bones, " like a potter's

[1] *Of Death and the Latter Times*, par. 9.

[2] Thomas of Margā, I. cxxv. *ff*.

sherd." His face was always sad and he never laughed. He died in A.D. 373. Of him it was said that "Ephraim of Edessa completed in worthy fashion the journey of the Spirit, without being diverted from the straight road, and was counted worthy of the grace of natural knowledge and afterwards of the knowledge of God and final blessedness."[1]

Meanwhile monasticism was spreading, and in A.D. 385 three Mesopotamian monks, Abdas, Ebedjesus and Jaballaha founded monasteries in Babylonia and Arabia. We find that in the fifth century "religion was established and propagated, not only in Mesopotamia, Assyria, and Arabia, but also in Media, Persia, Armenia, Bactria, and India, for in the year A.D. 530 among the Bactrians, Huns, Persians, Indians, Persamani, Medes, Elamites and in the whole region of Persis, were numerous churches, and also bishops and Christian people in large numbers, and many monks and hesychastæ—*i.e.*, silent ones, for thus they call the solitaries, the hermits and recluses."[2]

After the Persian war of 337–363, Nisibis and the provinces beyond Edessa were given up by Rome, and Edessa became the chief centre of Syriac Christianity. From 411 to 435, the Bishop of Edessa was Rabbūla, who after his conversion went to Jerusalem and was baptised in the Jordan. On his return he gave up his property to the poor, set free his slaves, separated from his wife, and sent his children to the convent schools, while he himself lived as a hermit in the desert and sought for martyrdom, but without success. After he was made bishop, Rabbūla made regulations for the clergy and for the Sons and Daughters of the Covenant,[3] and laid down rules for the monastic communities. These included the rule that those monks who had received ordination as priests or deacons, and had been entrusted with churches in the villages, should appoint superiors to rule the brotherhood, but should themselves remain in charge of their churches. This custom of monks serving churches in Mesopotamia seems to have been unique in the East, though we have noticed above that it prevailed in North Africa.

[1] *Hist. Laus.*, chap. xl. (1).

[2] Assem. *B.O.*, iii. 2, pp. 869, 872.

[3] See above, p. 27.

Abraham of Kashkar, who was baptised in A.D. 502, was an ascetic, who first studied at Nisibis, and then went to Jerusalem and to the desert of Scete, where he learnt something of the doctrine and principles of the Egyptian anchorites. He returned to his own country and lived at Mount Izla, near Nisibis, and wrote a treatise on the monastic life, in which he is described as being the head of the ascetics throughout Persia. His rules advocated a life of tranquillity, to be preserved by constant reading and prayer, as well as labour and meditation. " Therefore," he says, " let us be constant in our cells in quietness, and let us flee from idleness."[1] He also laid down a rule for fasting, as being agreeable to the example of the New Testament. " Let us therefore preserve fasting," he says, " inasmuch as it is the origin of a multitude of virtues and a guide to true life."[2] Prayer and reading and the offices were to be observed as being very profitable. Silence and meekness and solitude were all to be practised by the monks, for, says Abraham, " divine helps are hidden within them and without them we are not able to please God."[3] During Lent, the brothers were to keep to their cells, and at no time were they to go about in the neighbourhood or leave the monastery without the leave of the superior. The novices were to be tested for three years, and then to build cells for themselves or occupy empty cells. Rabban Abraham lived till after A.D. 604.[4]

Of the monastic life in Mesopotamia from this time onwards we have a full description by Thomas of Margā, who lived in the ninth century, and wrote a history of the great monastery at Bēth Abhē, some sixty or seventy miles to the north-east of Mosul. The common residence was called a cœnobium, and the inhabitants were " brethren." There were also other classes of ascetics, including solitaries, dwellers in the desert, recluses, weepers, anchorites and pillar-saints. Each novice had to work in the service of the monastery for three years and then might live in a cell. The monks wore a tunic, girdle, cloak, head-covering, sandals, and a cross, and carried a staff. In summer work was carried

[1] Thomas of Margā, p. cxxxv., Canon 1. [2] *Ibid.*, Canon 2.
[3] *Ibid.*, p. cxxxviii., Canons 5, 6.
[4] *Ibid.*, p. cxxxix., Canon 10.

on from dawn till the day grew hot, then until the sixth hour there was reading and meditation, from the sixth to the ninth hour food and rest, and from the ninth hour until evening, rest again.[1] Seven times of prayer in the day was the earliest rule. The monks were under the authority of an abbot and director.

The end and aim of all this asceticism and the renunciations involved in the monastic life were the same in Mesopotamia and Persia as elsewhere. It was contemplation and the life of communion with God that these monks sought after, and their asceticism was simply to fit them for the object of their search. Thomas of Margā, while writing of the means, remains always conscious of the end. " Certain of the fathers," he says, " have written in their books that there existeth in the heart a glorious intellectual mirror which the Creator of natures formed from all the visible and spiritual natures which are in creation for the great honour of His image, and as a means for discovering His invisibility ; and He made it a tie, and a bond and a completion of all natures. Now the fathers call it the ' beauty of our person,' and by St. Paul it is called the ' house of love,' and by the doctors the ' house of peace,' and by the wise the ' house of goodness,' and by others the ' house of joy,' in which dwelleth the spirit of adoption which we have received from holy baptism, and upon it shineth the light of grace. And whosoever hath cleansed this mirror of beautiful things from the impurity of the passions and from sin and hath renewed it and established it in the original condition of the nature of its creation, can see by the light of its glorious rays all spiritual things which belong to natures and to things of creation which are afar off, and which are near. And he is able by the secret power of the Holy Spirit to look into them closely as if they were all arranged in order, without any covering whatever, before his eyes. And when the working of God dawneth upon the souls of holy men there dwelleth and abideth upon it this gift of the Holy Spirit, and He bestoweth this gift upon the good, and maketh them to possess life and happiness for ever."[2]

[1] Thomas of Margā, I. cxlvii. *ff.*

[2] Thomas of Margā, *Book of the Governors*, V. xv.

The ascetic life represented the practical Way to be trodden by those who sought the mystical knowledge which should lead them to the Vision of God, and the life in union with Him, which is the goal of all mysticism.

CHAPTER III

ASCETICISM AND THE MONASTIC LIFE AMONG WOMEN

ASCETICISM and the monastic life found almost as many adherents among the women of the early Christian Church as among the men. There had been women recluses even in pagan times. The Roman vestals were an early example of women set apart to a life of chastity, and among the Pythagoreans, women consecrated to virginity attained to a high rank in the hierarchy. The celibate life became an ideal for women in the Christian Church earlier than for men, perhaps because married life was to them a greater hindrance to the pursuit of the life of devotion. Women held a high position in the early Christian Church; we note that St. Paul salutes fifteen women alongside of eighteen men.[1] Women exercised the prophetic office,[2] and Priscilla, whose name is twice mentioned before that of her husband by St. Paul, as if she held a more prominent position in the Church, was evidently a missionary and teacher of distinction,[3] and it has been suggested, with some reason, that she was the writer of the Epistle to the Hebrews.[4] The order of deaconesses (*ministræ*) is mentioned by Pliny, and there appears to have been an order of regular female ascetics, who formed an important part of the organisation of the Church in the first three centuries, and had their names enrolled on the list of church officials.[5] These virgins did not as yet live in communities, nor were they bound by vows, but remained, living a life of retirement, in their own homes. The *Acts of Paul and Thekla*, written about A.D. 170, which appears to contain some genuine information about St. Paul, gives a prominent rôle to women, as prophetesses, and above all to the "apostle"

[1] Rom. xvi. 1-15; Phil. iv. 2, 3; 2 Tim. iv. 19; Philemon i. 2.
[2] Acts xxi. 9.
[3] Rom. xvi. 3 and 2 Tim. iv. 19; Acts xviii. 26.
[4] *Cf.* A. Harnack, *Mission and Expansion of Christianity*, ii. 66.
[5] Socrates, *Hist. Eccles.*, i. 17.

Thekla of Iconium, who is said to have baptised, and to have enlightened many with the word of God. St. Clement of Alexandria gave it as his judgment that the virtue of man and of woman was one and the same. Since the God of both was the same, the Instructor of both was the same: they were members of the one Church; of both was required one temperate self-control and one modesty; they ate one common food, and to both marriage was an equal yoke; breath, sight, hearing, knowledge, hope, obedience, love—all things were alike to them. So Clement concluded that those whose life was common had also a common grace and a common salvation, and that their virtue and training were alike.[1] In his time, women studied the Scriptures and attended the classes of the great Christian teachers and apologists; Origen had a number of women pupils. So that up to the end of the second century or later, women appear to have been prominent in the Christian Church as deaconesses, prophetesses, teachers and missionaries, as they were prominent among the martyrs, for, in the persecutions, no distinction of sex was made. Women seem, indeed, to have been in the majority, at least among the upper classes, in the early Christian Church, and in the persecution of Licinius, about A.D. 322, special prohibitions were directed against women, as if the emperor realised that the strength of Christianity lay in its women members.

It is not surprising, then, that many women, at a time when asceticism and retirement from the world were felt to be the only means of attaining to the highest type of Christian life, should have been found ready to renounce all, and having turned their backs on home ties and the attractions of the world, should have sought the life of contemplation and communion with God. They took their part in every phase of the monastic movement in Egypt, and some lived the eremitic life as recluses in the desert, while communities of women came into existence earlier than those of men, and in Egypt these were to be found as early as the middle of the third century. This was made more possible in a country where the legal position of women had always been on an equality with that of men, and

[1] *Pædag.*, i. 4.

wives enjoyed the same rights as their husbands[1] and where women were therefore more free to devote themselves at their own choice to the religious life. In the time of Athanasius, who became Bishop of Alexandria in A.D. 327, there were houses of virgins in that city; St. Ambrose (born before A.D. 340) also says that there were many in his time in Alexandria and elsewhere in the East, and St. John Chrysostom (born A.D. 344) mentions associations of virgins in Egypt.[2]

We are told that St. Anthony, when he renounced the world, placed his sister, for whom he was responsible, in a "house of virgins," a nunnery, when as yet there were no similar institutions for men. Pachomius built a convent for his sister Mary, on the bank of the Nile opposite to Tabennisi, where his own monastery was, and there she established a nunnery, of which she was the abbess. Two other sisterhoods were formed a little later, according to the Pachomian rule, one being of four hundred sisters, situated near Panoplis (Akhmīm) and one at Tesminé,[3] and soon there were a dozen in existence. A large convent for women was founded at Atripé by the Coptic abbot Shenoudi, who had eighteen hundred women under his rule. There is a story given by Palladius[4] of Elias, an ascetic, who was a great friend of virgins, and who possessed some property in the city of Athribé: out of pity for the women ascetics, he built them a great monastery, and brought into it all the scattered recluses and cared for them, to the number of three hundred, providing them with gardens and everything that they could need. It is possible that this is to be identified with Shenoudi's convent.[5] The system of double monasteries seems to have been common in Egypt: the men, who worked at agriculture and other handicrafts, gave their surplus output for the needs of the women's convents, while the latter provided clothes for the men. There was an abbess for the women corresponding to the

[1] *Cf.* Amélineau, *op. cit.*, p. 7.
[2] Chrys., *Homil. in St. Matt.*, viii.
[3] *Cam. Med. Hist.*, p. 530.
[4] *Hist. Laus.*, xxix.
[5] Cf. *Hist. Laus.*, ii. Butler's note, p. 204.

abbot for the men, and some aged and discreet monk was appointed to give the nuns spiritual and Scriptural instruction, while a priest and deacon went to them on Sundays to celebrate the Sacrament. The convent was at a distance from the monastery, usually with the river Nile between. When a nun died, her sisters prepared her body for burial and laid it on the river bank and the monks came over and took the body back with them for burial in their cemetery.[1]

The number of these women ascetics was very considerable at this time. At Oxyrhyncus, a city in the Thebaïd, twelve miles south of Cairo, there were as many as twenty thousand nuns.[2] Palladius, during his visit to Egypt, saw much of the convents and of the holy women. He says that he finds it necessary to mention certain " manly " women, to whom God had appointed a contest equal to that of men, lest any should pretend that women are too feeble to attain to the perfection of virtue.[3] Many of the women whom he mentions led a life of asceticism as strenuous as that of the fathers, and the earliest monks showed a toleration of nuns and holy women, both married and single, which was less noticeable later; this toleration was probably due to the fact that the women who established the earliest nunneries were closely related to the founders of the monasteries. There are several accounts of women who disguised themselves as men and lived in monasteries, sharing the asceticism and the labours of the monks. One man who became a monk had a little daughter who begged that she might not be separated from him, so he disguised her as a boy and changed her name from Maria to Maryānā, and she remained in the monastery after her father's death and earned great commendation for her spiritual excellence, her sex remaining unknown. Later, she was accused of seducing a certain girl and being cast out of the monastery, took care of the girl's child and reared him, but constantly sat by the door of the monastery until at last, after four years, she was readmitted. Maryānā lived many years after that, and prevailed mightily in the great labours of spiritual excellence, and not until she died was found to be a woman.[4] We hear

[1] *Hist. Laus.*, xxxiii.
[2] *Paradise*, i. 337.
[3] *Hist. Laus.*, xli.
[4] *Paradise*, i. 248 *ff*.

also of Euphrosyne, who at the age of eighteen left her father and husband, and disguised herself as a man, went into a monastery of monks and there spent thirty-eight years without leaving her cell. Her father at one time visited the monastery, but without recognising her; later, when she was dying, she sent for him and revealed the secret of her sacrifice.[1]

In the city of Antinoë, Palladius tells us that he found twelve monasteries for women, among which was one ruled by an old woman named Amma Talis, who had spent eighty years in asceticism. With her lived sixty young women, who so loved her that it was unnecessary to have any key for the courtyard of the convent, because they were kept in by love of her. Palladius notes that she had reached such a state of "apathy" that when he entered, she came and sat by him and put her hands on his shoulders, with great boldness and freedom. One of her nuns was a certain Taor, who had lived for thirty years in the convent and would never accept any new garments, lest she should have to go out to church. She was very beautiful, but her chastity and modesty were her protection.[2]

Another stout-hearted old ascetic was Mother Sarā, who used to say to her brethren, "It is I who am a man and ye who are women."[3] She had lived in an upper room overlooking the river for sixty years, and never once looked out to see the river which passed by her cell. It was she who said, "If I were to pray to God that all men might be built up through me, I should be found expressing contrition at the door of each one of them: but I pray to God especially that my heart may be pure with Him and with every man."[4] An early anchorite of whom we hear was a young maiden named Alexandra, who left her home in Alexandria and enclosed herself in a tomb, and through an opening received whatever she needed, and saw neither woman nor man for ten years. Then, having adorned herself in readiness for her death, in the tenth year she died.[5] Another virgin had lived the ascetic life in her village for thirty years and never tasted food except on Saturday and Sunday, and

[1] Montalembert, *op. cit.*, p. 242.
[2] *Hist. Laus.*, lix.
[3] *Paradise*, ii. 257.
[4] *Ibid.*, ii. 173.
[5] *Hist. Laus.*, v.

spent her time praying. We are told how certain of the fathers of Scete while travelling in the desert came across a holy woman who had lived in a cave for thirty-eight years eating only grass, and had never looked upon a man. She died in their presence, and the fathers who had found her buried her.[1] One of the holy fathers told of a blessed widow, who had lived a life of chastity, both before and after her husband's death, and had waged a successful war with Satan, and he adds: "If such things as these are to be found in Eve, how much more ought they to be found in the Adam which hath been redeemed by the second Adam?"[2]

Amongst the women who embraced the life of asceticism were a class of whom it might have been least expected. We are told that among those who came to the convents, the sanctuaries of virginity, were the courtesans and dancers. They had pursued the monks to the deserts, seeking to tempt them, and had themselves been vanquished by the power of holiness; they had retired into the convents or remained in solitude, working out their repentance, and seeking the Divine forgiveness. Such were Mary of Egypt and Pelagia. The latter visited the monks in the desert, displaying all her beauty and her jewels. They turned away their eyes, but their bishop, who was with them, told them after she had gone that he had taken great pleasure in her beauty, for God had destined her to judge them. "I see her," he said, "like a dove all black and stained; but that dove shall be bathed in the waters of baptism and shall fly towards heaven white as snow." A little while after she returned for baptism, gave away her goods to the poor, clothed herself in haircloth, and went to live in a cell on the Mount of Olives. Another famous courtesan was Thais, who led many astray by her great beauty, "because she burned like a flame of fire into the hearts of those who saw her." She was converted by Abbā Bessarion, and burnt all that she had gained by her manner of life. She entered a convent, and remained in her cell for three years, living on dry bread and water. Then Paul, the disciple of St. Anthony, had a vision in which he saw a couch prepared in heaven, attended by angels, with a crown of glory laid thereon.

[1] *Paradise*, i. 240. [2] *Ibid.*, ii. 270.

This, he thought, must be for some great saint, but a voice told him that it was for Thais, whose sins were forgiven, and fifteen days later she died.[1]

In North Africa we also find convents for women in the early centuries of Christianity. In the time of Tertullian and Cyprian, veiled virgins were recognised, and in St. Augustine's time there were many nuns established in convents, one of which was ruled by his sister. One of his letters was written for a nunnery, and women evidently took their full share in the development of monachism during the fourth and fifth centuries in Africa.

In Syria and Asia Minor, too, we find women ascetics at an early stage. Eusebius speaks of one named Ennathis, a woman adorned with the chaplet of virginity, who lived in Syria in the third century; and Theodoret tells us of Publia, the deaconess, in the fourth century, who apparently lived at Antioch, and who had at her house a group of young women vowed to perpetual virginity. Palladius in the course of his travels met with another of these virgins, Photina of Laodicea, who was greatly revered, and in Antioch he met Sabiniana the deaconess, a woman very venerable, who, he says, held intimate converse with God.[2]

Many great ladies of European birth, who had been attracted towards the ascetic life, were to be found at this time in the Holy Land, living a life of seclusion and piety. Among these was Melania, whom Palladius calls "ἡ ἄνθρωπος τοῦ θεοῦ," whom he first met in Nitria.[3] She was Spanish by origin, but had lived in Rome. Having been widowed at twenty-two, she was deemed worthy of the Divine love, and taking her possessions with her, she set sail for Alexandria, with other well-known women, and a number of children. Thence she went first to Nitria and met several of the Egyptian fathers, and later went to Palestine, and ministered of her substance to the saints. She founded a monastery at Jerusalem, and was there for twenty-seven years, having a group of fifty virgins under her charge. Rufinus of Aquileia also lived there, and the two exercised hospitality to many visitors to Jerusalem and settled dis-

[1] *Paradise*, i. 140 *ff*. [2] *Hist. Laus.*, xli.
[3] *Ibid.*, ix.

putes and combated heresy.[1] We are told that her charity extended even as far as the dwellers in Persia. She persuaded her grand-daughter Melania and her daughter-in-law Albina to embrace the monastic life, going even to Rome to fetch them. Then she came back to Jerusalem and died there at a ripe old age.[2] Palladius travelled with both Melania and Silvania, the latter being a virgin, sister-in-law to Rufinus. She never washed, or rested on a bed, or used a litter. She seems to have travelled for about three years in and about Palestine. She visited Sinai and the monks there, and also went to Mesopotamia and Edessa, and there read *The Acts of Thomas*, in which asceticism was upheld. From there she travelled to Harān and thence to Antioch and across Asia Minor. She had apparently held office in some convent, to the sisters of which she wrote. She was learned in sacred literature and had read a great deal of the writings of Origen, Gregory and Basil. She was thus enabled to rise, as on wings, above mere earthly knowledge, and by fair hopes, making herself a "spiritual bird," to pursue her journey towards Christ.[3]

Another of these holy women was Olympias, married, but a virgin, living with the Word of Truth. She gave away her goods and gave instruction to many women, and she was reckoned as a confessor.[4] Another, conspicuous for her sanctity and her asceticism, was Candida, wife of a Roman general. She gave up her daughter to the life of virginity, and she herself used to work all night at the mill in order to subjugate her body, feeling that watching was necessary, in addition to fasting.[5] Paula, the well-known disciple and companion of St. Jerome, was amongst those whom Palladius came across, and whom he considered to have great capacities and to be conspicuous in the spiritual life. She built three convents for women at Bethlehem, and provided cells and lodgings there for pilgrims. St. Jerome held that the Christian woman who would live the perfect life must be a virgin and live the cloistered life apart from the world, knowing only her convent and the church, and he influenced many women to take up monastic life in Palestine.

[1] *Hist. Laus.*, xlvi. [2] *Ibid.*, liv. and lxi. [3] *Ibid.*, lv.
[4] *Ibid.*, lvi. [5] *Ibid.*, lvii.

Among the women ascetics of Syria, as among the men, there were many who went to excess in their austerities. Theodoret in his *Philotheus* gives instances of women who withdrew from the world and lived in a state of perpetual bodily mortification, and he himself had met with two women hermits who lived in the most rigid solitude within a narrow cell, which they allowed him to enter: he found them weighed down with heavy chains and unable to move, and they passed their days in this state. But this kind of asceticism represented an extreme. The women ascetics of Syria for the most part lived in convents and divided their time between good works and the life of prayer and contemplation, and were a force for spiritual progress and vitality within the Christian Church.

The development of Montanism in Asia Minor in the second century, already referred to,[1] gave a prominent place to women. Two women, Priscilla and Maximilla, claimed, with the founder Montanus, the gift of prophecy, and became leaders of the new sect. Women were admitted to high office in the Montanist Church, acting as bishops and priests, and celebrating the Sacraments, the first condition required of those who held office being the possession of spiritual power, which was never limited to one sex. As noted above, the Montanists practised an extreme asceticism, made a second marriage unlawful, and fasted rigorously. Many Christians in Phrygia became Montanists, and their teachings doubtless prepared the way for the acceptance by women of the ascetic life, and later the monastic life, in Asia Minor. There were Basilian nuns from the foundation of the Basilian rule. As we have seen, St. Basil's mother Emmelia and his sister Macrina lived at Annesi, on the bank of the Iris, opposite the place of his own retreat. There, with their household, they lived a life of true asceticism, and Macrina may be considered the founder of the conventual life for women in her country.[2] Her brother, when he became bishop, opened numerous convents for nuns. We have seen that he inaugurated a system of double monasteries, following the example which Pachomius had

[1] See above, p. 23.
[2] *Cf.* W. K. L. Clarke's *The Life of St. Macrina.*

set in Egypt. The abbot and abbess of such a double monastery worked in close touch with each other, and the abbot's authority over the women was exercised through the abbess. In addition to the nuns, there were women devoted to the religious life called canonesses (*canonicæ*), who were devout women members enrolled to devote themselves to works of charity, such as taking charge of funerals, and other similar works of piety. They were not bound by a vow, nor compelled to live in a regular convent, but they lived apart from men, in a cœnobium of their own. One of St. Basil's *Letters* was written to Theodora, a Canoness, about the year A.D. 374, and in it he admonishes her to be modest in dress, discreet when in the society of men, abstemious in regard to food, ready to limit herself in the necessities of life, humble, self-controlled, and given to prayer, charity, generosity, contrition and sincere faith.[1] Another of St. Basil's *Letters* was written to certain deaconesses, the daughters of Count Terentius. It was fitting that Basil, who himself owed so much to the women of his own family, should have found a prominent place for women in his efforts to revive and develop the spiritual life among the Christians of Asia Minor.

We have seen how St. Basil's one-time friend Eustathius of Sebaste[2] condemned marriage and encouraged the celibate life for both sexes. He persuaded many married women to leave their husbands and enter the monastic life; such women cut their hair short and adopted male attire, apparently with the idea of getting away from sex as far as possible. This form of asceticism was condemned by the Council of Gangra in A.D. 340, which anathematized those who condemned marriage as inconsistent with salvation, and forbade virgins to exalt themselves above the married. But the very fact of the condemnation proves that the celibate life was in practice held to be the highest type of religious life, and that it had been widely adopted by women.

Palladius, at the beginning of the fifth century, in the city of Ancyra, in Galatia, found virgins to the number of two thousand, women distinguished both for their chastity and their ability. Among these was Magna, greatly revered for

[1] *Letter* CLXXIII. [2] See above, p. 23.

her piety, whom Palladius is at a loss to describe, whether as virgin or widow. She had been married to a husband, but had remained a virgin, and after his death she gave herself up wholly to the service of God, being held in veneration by all, including the bishops of the Church, for her devotion. She dispensed much kindness to the sick and the poor and to travellers, and laboured with her own hands, and spent her nights in vigil in the church.[1]

In the Syriac-speaking Church we find women ascetics also to the fore. The " elect " of the Manichees, who abstained from marriage and renounced their property, included women as well as men, and in the Christian Church of the third century we find " Daughters of the Covenant " (*B'nāth Q'yāmā*) alongside of the Sons. In the *Martyrdom of Shamōna and Guria*, written in A.D. 297, is an account of the persecution of Diocletian against the Churches in which the *B'nāth Q'yāmā* and the cloistered nuns are described as standing in bitter exposure, and all the Christians as being in affliction and grief.[2] At this same period there was at Nisibis a convent of fifty virgins, including Febronia, a maiden famed for her beauty and her austerity, no less than for her spiritual knowledge and teaching, who suffered martyrdom.[3]

Aphraates writes to both the Sons and Daughters of the Covenant, upholding celibacy. Woman with woman ought to dwell, he thinks, and man with man. He writes to solitaries that take no wives and virgins that are not taken to wife, and they that love holiness, saying : " The fruits of the Tree of Life are given as food to the virgins and those that do the will of God, . . . those that keep holiness rest in the sanctuary of the Most High ; all the solitaries doth the only One from the bosom of His Father make to rejoice. And all the pure virgins that have been betrothed to the Messiah, there they light their torches and with the Bridegroom do they enter the marriage chamber . . . theirs is the Bridegroom that doth not withdraw for ever."[4] Ad-

[1] *Hist. Laus.*, lxvii.
[2] F. C. Burkitt, *Early Eastern Christianity*, pp. 131, 132.
[3] Montalembert, *op. cit.*, p. 221.
[4] F. C. Burkitt, *Early Eastern Christianity*, p. 138.

dressing the Daughters of the Covenant, Aphraates says: "O virgins who have betrothed yourselves to the Messiah, when one of the Sons of the Covenant shall say to one of you, 'I will dwell with thee and thou minister to me,' then shalt thou say to him: 'To a royal Husband am I betrothed and to Him do I minister; and if I leave His ministry and minister to thee, my Betrothed will be wroth with me and will write me a letter of divorce and will dismiss me from His house, and while thou seekest to be honoured by me, and I to be honoured by thee, see lest hurt come upon me and thee. Take not fire in thy bosom lest it burn thy garments, but be thou in honour by thyself, and I will be by myself in honour.'"[1] Rabbūla also drew up regulations for these Daughters of the Covenant, who seem to have corresponded to the Canonesses already mentioned in connection with the Church in Syria and Asia Minor,[2] and these regulations were the same as those for the men living under this rule. A layman who dared to marry a Daughter of the Covenant, and the maiden who consented, were to be arrested and judged and sent to monasteries for penance.[3]

Evidently convents for women were already in existence in Rabbūla's time, and at a later period a "convent of Daughters of the Covenant" is mentioned as existing in the village of Bēth Ṭĕḥūnai.[4] Ḥīra, on the border of the Persian Empire, was a centre of Christianity, but was ruled by a heathen king. In the sixth century, we read, the king al-Mundhir sacrificed a number of Christian nuns to his god al-'Uzza. We hear also of a virgin nun and recluse of the sixth century in Mesopotamia, of whom one of the fathers, Mār-yahbh, related that in the mountains he found a holy woman, whose garment was made of dried grass, and who fed upon roots and fruit, and she had a child. Mār-yahbh, speaking of this child, says: "Now the girl whom the Guardian of all mankind raised up from her was, like Mary, in the stead of Eve, heaven instead of earth, and a life-bearer instead of a death-bearer. And it came to pass not long after this that the holy woman, her mother, died,

[1] F. C. Burkitt, *op. cit.*, p. 139. [2] See above, p. 43.
[3] F. C. Burkitt, *op. cit.*, pp. 146, 147.
[4] Thomas of Margā, ii. 325.

having led a life of good deeds which were pleasing to God, and she left the divine woman, her daughter, in her place." Mār-yahbh sometimes visited the daughter, and he used to say of her that, " Although she was in the world, she was not of the world. And I know not at all if she ever lifted her eyes and looked in my face, for her mind was led captive by the vision of God."[1]

We find, then, that women, no less than men, in these early centuries of the Christian era, were prepared to renounce the world and all its attractions, and to embrace the life of solitude and seclusion. The religious life for women was held in great honour, and holy women were held to be saints, and received the reverence due to their sanctity, both during their lifetime and, as we have seen, at shrines after their death. The Nestorian controversy in the fifth century raised the Blessed Virgin to a rank above all the saints, in giving her, in all save the Nestorian Church, the title of Mother of God (θεοτόκος), and the idea of a woman mediator was welcomed. So the cult of the saints, women as well as men, was developed. But the aim of the women ascetics and nuns was, first and foremost, holiness of life, to be attained, partly by service to mankind—for many of these religious women gave themselves to the care of the poor and sick—but still more by prayer and meditation, so that in the end they might attain to the mystic's goal, and like the blessed woman whom Mār-yahbh visited, they might be led captive by the Vision of God.

[1] Thomas of Margā, ii. 73-75.

CHAPTER IV

EARLY MYSTICISM IN THE NEAR EAST

SINCE the ideal of Mysticism is the direct intercourse of the soul with God, we can well understand that it was among the ascetics and in the monasteries that the mystics were to be found. The aim of asceticism and the monastic life was the conquest of self, and renunciation, in order that the ascetic, having purified himself from all that would hinder his approach to the Divine, might live the perfect life of the soul, face to face with God, in direct intercourse with Him. In the silence of the desert, and in the solitude of his cell, the mystic could ascend, freed from the entanglements of matter, to the mountain-tops, where he could contemplate and hold communion with the Absolute.

Mysticism had indeed been inherent in the teaching of Christianity from the beginning. St. Paul was himself a mystic and a teacher of mystical doctrine. The soul, to him, was the " image and glory of God," but if it was to return again to God, there must be a cleansing from all defilement both of flesh and spirit. " To be carnally minded," he says, " is death, but to be spiritually minded is life and peace."[1] By self-mastery and enlightenment and love, the seeker might attain to the Vision of God, to be spiritually discerned only by those fitted to receive it, not by the finite, human understanding. " Eye hath not seen, nor ear heard, neither have entered into the heart of man the things which God hath prepared for them that love Him. But God hath revealed them unto us by His Spirit."[2] Those who have known and seen become the children of God, in whom and with whom He dwells, and through whom He works, and thenceforth they live in conscious union with Him. " As many as are led by the Spirit of God, they are the sons of God."[3] Here we have in germ the doctrine of deification, and in the most beautiful of all the mystic images which he

[1] Rom. viii. 6. [2] 1 Cor. ii. 9, 10. [3] Rom. viii. 19.

uses, St. Paul shows how those who gaze upon the Divine Beauty themselves become Godlike: "We all, with open face beholding as in a glass the glory of the Lord, are changed into the same image from glory to glory, even as by the Spirit of the Lord."[1]

St. John, though he gives us no account of his own religious experience, includes much mystical teaching in his theology, which was plainly influenced by Platonism. To him God is Light and Love and Spirit, but since the Absolute Godhead cannot be seen or known, He is manifested through God revealed, the Logos. To St. John, religion is essentially an inward process of growth, depending upon direct experience. The end is Eternal Life, and the way thereto is by rebirth, the way of purgation, and the death of the carnal self, that the spiritual self may come to life. "It is the Spirit that quickeneth, the flesh profiteth nothing."[2] Faith is shown in self-sacrifice, and this is inspired by Love; "Love is of God," he writes, "and everyone that loveth is born of God and knoweth God. He that loveth not knoweth not God; for God is Love."[3] To those who, in faith and love, have died to self, God grants the mystic union, whereby they partake of His divine Life, and abide in Him. "If a man love Me," says the Logos, "he will keep My words and we will come unto him, and make our abode with him."[4] This unitive life, lived in God, means an ever-present sense of the Divine power working within; "Hereby we know that we dwell in Him and He in us, because he hath given of His Spirit."[5]

(*a*) St. Clement of Alexandria

St. Clement of Alexandria,[6] in the second century, aimed at constructing a Christian "gnosis," whereby the Christian who was fitted for it might be initiated into the higher mysteries of his faith. He conceives of God as the One Reality, Alone Almighty, the Creator and Ruler of the World. "If there is manifest round about us," he writes

[1] Eph. iii. 19. [2] John vi. 63. [3] 1 John iv. 7, 8.
[4] John xiv. 23. [5] 1 John iv. 13.
[6] Born A.D. 150, died before A.D. 216.

in his *Exhortation to the Greeks*, " a certain perception of Divine Power, then nothing else is left but to confess that the one true God is the Only One Who really is and is Self-existent."[1] Again he writes : " Regard the whole universe ; that is His handiwork. Heaven, the sun, the angels and men are the works of His fingers. How great is the power of God ! His will alone is creation ; for God alone created, since He alone is truly God. By the expression of His will alone His work is accomplished, and the existence of the world results from a single act of that Will. Let none of you worship the sun, but let him rather long after the Maker of the sun."[2] God is the Lover of all He has made ; He is Perfect Goodness, and man may be made like to God by learning to know Him, by the indwelling of the Word in him, by purity, and by freedom from passion (ἀπάθεια). In *The Rich Man's Salvation* St. Clement writes : " We must therefore store up in the soul from the very beginning the greatest and most valuable of the doctrines leading to life, namely to know the eternal God as both the Giver of eternal gifts and the First and Supreme and the Only Good God. And we can come to possess God (only) through knowledge and apprehension, for this is the fixed and immutable beginning and foundation of life . . . the knowledge of God Who is Self-Existent, the Giver of all existence, that is, of all that is eternal, from Whom it is that all else derives both its origin and its subsistence. Ignorance of Him is death, but full knowledge of Him and appropriation of Him, and love to Him, and growth in His Likeness, this alone is true life."[3]

It follows from this conception of God as the Sole Reality that man, if he is also real, must be a partaker in the Divine Nature. " There is a certain Divine emanation instilled into all men without exception, but especially does it enter into those who spend their time in meditation ; it is for this reason that they admit, even though against their will, that God is One, unbegotten and immortal, and that somewhere on high He truly exists unto eternity. Not even the sun could ever reveal to us the true God. The life-giving Word or Reason, Who is the Sun of the soul, alone is able to do

[1] *Protrepticus*, x. [2] *Ibid.*, iv. [3] *Quis dives salvetur*, vii.

it; through Him and Him only, when His rays have shone upon the inmost recesses of the mind, the soul's eye is illuminated."[1] The last words show that St. Clement recognised that the soul possessed a spiritual sense, whereby it was able intuitively to receive the revelation of God. The soul itself is conscious of its high destiny, and knows itself to be distinct from that which is merely temporal and perishes. "From the beginning," says St. Clement, "ye have been immortal and children of eternal life, and ye desired to take death upon yourselves, so that ye might drain it to the dregs, and destroy it, that Death might die in you, and through you: for if ye destroy the world, without yourselves being destroyed, ye are lords of the universe and of all that is mortal."[2] To him, the gnostic soul is a divine image, made like unto God Himself, adorned with perfect virtue, due to the formative action of nature, discipline, and reason, and the soul, thus beautified, can, and does, become a temple of the Holy Spirit.[3]

He urges men to enter upon the mystic Path which leads unto eternal life, the life of God. "Do you still remain blind," he asks them, "and unwilling to look up to the Master of all and the Lord of the Universe? Will you not flee from the prisons of this earth and escape to the pity which comes from heaven? For God, out of His great love to the human race, still keeps hold of man. He is a Father, Who seeks after His creature. Why do we not receive the Word with open ears and entertain God as guest in souls made pure from stain?"[4] In the search after salvation and eternal life, which is the unitive life in God, the gnostic has the fellowship of others like-minded with himself; he with them is to be builded up into a holy temple, the Church Invisible, the Communion of the Saints. "Let us strive," St. Clement writes in his *Exhortation to the Greeks*, "after salvation and the new birth. Let us, who are many, strive to be united into one love, corresponding to the Unity of the One Being. So also, let us follow after unity by the practice of good works, seeking the good Monad. For the union of many into one, bringing a divine harmony out of

[1] *Protrepticus*, vi.
[2] *Strom.*, iv. 89.
[3] *Strom.*, vii. 64.
[4] *Protrepticus*, x, ix.

many diffused sounds, becomes one symphony, following one leader and teacher, the Word, until it reaches the Truth itself."[1] But the gnostic, before he can attain unto salvation, must tread the Way of Purgation, being purged as by fire, not the all-devouring flame of common life, but the discerning flame which penetrates the soul that walks through fire.[2] St. Clement tells us of what sort this purification must be; it is the cleansing of the soul from its vices and the adornment of it with the virtues acceptable to God. "If you desire to see God in truth," he writes, "partake of purifications meet for Him, not of laurel-leaves and fillets decked out with wool and purple, but being crowned with righteousness, let your wreath be wrought from the leaves of self-control and seek ye diligently after Christ. 'For I am the door,' He says somewhere, and I know well that He Who opens this door, so long closed, will afterwards unveil what is within, and bring to light what could not have been known, had we not entered through Christ, through Whom alone the vision of God is revealed. He is the Word of Truth, the Immortal Word, Who has built His temple in man, that in man He may establish God. Cleanse the temple and cast aside pleasure and heedlessness, like the flower that lives but a day, to the wind and fire, but strive in all wisdom for the fruits of temperance, and offer yourselves as first-fruits to God, so that you may be not only His work, but also a source of joy to Him."[3]

By constant self-discipline and the cherishing of that which is Divine within him, the gnostic seeks to serve God, caring for none of the fair things of this world, lest they should tie him down to earth. He is temperate and passionless, unaffected by pleasures and pains, as the diamond is said to be against the fire, knowing that he who holds intercourse with God must have his soul undefiled and spotlessly pure.[4] In seeking for the "apathy" which is essential to the gnostic's aim, "for salvation belongs to pure and passionless souls," the gnostic knows that he will have the Divine help. "When exercising discipline and striving after the passionless state by himself man accomplishes nothing,

[1] *Protrepticus*, ix.
[2] *Strom.*, vii. 34.
[3] *Protrepticus*, i, xi.
[4] *Strom.*, vii. 67, 49.

but if it is evident that he is eagerly longing after this, and is making every effort thereto, he prevails by the help of the power that comes from God. For God breathes His own power into willing souls, but if ever they cease to be willing, then, too, the Spirit given from God is withheld."[1] St. Clement urges the would-be gnostic to practise quiet of word and deed, of speech and gait, so that the mind may remain steadfast. The mind, he says, ought to prevail over the passions, since " it is seated on high on a quiet throne, gazing only upon God."[2]

The gnostic must give much time to prayer, because through prayer he seeks converse with God. Therefore he must constantly turn his soul to God and communicate his inmost thoughts to Him, by night as well as by day. Sleep should not be allowed to keep him from his prayers and hymns to God, for overmuch sleep is a rival to death, and instead of such fleshly indulgence the gnostic should choose the joys which God seeks to bestow, and let meditation upon the Divine lead him ever upward to heaven.[3] St. Clement gives a place to mental prayer, saying that it is possible to send up a voiceless prayer, if only the one who prays brings his whole spiritual effort to bear upon the inner voice of the mind, in undistracted turning to God.[4] Prayer, he says, is intercourse with God, and though we may address Him without opening the lips, in silence, yet our cry will reach Him from the innermost recesses of the heart, and while we are thinking upon God, He will be near us and with us.[5]

In all his upward striving, the mystic is inspired by Love, for before all things the gnostic is a lover of God ; he is distinguished from the ordinary believer in being actuated solely by love, and love, says St. Clement, surpasses all knowledge in holiness and sovereignty. By it, the gnostic becomes a truly perfect man and the friend of God.[6] " Love goes with us," St. Clement writes in *The Rich Man's Salvation*, " into the fullness of God and increases the more when perfection has been granted. For if anyone admits love into his soul, even though he be born in sins and have allowed

[1] *Quis dives salvetur*, 21.
[2] *To the Newly Baptised*, p. 371.
[3] *Ibid.*, p. 370.
[4] *Strom.*, vii. 43.
[5] *Strom.*, i. 7.
[6] *Strom.*, vii. 68.

many things to hinder him, he is able, by increase of love and the admission of pure repentance, to retrieve his errors. For in proportion as a man loves God, does he penetrate further into the inmost shrine of God."[1]

So the gnostic is led on to that perfect end which knows no end, and learns what is that future life, lived according to the will of God, among those who are Divine, and he becomes transformed into that divine and holy state which is really natural to the soul. As he passes through the mystic stages, he receives more and more illumination and enlightenment, until at last love, which teaches the pure in heart to look upon God face to face, restores him to that supreme place of rest, and once again he is possessed of complete certainty and perfect comprehension.[2] St. Clement uses the language of the Greek mysteries to describe the process of initiation by which the gnostic is at last admitted into that pure Light, which is the radiance of the very Presence of God. It is in the "blaze of torches" that the mystic sees the vision of God, when the Lord reveals the sacred mysteries, and marks the worshipper with His seal, and gives him light to guide him on his way into the very Sanctuary of God, where he shall be safe for evermore. It is Jesus, the great High Priest, Who calls to the gnostic to come to initiation, saying: "To you alone of all mortal beings, I give the joy of immortality. And I give unto you the Divine Word, the true knowledge of God, I give unto you Myself in perfection." So St. Clement bids the initiate hasten to accept the gift and to take upon himself immortality.[3] Elsewhere he gives us a wonderful picture of that mystic experience which confers immortality, even deity, upon the purified soul. "Those gnostic souls are carried away by the splendour of the Vision, and being reckoned as holy among the holy, and rapt away, they attain to the highest of all regions, and then, not in or through mirrors do they greet the Divine Vision, but with loving hearts they feast eternally upon that never-ending sight, pure and radiantly clear, enjoying a delight that never cloys, unto unending ages. This is the apprehensive vision of the pure in heart, and this is the work of the perfected gnostic, to

[1] 38, 27. [2] *Strom.*, vii. 56. [3] *Protrepticus*, xii.

hold intercourse with God, being made like, as far as possible, unto the Lord, . . . he is indeed making and forming himself like unto God, assimilating, as far as may be, to that which is by nature passionless, that which has been subdued by discipline to apathy, and this by holding undistracted intercourse and communion with the Lord."[1]

It is thus that the mystic enters upon the unitive life; knowing God, he shall be made like to Him, and he becomes God, for God so desires it. By being deified into apathy, the soul becomes Monadic without stain.[2] Now the gnostic abides in the rest of God, being already holy and divine, bearing God within him, and being borne by God.[3] So, finally, St. Clement brings into Christian mysticism the idea of deification, the logical conclusion of the doctrine of union with the Divine, as the goal of the mystic's quest.

(*b*) St. Basil the Great

St. Basil undoubtedly owed much of his mysticism to the teachings of Origen (A.D. 185-254), who had held that the world, since it was the work of God and bore His impress, could be the means of ascent for the soul, which at first was perfect, but had fallen from its high estate. The soul, by means of earthly things, could rise to understand spiritual mysteries and be raised to the contemplation of the invisible and eternal, when it would see the nature of the Ideal, and look upon the beauty of Truth itself. St. Basil, too, regarded the mystical contemplation of God as the end and aim of the ascetic and solitary life, which he advocated so ardently, and which, as we have seen, he made possible for so many devoted Christians of both sexes, in his own country. He is chiefly concerned with teaching the mystic way. There is only one means of securing the tranquillity needed for contemplation, and that is separation from the world altogether, and that not simply by bodily separation, but by the severance of the soul from sympathy with the body, renunciation of all possessions, and retirement into solitude. The beginning of the soul's purgation is tranquillity, for when the

[1] *Strom.*, vii. 3. [2] *Strom.*, iv. 152.
[3] *Strom.*, vii. 13, 82.

mind is not distracted by extraneous things, nor dissipated over the phenomenal world through the senses, it withdraws into itself, and of its own initiative ascends towards the contemplation of God, and being enlightened without and within, when that Divine Beauty shines about it, the soul becomes oblivious of its own nature and devotes all its efforts to the attainment of that which is eternal.[1]

Prayer is a means towards this end, and St. Basil commends it, as giving rise within the soul to a distinct conception of God. But prayer is not a matter simply of requests, nor is it limited to words; it represents rather an attitude towards God, the attitude of adoration and of loving intercourse. "Prayer," he writes, "is a petition for good addressed by the pious to God. But we do not by any means limit our petition to words. Nor do we suppose that God requires to be reminded by our speech. I say, then, that we ought not to regard our prayer as completed by the syllables we utter. The strength of prayer lies in the purpose of our soul, and in deeds of virtue affecting our life at every point. When you seat yourself at table, pray. As you lift up the loaf, offer thanks to the Giver. When your need for taking food has passed away, let not the thought of the Benefactor pass away too. Is the day finished? Give thanks to Him Who has given us the sun for our daily work, and has provided for us fire with which to light up the night and to serve the other needs of life. Let night provide fresh occasions for prayer. When you gaze at the heavens and fix your eyes upon the beauty of the stars, adore the Lord of the visible world, God, the Arch-Artificer of all things, Who in wisdom hath made them all. When you behold all animate nature wrapt in sleep, then again worship Him Who by sleep releases us, even though we be unwilling, from the strain of continuous toil, and, by a brief repose, restores our strength once more. Let not the whole night be the special and peculiar property of sleep, but let it be divided between sleep and prayer. Nay, let sleep itself be an exercise in piety, for such as our life and conduct have been, so also of necessity will be our dreams. So shall we pray without ceasing, if we pray not only in words, but unite ourselves to God

[1] *Epis.* II., *Gregorio*, par. 2.

through all the course of life, and so will our life become one ceaseless and uninterrupted prayer."[1]

Again, St. Basil writes of the need of purity for those who would see God, and this is to be obtained by the true asceticism, abstention not merely from that which might defile the body, but from all evil which may assault and hurt the soul. Fasting he commends because it "begets prophets and strengthens the strong. Fasting makes law-givers wise, is the soul's safeguard, the body's trusty companion, the armour of the champion, the training of the athlete."[2] But the true fast is alienation from evil, just as real abstinence is not abstention from earthly food, but is complete abandonment of one's own wishes. We have always to remember that the body which is given to man's soul for it to dwell in is called the tabernacle of God, and is therefore not ours but His. As those who live on land not their own, cultivate the estates for the owner, so we too, entrusted with the flesh, must tend it with care and make it bear fruit for Him Who gave it. If it thereby become worthy of God, it becomes in truth His tabernacle, for He makes His dwelling in the saints. Then comes progress to that which is more perfect, for the sojourner in this body shall come to that heavenly country, bright and adorned with splendour, which is the city of the living God, the assembly of the saints, for he has become "the perfect man, that is, he who is ordained to ascend to the life of everlasting peace."[3] St. Basil regards contrition as a mark of grace. "The lamentations and tears of the saints are caused by their love to God. So, with their eyes directed always towards the Object of their love, and thence increasing their own joy, they devote themselves to the interests of their fellow-servants, weeping over sinners, in order to bring them to better ways by their tears."[4]

The self must be conquered by those who aim at spiritual perfection, and this can only be accomplished by those who, impelled by love, look ever towards their goal.

[1] Hom. V., *In martyrem Julittam*, par. 3.
[2] Hom. I., *De Jejunio*, pars. 6 and 10.
[3] Hom. I., *In Psalmam XIV.*, par. 1.
[4] Hom. IV., *De Gratiarum actione*.

"Hold fast," says St. Basil, "to the rudder of life. Guide thine eye, lest at any time through the eyes there should beat upon thee the impetuous wave of lust. Guide ear and tongue, lest the one receive anything hurtful or the other speak forbidden words. Beware lest the tempest of passion overwhelm thee, or any terrors of the future beat thee down, or any weight of sorrow submerge thee in its depths. Our states of mind are like the waves: if thou dost rise above them, thou wilt be a safe steersman of life. Hear, then, how it is possible to acquire the steersman's skill. It is customary for those on the sea to lift up their eyes to the heavens. So also do thou raise thine eyes to heaven and look upon the sun of righteousness. Guided by the commandments of the Lord, as by some shining constellations, keep thine eye sleepless. Truly, if thou dost never slumber at the helm, whilst thou livest here, amid the unstable circumstances of this world, thou shalt receive the help of the Spirit, Who shall conduct thee ever onward. He shall carry thee safely by the gentle winds of peace, till thou shalt come safe and sound to the calm and serene haven of the Will of God."[1] Such self-discipline and self-purification will fit the soul to become the companion of God, for not to be corrupted is to have part with God, just as to be corrupted is to have part with this world. Self-discipline is the denial of the body and the self and the confession of God, for it means the withdrawal from what is mortal and from all rival claims to Him, and life in His Spirit, and in union with Him. That one who has not admitted impurity into his heart is henceforth strong enough to endure all labours, and though he have died to the body, he is alive for ever in the Spirit. He has become, through self-purification, like unto God Himself, for God desires nothing, having all things in Himself. He seeks after nothing, for He has no sense-experiences through eyes or ears: He needs nothing, for He is in all respects complete and perfect. If we have the patience to undergo such a purification, and set our love not on this world, says St. Basil, but on the life above, we shall be found there, in that abode towards which we direct

[1] Hom. XII., *In principium Proverbiorum*, par. 17.

our mind. For the mind is the eye whereby we see the unseen things of God.[1]

St. Basil holds that the kingdom of Heaven is not to be considered as anything else but the true contemplation of Reality, which the Holy Scriptures call " blessedness," for the kingdom of Heaven is within the soul, and as for the inner man, it consists of nothing but contemplation. So it follows that the kingdom of Heaven must be contemplation. " For as the senses perceive things sensible, so does the mind lay hold of things mentally perceptible. So also the mind, being bound in the fetters of the flesh, and filled with the phantasies of the same, needs faith and right conduct, and then it shall do all that is necessary to make its feet like hart's feet, and to set it upon high places."[2] Through this mystic contemplation, the soul attains to the unitive life, and of the means by which this is effected, St. Basil says, " The Divine Spirit is not brought into communion with the soul by local approximation, for how could there be a corporeal approach to the incorporeal ? " This association results by withdrawal from the passions which have taken possession of the soul through its friendship to the flesh, and which have alienated it from its close relationship with God. And so, after a man is purified from the shame by which he was defiled through his evil-doing, and has returned to his natural beauty, as it were cleansing the Royal Image, and restoring its ancient form, it is possible for him to draw near to the Spirit of God. And He, like the sun, having found a purified eye, will show to it in Himself the image of the Invisible, and in the blessed contemplation of the image will be seen the unspeakable beauty of the Archetype. " Through His aid, hearts are lifted up, the weak are led by the hand, and they who are advancing are brought to perfection. By His illumination of those who are purified from all defilement, He makes them spiritual by fellowship with Himself. Just as bright and transparent bodies, in contact with a ray of light, themselves become translucent, and emit a fresh radiance from themselves, so souls wherein the Divine Spirit dwells, being illuminated thereby, themselves

[1] *Epis.* CCCLXVI., *Ad Urbicium monarchum.*
[2] *Epis.* VIII., *Apologia ad Cæsarienses*, par. 12.

become spiritual and give forth their grace to others. Hence comes their foreknowledge of the future, the understanding of mysteries, the comprehension of what is hidden, the distribution of good gifts, the heavenly citizenship, a place in the choirs of angels. Hence comes to them unending joy, abiding in God, being made like unto God, and, which is highest of all, being made God."[1]

Now is the soul deified, made one with the Divine, because the Divine is within it, and of the effect of the unitive life, St. Basil says, " the indwelling of God is this—to have God ever in mind, established within us. We thus become temples of God whenever our recollection of Him is not interrupted by earthly thoughts, nor the mind disturbed by unexpected passions, but escaping all these, the lover of God withdraws to Him."[2]

(*c*) St. Gregory of Nyssa

St. Basil's brother, Gregory of Nyssa, has left mystical teaching of a still more comprehensive type. Gregory was born probably in 335 or 336 A.D. at Cæsarea, in Cappadocia, and for his sanctity, and his work in teaching others, was given the name of the " Father of the Fathers " and the " Star of Nyssa." Basil gave him his first secular instruction, while his mother and his sister Macrina were responsible for his religious education. To his sister also he owed his conversion, after which he retired to Basil's monastery, and gave himself up to the study of the Scriptures and of the writings of Origen. Basil made him Bishop of Nyssa, much against his will. He died probably in 395 A.D.

In Gregory's theosophy, God is the Self-Existent One, Infinite, Changeless, Transcendent, Eternal. God is the First Cause, to which the whole universe owes its existence, for it is impossible to contemplate anything as being quite outside the Divine Nature, since that would presuppose two Creative Principles.[3] The Godhead is Reason and Wisdom and Perfect Goodness and Truth and Love. " For," says St. Gregory, " the life of the Supreme Being is

[1] *De Spiritu Sancto*, ix. 23. [2] *Epis.* II., par. 4.
[3] *De Infantibus qui præmature abripuintur.*

Love, since the Beautiful is of necessity beloved by those who recognise it. For the Divine does recognise it and this recognition becomes love, because that which is recognised is essentially Beautiful. Presumptuous satiety cannot touch the True Beauty, and the capacity to love the Beautiful not being disturbed by satiety, the Divine Life will for ever manifest itself in Love."[1]

It was because of this superabounding love, which is the life of the Godhead, that man was created, that God might be manifested in a being who should participate in the Divine perfections. "For it was needful that the Light should not be unseen, nor the Divine Glory without witness, nor Its goodness unenjoyed, nor all the other attributes which are to be seen in the Divine Nature become inoperative, with none to share in them or profit by them. If, then, man comes into existence, for the sake of these things, in order to become a partaker of the Divine bounty, it is necessary that he should be fashioned in such a way that he may be fit to share in these good things. For as the eye, through the bright rays which by its nature are contained in it, comes into fellowship with the light, and attracts to itself, by its innate power, that which is akin to it, so it was necessary that there should be mingled in human nature something of the Divine Nature, in order that by means of this affinity it should aim at that which is proper to it."[2]

Man was therefore created to be the incarnate likeness of the Divine transcendent Power. Man was made in the image of God that like might be able to see like, and to St. Gregory to see God is the very life of the soul. The soul of man, then, though created and therefore not identical with the Creator, is possessed by nature of a godlike beauty and is, by its affinity to the Deity, of necessity attracted towards the One. "Since of all that is good, the most Beautiful and Perfect is the Godhead Itself, to which all things that desire the beautiful tend, for this reason we say also that the mind, which is made in the image of the Supremely Beautiful, so long as it partakes, as far as may be, of the likeness of the Archetype, also itself abides in beauty, but if it departs from

[1] *De Anima et Resurrectione.*

[2] *Oratio catechetica magna*, c. v.

this, it is stripped of the beauty in which it was."[1] It is when the soul recedes from that Perfect Beauty, that evil is engendered within it and takes possession of the will. "Then that godlike beauty of the soul, which was displayed in accordance with its Archetype, like iron blackened with vile rust, no longer preserves the grace of that image which belongs to it, but is transformed to the ugliness of sin."[2]

When the image has been thus disfigured, it is only by purification that the soul can be freed from its hindrances and again be drawn towards the Divine Spirit. For none can come near the purity of the Divine Being who has not first himself become such. "It is not possible for the soul to be united with the incorruptible Godhead unless it become itself, through its virginity, as pure as possible, so that, by means of that likeness, it may be able to apprehend that to which it is like, placing itself like a mirror beneath the purity of God, so that it may mould itself upon the Archetypal Beauty, by its fellowship therewith and its vision thereof."[3] Therefore the soul which seeks to gaze upon heavenly delights and to attain to union with God must turn itself aside from earth and all worldly business. The mind which "pours itself into many channels" cannot win its way to knowledge and the love of God. The heart must be disengaged from the affection of material things if it is to give itself to the contemplation of the immaterial Beauty. The beauty of natural things must be regarded as but a hand to lead us to that Divine Beauty "of whose secret the whole creation sings." In his treatise *De Virginitate* St. Gregory shows how "virginity" is to be interpreted as singleness of heart and purity of soul. "For if the right accomplishment of this holy Virginity is to make us blameless and holy, and these epithets properly and primarily are reserved for the glory of the incorruptible Godhead, what greater praise of Virginity can there be than to be shown through these things as in a manner deifying those who are partakers of its pure mysteries, so that they become sharers of the glory of the One truly Holy and Blameless God, being made akin to Him by their purity and incorruptibility?"[4] It is love

[1] *De hominis opificio*, c. xii.
[2] *De Virginitate*, c. xii.
[3] *Ibid.*, c. xi.
[4] *Ibid.*, c. v.

that will lead the soul onward to perfection, the love that is called forth by the sight of that Divine Beauty, and the soul which by purification has made itself like again unto its Archetype, will be raised above the whole universe and find that which alone is worth loving, and will itself become as beautiful as the Beauty into which it has entered, and will become radiant itself in fellowship with the true Light.[1]

So purification, the true "virginity," will end in the attainment of the goal, the power to see God and be united with Him. This is the true spiritual marriage, in which the soul cleaves to the immortal Bridegroom, and has fruition of her love for the True Wisdom, that is, God.[2] Now the soul dwells for ever with God, contemplating the Divine Beauty in unspeakable bliss. For now that the soul is made pure, even as He is pure, "there will be nothing to hinder its vision of the Beautiful: for this Beauty is able by its own nature to attract by some means everyone who looks towards it. If, therefore, the soul is cleansed from all defilement, it shall dwell wholly within the Beautiful. The Divine is Beautiful in its own Essence, and to It the soul, when purified, will be united, being joined unto its like."[3] The soul is now conformed to the Divine nature and nothing is left of itself save the love by which it cleaves unto the Beautiful. So the soul and God are become one again, that God at last, having drawn back to Himself that which He sent forth from Himself, may be All in all.

(*d*) St. Macarius of Egypt[4]

St. Macarius lived for some sixty years in the desert of Scete, and he was himself a mystic. It was related of him that "he was at all times in a state of wonder at some divine Vision, and he used to become like a drunken man by reason of some hidden vision, and his mind was more often exalted unto God than it was concerned with the things which are in this world, and those which are under the heavens."[5] He was the reputed author of certain epistles and spiritual

[1] *De Virginitate*, c. xi.
[2] *Ibid.*, c. xx.
[3] *De Anima et Resurrectione*.
[4] Born *c*. A.D. 300, died A.D. 389.
[5] *Paradise*, i. 115.

homilies, addressed to the ascetics of his time, the theme of which is the relation of God and the soul, and which contain a very complete mystical doctrine. In his view God is both transcendent and immanent: the whole of God's creation is governed by Him alone, the God Who is in all things: "If you seek God in the depth, you find Him there—if you seek in the water, there you find Him—if you seek Him in the fire, you will find Him there also. He is everywhere, both under the earth and above the heavens and within us, too."[1] Again he says: "The Godhead comprehends all creatures . . . and everywhere is fulfilled in the creation, although It is outside the creatures, because It is infinite and incomprehensible."[2]

The soul is made in the Divine likeness; in itself it is neither of the nature of the Godhead, nor of the nature of the darkness, but is "something created, with the power of thought, beautiful, great and wonderful, a fair likeness and image of God."[3] There is no tie of blood or affinity like that between the soul and God, and between God and the soul. The chief faculties of the soul are the will, the conscience, the intelligence and the power to love. By bringing these to bear, the soul can be purified, and attain to the unitive life, but only with labour and pains, and much contention. "The soul that desires to live with God in rest and eternal light," Macarius says, "must come . . . and be slain and die to the world and be rapt away into another life and to an intercourse that is divine—into the city of the Light of the Godhead."[4] The attractions of the world must be resisted, lest they tie a man down and prevent him from rising to the spiritual heights.[5] The mystic must also war against passion and the snares of earthly desires, which, unless they are conquered by his faith and love, will hinder him from obtaining eternal life and possessing, even here, the heavenly treasure which is the earnest of the kingdom. "Those who desire in truth to come to the end in good living, ought not willingly to admit any other love or affection with that Heavenly joy, lest they should be hindered from spiritual

[1] *Homilies*, xii. 10, 12.
[2] *Ibid.*, xl. 3.
[3] *Ibid.*, i. 7.
[4] *Ibid.*, i. 8.
[5] *Cf.* Clement of Alexandria, p. 51 above.

things and be turned backward and at the last should be excluded from life."[1] This Purgation must be as by fire, which burns up all the dross within the soul, that burning of the Spirit, which burns hearts into flame—but is a power bringing resurrection and immortality, which removes the beam from the eye of the soul, that it may see clearly the wonderful things of God.[2]

This idea of the cleansing power of the Divine fire is a favourite one with the mystics, and Macarius develops it further. " As iron or lead or gold or silver, being cast into the fire, are melted from the hardness which belongs to them by nature, and are changed into softness, and so long as they are in the fire, their natural hardness continues to melt and be altered on account of the vigorous heat of the fire, in like manner also the soul which, having renounced the world, is possessed by the desire for God alone, in great searching and pains and conflict of soul, maintains an unceasing watch for Him in hope and faith, and having received that celestial fire of the Godhead and of the love of the Spirit, it is then in truth freed from all love of the world and is set at liberty from all evil affections and casts all things out of itself and is changed from its own natural habit and hardness of sin and sets aside all other things for the sake of the heavenly Bridegroom alone, Whom it receives, at rest in His fervent and ineffable love."[3]

St. Macarius has much to say on the value of the prayer-life; it is perseverance in prayer that will bring a man into fellowship with God in love. This is the prayer, not of petition, but of concentration upon God in quietness and peace, free from all distracting thoughts. Through contemplative prayer the mystic is rapt into ecstasy, into the unfathomable deep of that other world: his mind is carried beyond all material things, and he becomes oblivious to the interests of the understanding, for his thoughts have been taken captive by divine and heavenly things, by the infinite and the incomprehensible, by things beyond all human power of expression. In this state of ecstasy, when the light shining in the heart discloses the inner, deeper, hidden light,

[1] *Homilies*, v. 5, 6. [2] *Ibid.*, iv. 10, xxv. 9.
[3] *Ibid.* iv. 4.

the mystic is no longer master of himself, because of the surpassing love and delight of the hidden mysteries; for that brief space the mystic is set at liberty, and comes to perfect light and sinlessness.[1] The soul, thus rapt away and inflamed by the fire of love, is granted the heavenly Vision, when the soul, with no veil between, gazes upon the heavenly Bridegroom, face to face, in unclouded Light, having communion with Him in full assurance, and thus it is made worthy of eternal life.[2]

The soul now lives the unitive life in God: the perfect Bridegroom has accepted the perfect bride, and receives her into the mystical and sanctified fellowship of marriage, an unending union.[3] Here and now the soul partakes of the Divine substance and is deified. "For when the soul reaches the perfection of the Spirit, being completely purified from passion, and is joined and commingled with the Holy Spirit by that secret communion, and being united with the Spirit is deemed worthy to become spirit itself, then it becomes all light, all eye, all spirit, all joy, all rest, all exultation, all heartfelt love, all goodness and lovingkindness. Such souls as these are strengthened within themselves by the virtues of the Spirit's power, for ever, being blameless within, and spotless and pure."[4]

So Macarius points out the Way which he had himself trodden to the mystics who came after him, seeking to lead them to newness of life, and to become partakers, while still in this world, of immortal life and glory incorruptible.

(*e*) John Cassian and the Egyptian Fathers

John Cassian, born about A.D. 360, was probably of Western origin, but he passed much of his life at Scete, and may thus be reckoned among the teachers of mysticism in Egypt. While still quite young, he forsook the world and went into a monastery at Bethlehem, and there spent several years. Thence he went to Egypt and visited the desert hermits, and remained there for seven years. Coming back for a second visit, he went to Scete and the Nitrian valley and died some

[1] *Homilies*, viii. 1, 3.
[2] *Ibid.*, x. 4.
[3] *Ibid.*, xlvii. 17.
[4] *Ibid.*, xvii. 10.

time after A.D. 432. His Institutes and Conferences deal with the ascetic life and its aim, and contain some definitely mystical teaching.

God is to him the sole Cause, nothing whatever is done in this world without Him, all good is done by His will, and evil by His permission.[1] He is also the Giver of all good and perfect gifts, including faith and patience and godly fear. The Way to attain to the end of all good life, that is, to purity of heart and the contemplation of God, is by renunciation, of all external hindrances, then of all internal hindrances, and finally of all present and visible things, for the sake of the contemplation of things to come and the desire of the invisible.[2] In vain, he says, does anyone strive for the vision of God, who does not shun the stains of sin, and therefore the beginning must be by repentance from sin. Perfect penitence, he tells us, is never again to yield to those sins for which we do penance, and the proof of satisfaction and pardon is for us to have expelled the love of them from our hearts. In true penitence, sins are forgotten, " by the obliteration of former sins and likings and by perfect and complete purity of heart."[3] Cassian sets forth the stages of progress along the Way towards perfection. The beginning of our salvation and of wisdom is the fear of the Lord. " From the fear of the Lord arises salutary compunction. From compunction of heart springs renunciation—*i.e.*, nakedness and contempt of all possessions. From nakedness is begotten humility: from humility the mortification of desires. Through mortification of desires, all faults are extirpated and decay. By driving out faults, virtues shoot up and increase. By the budding of virtues, purity of heart is gained. By purity of heart the perfection of apostolic love is acquired."[4] This is the disinterested love of God which is the mark of the true mystic, and beside which all baser motives count for nothing. " There is a great difference," Cassian observes, " between one who puts out the fire of sin within him by fear of hell or hope of future reward, and one who from the feeling of Divine love has a horror of sin itself and of uncleanness, and keeps hold of the virtue of purity and

[1] *Conf.*, iii. 20.
[2] *Ibid.*, iii. 6.
[3] *Conf.*, xx. 5, 7.
[4] *Insts.*, iv. 43.

looks for no reward from a promise for the future, but . . . does everything from delight in virtue."[1]

Prayer is one of the means towards the end, as the mystic strives to attain the goal. There must be continued and unbroken perseverance in prayer, in order to secure unmoved tranquillity of mind and perpetual purity. Pure and sincere prayer is only obtained by laying aside all anxiety about material things, and all distractions. When purification and cleansing have done their part, there must be no self-satisfaction, but only a deep humility : then the soul must concentrate its thoughts and little by little it will begin to rise to the contemplation of God and to spiritual insight.[2] The highest and most sublime form of prayer is mental prayer, the prayer of Quiet, which transcends all human thoughts and is distinguished by no utterance of words. " Sometimes the mind hides itself in complete silence within the secrets of a profound quiet, so that the amazement of a sudden illumination chokes all sound of words and the overawed spirit either keeps all its feelings to itself, or loses them and pours forth its desires to God with groanings that cannot be uttered."[3] It is thus that the true knowledge of God, which depends on no earthly learning, can be obtained. It is one thing to have a ready tongue, and quite another thing to have the power of penetrating into the very heart of the divine utterances, and to gaze with the pure eye of the soul on profound and hidden mysteries, for this comes by no human learning nor worldly state, but only by purity of soul, through the illumination of the Holy Spirit.[4] It was to obtain this ever-deepening insight into heavenly things that the solitaries entered the desert, in order that there, having attained to perfection in solitude, they might occupy themselves with divine contemplation.

Through purification the soul of the mystic has reached illumination and is fit to look upon the heavenly Vision, for the contemplation of God is granted only to those in whom nothing of carnal affections still remains. Thou canst not see My face and live, says the Lord, to this world and to earthly affections. But, for those who are purified, the end

[1] *Conf.*, xi. 8.
[2] *Ibid.*, ix. 2, 3.
[3] *Ibid.*, ix. 27.
[4] *Ibid.*, xiv. 9.

is certain. "Then," says Cassian, "we shall succeed in reaching perfection, whenever our soul is sullied by no stain of carnal coarseness, but all such having been carefully eliminated, it has been freed from every earthly quality and desire, and by constant meditation on things Divine, and spiritual contemplation, has so far passed on to things unseen, that in its earnest seeking after things above and things spiritual, it no longer feels that it is prisoned in this fragile flesh and bodily form, but is caught up into an ecstasy."[1] The mystic who looks upon that vision will enter into union with That which he sees, for he has offered a sacrifice acceptable to God, and has become fit to be a shrine of holiness in the pure and undefiled innermost chambers of his heart; for it is not the corruptible flesh, but the clean heart which becomes a shrine for God and a temple of His Holy Spirit.[2] So the mystic enters upon the Unitive life: "This will come to pass when God shall be all our love and every desire and wish and effort, every thought of ours, and all our life and words and breath, and that unity which already exists between the Father and the Son and the Son and the Father, has already been shed abroad in our hearts and minds, so that as He loves, so we also may be joined to Him by a lasting and inseparable affection, since we are so united to Him that whatever we breathe or think or speak is God."[3] This, then, to Cassian, was the destination to which all asceticism, the life of the solitary and of the monk, should lead; this should be all the aim of the seeker after God, that he should, even while in the flesh, possess an image of future bliss, and should begin in the world to have a foretaste and an earnest of the life and glory of God.

Palladius, who was contemporary with Cassian, includes a good deal of mystical teaching in his accounts of the ascetics whom he visited. He naturally lays stress on the Purgative life, beginning with the subjugation of the body, and quotes Abbā Daniel as saying, "In proportion as the body groweth, the soul becometh enfeebled; and the more the body becometh emaciated, the more the soul groweth."[4] Again he gives the words of certain of the brethren, "Fast-

[1] *Conf.*, iii. 7.
[2] *Insts.*, v. 21.
[3] *Conf.*, x. 7.
[4] *Paradise*, ii. 22.

ing and strict vigil in the fear of God, with the crucifying of the body throughout the night against the pleasures of sleep, are the foundation of the holy path of God and of all the spiritual excellences."[1] He states also that the saints of old triumphed through the fervour of their supernatural love, through the death of the corruptible man, through the promise of certainty: through the desire for these glorious things, the saints had acquired in the soul the spiritual body.[2] Again on the same theme he gives the teaching of Abbā Mār John: "He who believeth in the promises and threats, goeth hungry and he denieth himself and he watcheth in prayer, and he humbleth himself, and he layeth hold upon abstinence and restraineth himself from the gratification of his pleasures, and he inheriteth the purity which is promised to those who are blessed."[3] The true Way of life for the mystic is to go forth from this temporal world into that invisible world, and it is not possible to go forth from this world except by being remote from it. The motive which leads the mystic towards the life in God and the force which urges him on to tread the way is Love. "True and pure love is the way of life and the haven of promises and the treasure of faith, and the interpreter of the kingdom, and the herald of that which is hidden."[4] Love is therefore to be sought after by the mystic, for it is impossible to partake of the nature of God, and not to love, and love can only be fostered and kept constantly fervent and established within the soul by Prayer, and especially by the prayer of Quiet, that pure prayer which is little in words and great in deeds. By such prayer the saint keeps the remembrance of God always within his heart, but this can only be secured by complete abstraction from all thought of the earthly and the material, and concentration of the powers of the mind on spiritual things alone. Palladius gives us the teaching of the blessed Mār John, of Lycus in the Thebaïd, on Prayer and the knowledge of God to which it leads. He warns those who would pray to God in very truth against remembering anything at all of the world, "for if the man who holdeth converse with his Lord be reduced or drawn aside . . . his labour

[1] *Paradise*, ii. 308.
[2] *Ibid.*, ii. 264, 265.
[3] *Ibid.*, ii. 282.
[4] *Ibid.*, ii. 262.

is emptiness. Now this falling away happeneth to the mind of man after man who doth not deny the world absolutely . . . for his mind is divided among many kinds of thoughts, both of the body and of the earth, and thereupon he is obliged to strive against his own passions and is not able to see God. . . . It is right therefore that the mind of every man who loveth God should be remote from all these things, for he who in truth seeketh after God with all his heart will remove his mind far away from every earthly thing and he will direct the gaze of his understanding towards God."[1]

By prayer and contemplation, the mystic will attain to the knowledge of God and will be permitted to see unspeakable things and to receive the glorious revelations made to the saints. For a man is held capable of revelation to the same extent that he is capable of stripping off sin and purifying himself in body and in soul. "For when a man dieth by spiritual sacrifice, he dieth to all the words and deeds of this habitation of time, and when he hath committed his life to the life which is to be, Divine grace bestoweth itself upon him and he becometh capable of Divine revelations. For the impurity of the world is a dark covering before the face of the soul and it preventeth it from discerning spiritual wisdom."[2] Now to the mystic is granted the vision of God, and he is with Him Who cannot be seen, as if he saw Him, for when he has become constant in pure prayer, he shall be worthy to see within his heart, even as in a polished mirror, the light of the revelation of the Godhead shining upon it.[3] And when once the Vision has been granted, though it may be but briefly, it will be given again to the loving soul. "Although the mind cannot be occupied with and stay with the divine Vision continually, still when it is pressed by the thoughts it can fly to God, and it shall not be deprived of the divine Vision. But I say unto thee that if the mind be made perfect in this respect, it shall be easier for thee to move mountains than to bring it down from above. For as the blind man who is shut up in darkness, if his eyes be opened and he go forth into the light, will be unwilling for the darkness to overtake him again, so the mind having

[1] *Paradise*, i. 325.

[2] *Ibid.*, ii. 265.

[3] *Ibid.*, ii. 320.

begun to see the light of its own person, hateth the darkness and is unwilling to remember it again."[1]

As the mystic travels along the path to meet his Lord, so the Lord advances to meet him with the Divine Light, until they meet and then the mystic remains dwelling in God and God in him. Now the mystic has attained to the unitive life, for Palladius tells us that " the believing mind is a temple of God, which it is meet for a man to adorn daily and to burn incense therein, inasmuch as it is God Who dwelleth there."[2] The mystic is with God and holdeth converse with God continually, for God dwelleth in His saints and walketh in them by means of the Vision and the revelations granted to them, and so they live in union with Him, marvelling at His majesty and rejoicing continually in His love.[3]

Thus Palladius traces out the mystic Way for his readers and gives them the mystical teaching which he had heard from the lips of the mystics themselves, those who had seen the invisible God in the mirror of their hearts, who had been exalted to heaven and had stood before the Presence of God, who, because they were pure in heart, had seen God, and been made one with Him.

(*f*) St. Augustine of Hippo

St. Augustine has been called " the prince of mystics," and, while his influence upon Western mysticism has been more frequently emphasised, it was hardly less effective in regard to the development of mysticism in the Near East. He was born at Thagaste in North Africa, not far from Carthage, in A.D. 354. From his pagan father Patricius he in-

[1] *Paradise*, ii. 274. *Cf.* also Plotinus : " Suppose him to fall again from the Vision, he will call up the virtue within him and seeing himself all glorious again, he will take his upward flight once more through virtue to the Divine Mind, through the Wisdom there to the Supreme." (*Enn.*, vi. 11.)

[2] *Paradise*, i. 81. *Cf.* C. Sorley, *Expectans Exspectavi :*

" This sanctuary of my soul
Unwitting I keep white and whole
Unlatched and lit, if Thou shouldst care
To enter and to tarry there."

[3] *Paradise*, ii. 304.

herited a nature prone to passion and sensuality, from his Christian mother Monica, his strong yearning towards God. He studied at Madaura and Carthage, and for a time was attracted towards Manichæism, and then travelled to Rome and lived in Milan as a teacher of rhetoric. There he made acquaintance with academic scepticism, and also with the ideals of the Neo-Platonists, and it was by these that his mind was turned towards Catholic Christianity, as it was by the mysticism which he found in their writings that his own doctrines were so profoundly influenced. The sermons of St. Ambrose combined with the prayers of his mother to effect his conversion; he accepted Christianity as a way of life, and was baptised in A.D. 387. He was ordained five years later, and in A.D. 396 became Bishop of Hippo, where he lived a simple and ascetic life with his clergy in a community house, which he developed into a theological seminary. He lived an active life, preaching and writing continually, but at the same time he found his greatest joy in contemplation. Through his dominating personality, Hippo became the centre of the intellectual life of Western Christianity, and there he died in A.D. 430, at the age of seventy-six. In his *Confessions*, written about A.D. 400, St. Augustine gives us the clearest account of his own mystical experience and of the way of the mystic, but there is much teaching of a mystical character to be found in his other writings.

St. Augustine is a true monist; for him, God is the only Reality. Everything which was not God, to him was unreal, transient, non-existent: God alone exists. "Why do I desire," he asks himself, "that Thou shouldst come into me, who were not, unless Thou wert in me? I should not be, therefore, O my God, I should not be at all, unless Thou wert in me. Or rather, I should not be unless I were in Thee, from Whom are all things, by Whom are all things, in Whom are all things. Whither do I call Thee, since I am in Thee? or whence mayst Thou come to me? For whither shall I go beyond heaven and earth, that my God should come thence to me, Who said, "I fill heaven and earth"?[1] God is the One Invisible, from Whom, as Creator and First Cause, all things visible derive their being; He is the One Supreme,

[1] *Conf.*, i. 2.

Eternal, Unchangeable, comprehensible to none save Himself alone, possessed of Majesty sublime, Holy and the Sanctifier of all that is sanctified.[1] In his earlier days St. Augustine had held a very pantheistic conception of God. "For thus did I conceive of Thee, O Life of my life," he writes in his *Confessions*, "as vast, penetrating the whole mass of the universe through endless spaces everywhere . . . so that the earth should have Thee and the heavens have Thee, all things should have Thee and be bounded in Thee and Thou be bounded by nothing . . . I thought of Thy finite creation as being full of Thee, Infinite, and I said, 'Behold God and behold what God created, and God is good and incomparably higher than these; yet He, being good, He has created them good and behold how He surrounds and fills them.'"[2] Later, he gives a more spiritualised form to this conception. God is wholly present everywhere, as the Truth is, for the Truth is God Himself. Whatever has Reality, that is, whatever partakes of Truth, must partake of the Divine. In his *Soliloquies* we find a magnificent declaration of his conception of the nature of God. "O God, the Founder of the Universe," he prays, "help me, that, first of all, I may pray to Thee aright, and then, that I may bear myself as worthy to be heard by Thee, and finally that Thou mayst set me free: God, through Whom all things have their being, which of themselves could not exist: God Who has created out of nothing this world which all who look upon it see to be most beautiful: God through Whom the universe, though part of it be perverse, is made perfect: God, Who art loved, whether consciously or unconsciously, by every creature with the capacity to love . . . God, in Whom are all things: God Who dost not will that any save the pure should know the truth: God, Father of Truth, Father of Wisdom, Father of the True and Highest Life, Father of Blessedness, Father of the Good and Beautiful, Father of Intelligible Light, Father of our awakening and enlightening, Father of that pledge of love by which we are admonished to return to Thee!

"Thee do I invoke, God the Truth, in Whom and by Whom and through Whom are all things true which are

[1] *Ep.* CCXXXII., *Madaurensibus*.
[2] *Conf.*, vii. 1.

true: God, the Wisdom in Whom and by Whom and through Whom are all wise who are wise: God, the true and perfect Life, in Whom and by Whom and through Whom live those who truly and perfectly do live: God, the Source of Blessedness, in Whom and by Whom and through Whom are all blessed, who are blessed: God, the Good and the Beautiful, in Whom and by Whom and through Whom are all things good and beautiful, which are so: God, Intelligible Light, in Whom and by Whom all shine intelligibly who do so shine: God, Whose kingdom is the whole universe unknown to sense: God, to turn away from Whom, is to fall: to turn towards Whom, is to rise; to abide in Whom, is to stand: God, Whom no one loses, unless led astray; Whom no one seeks, unless admonished thereto; Whom no one finds unless he is purified: God, from Whom to be separated is to perish; Whom to incline towards is to love; Whom to see is to possess: God, to Whom Faith urges, Hope raises us, Love unites us: God, by Whom we are stripped of that which is not, and clothed upon with that which is. O Thou, the one true Eternal Substance, where there is no discord, no confusion, no change, no lack, no death: where all is concord, all illumination, all subsistence, all abundance, all life. Hear me, after that manner of Thine, known but to the few."[1]

So, to St. Augustine, God is Goodness, Beauty, Truth, Life and Love. From his earliest days, he confesses, he had longed for the truth in the innermost recesses of his heart: "I hungered and thirsted after Thee Thyself, the Truth," and in the *Confessions* he tells how he had attained to what he sought and therein found rest for his soul, for the home of God is in the soul, which was made for Him. "God is not only the Creator, but the Country of the soul." It is in the rational, human soul that we find that image of the Creator "which is immortally planted in its immortality." The human soul is never otherwise than rational and intelligent, and since it is made in the image of God in this respect, that it is able by means of reason and intellect to understand and look upon God, then from the moment when this great and wonderful nature began to be, whether the image be so

[1] *Solil.*, i. 2, 3.

faint as to be almost non-existent, or whether it be darkened and defaced, or clear and beautiful, certainly it always exists.[1] St. Augustine is perpetually conscious of this kinship between the soul and God. "Now," he says to his own soul, "thou art my better part, since thou dost quicken the mass of thy body, giving it life, which no (mere) body can do for a body. But thy God is even the Life of thy life."[2] Again he says, addressing his Lord, "Thou my Love, Thou art the Life of souls, the Life of lives, having life in Thyself . . . and Thou dost not change, Thou Life of my soul. Thou art more inward than my inmost part, and higher than my highest."[3] There is some evidence that St. Augustine accepted the Platonic idea of Recollection, that souls in this life are conscious, however dimly, of a state of pre-existence, in which they lived the life of beatitude with God, and it is this sense of recollection which leads them to seek to return once more to that state of blessedness. "How then do I seek Thee, O Lord?" St. Augustine asks. "For when I seek Thee, my God, I seek the blessed life. I will seek Thee, that my soul may live. For my body lives by means of my soul, and my soul by means of Thee. How therefore shall I seek the blessed life, because it is not mine, until I can say, 'It is enough,' where I ought to say it? How do I seek it? Is it by remembrance, as if, having forgotten it, yet I realise that I have forgotten it? Or by seeking to learn it as a thing unknown, whether as something I have never known, or as something so forgotten that I do not remember that I have forgotten it? For is not the blessed life that which all desire, and there is none who does not desire it? Where have they known it, that they so desire it? Where did they see it, that they love it? Assuredly we have it, but I know not how."[4]

Therefore the human soul yearns for that blissful state again, and this earthly life should be spent in the quest for that blessed life. St. Augustine urges men to follow the quest and to tread in the mystic Way which leads to Eternal Life, the Way to which Christ, the Word by Whom God manifested Himself, has pointed us. "For He did not linger, but hastened away, crying out by His words and deeds, His

[1] *De Trinitate*, xiv. 46.
[2] *Conf.*, x. 6.
[3] *Ibid.*, iii. 6.
[4] *Ibid.*, x. 20.

death and life, His descent and ascension, crying out to us to return to Him. And He vanished from our eyes, that we should return unto our own heart and find Him there. For He went away, and behold He is here. He willed not to be long with us, and yet He did not leave us. For He went thither, whence He had never departed, because the world was made by Him. Nay, but since Life has descended, will ye not ascend and live? Descend, that ye may ascend and ascend to God."[1]

In its journey along the Way the soul has not to depend on its own strength, for it is from God that it derived that nature, whereby it is made in His image, that reason, whereby it knows Him, and that grace, whereby it is blessed in being united to Him, for union is the end of the quest. Reason will not help the soul on its way, it cannot take the place of faith, the gift of grace, for faith includes love, and without this the stubborn will of man will never surrender itself to God, and the consecration of the will is essential before the journey Godwards can begin; "not only to journey, but also to arrive there, is nothing else than to will to go, but to will vigorously, and wholeheartedly, not to turn and toss this way and that, a will maimed and struggling, one part rising and the other falling."[2] When the soul has turned to God, then it must be purified, and so be made fit to perceive the Divine Light and to rest in it when it is perceived. This process of purification is to be regarded as a kind of journey or voyage to the soul's native land. For it is not by a change of place that the soul can come near to Him Who is present everywhere, but by means of pure desires and virtuous habits.[3] St. Augustine has left us a beautiful prayer for the purity which means freedom from the desire of all save God. "Thee do I seek after, and by whatsoever means Thou mayst be sought these I ask from Thee! If I desire nothing beside Thyself, I beseech Thee, that I may find Thee now, but if there is in me a desire for something beside Thyself, do Thou purify me and make me worthy to look upon Thee! This I do beseech of Thee, that Thou convert me wholly to Thyself, let nothing hinder

[1] *Conf.*, iv. 12. [2] *Ibid.*, viii. 4.
[3] *De Doctrina Christiana*, I. ix. 10.

me from reaching unto Thee, and grant that I may be pure and high-souled, just and wise, a perfect lover, apprehending Thy wisdom, and worthy to dwell in Thy most blessed Kingdom!"[1] Only when the seeker is pure from every fleshly taint and purged from the desire of mortal things, will the eyes of the soul be fit to look upon the Divine mysteries, and when this fitness is attained, the first stage of the Way is past. Yet though able to look, the soul needs faith, hope and love, before it can apprehend, and of these love is that which will lead it on to know God when it sees Him. "Too late have I loved Thee, Beauty so old and yet so new," Augustine cries out in bitter remorse for wasted years apart from God, "too late I have loved Thee," but when that love at last took possession of his soul, it consumed all desire for the lesser beauties of earth and kindled within him a passionate longing to look upon and apprehend the "Beauty of all things beautiful," the Divine Loveliness Itself.

Of that Vision he had talked with Monica, his mother, before her death, and he tells us, "We were saying then: 'If to anyone were hushed the tumult of the flesh, hushed the images of earth and the waters and the air, hushed the heavens, and if the soul were hushed unto itself and were to pass beyond itself by cessation of the thought of self, if hushed were dreams and images, if every tongue and every sign and all that is subject to change were hushed . . . and He Himself by Himself should speak, not by them, but by Himself, so that we should hear His Word . . . Himself, Whom in these we love, if we should hear Him without these, as if now we strove and in the flight of thought we attained to the Eternal Wisdom that broods over all things, if this were sustained, and other visions far inferior were withdrawn, and this alone should ravish and absorb and enwrap the one beholding it, in spiritual joys, so that eternal life might be such as was this moment of apprehension for which we sighed . . . were not this an 'Enter thou into the joy of thy Lord'?"[2] That mystic experience for which he longed was granted to his soul when, as he tells us, "with the flash of a trembling glance, it arrived at That

[1] *Solil.*, i. 6.

[2] *Conf.*, ix. 10.

Which Is," when he entered into the inner sanctuary of his soul, and beheld with the eye of his soul, above that same eye of the soul and above the mind, the Light Unchangeable. Whoso knows the Truth, he says, knows that Light, and he who knows It, knows Eternity: Love knows It.[1] "I awoke in Thee," he writes, "and found Thee infinite, yet otherwise than I had thought, and this vision came not from the flesh. . . . And I was amazed, because now I loved Thee, and no phantom instead of Thee, and I was rapt away unto Thee by Thy Beauty. . . . Thou didst beat back the weakness of my sight, shining radiantly upon me, and I trembled with love and awe, and I heard, as it were, Thy voice from on high: 'I am the food of the full-grown: grow and thou shalt feed on Me. Nor shalt thou transmute Me into thyself, as the food of thy mortal body, but thou shalt be transmuted into Me!'"[2] So vision passes into union, and the soul becomes one with That which it beholds. Henceforward it lives the life in God, a life which is the true life indeed. No longer is the carnal body an encumbrance to the soul, by corruptibility, but it too is now become spiritual, perfected, and entirely subject to the will, which is merged now in the Eternal Will.[3] The soul, made one with the Divine, is deified, for it is a partaker of God, become godlike by participation in Him. "Then shall we know this thing perfectly, and we shall perfectly rest and shall perfectly see. There we shall rest and see, we shall see and love, we shall love and praise. Behold what shall be in the end without end! For what other thing is our end, but to come to that Kingdom of which there is no end?"[4]

After this manner St. Augustine showed the Way which he himself had followed, to those who came after, and told them of the joy awaiting those who followed it to the end, but he was no mere visionary, advocating solitude and contemplation to the neglect of the duties of common life. Most men, he knew, must live an ordinary human life in the world, but this could be, and should be, brought into relation with the heavenly life, "quod ita nos vivere oportere censemus in hac vita mortali, ut vitæ immortali quodammodo co-

[1] *Conf.*, vii., 10.
[2] *Ibid.*, vii. 14, 17, 10.
[3] *De Civitate Dei*, XIX., xvii.
[4] *Ibid.*, XXII. xxx.

aptemur."[1] Man must live for God, but also for his neighbour; no one should be so given to contemplation as to neglect the good of his fellow-man, nor, on the other hand, so concerned with active affairs as not to seek after the contemplation of God. Contemplation aims not at idleness, but at truth; it is to benefit the one who contemplates by the knowledge which he gains thereby, but he must be ready to impart of his spiritual riches to others. It is by fellowship that men will attain to the fruition of God and of one another in God. So St. Augustine, like the other great mystics and contemplatives, advocates the universal life lived Godwards and manwards; that which has been given in such full measure to the mystic who has attained, must be shared with others. The soul which has partaken of the Divine Life, must, and will, live a fuller, richer life in contact with other human lives. St. Augustine would have agreed with Plato that the perfect life "is a life of perfect communion with other souls, as well as with the Soul which animates the universe."

(*g*) Dionysius the Areopagite

A mystical writer who had a far-reaching influence on the development of mysticism in both East and West was Dionysius, the pseudo-Areopagite. He was probably a monk of Syria and a pupil of the heretical Stephen Bar Sudayli. He seems to have written about the end of the fifth or beginning of the sixth century. Dionysius develops a mystical theosophy based on Hellenistic sources in the main, though he also makes use of Jewish ideas, and the whole is adapted to form a highly developed system of Christian mysticism.

His conception of the nature of the Godhead is derived from the Neo-Platonic Monad. The Absolute is conceived of as Super-Essence, and therefore Supra-Personal; He is the Ultimate, Undifferentiated Unity, sublimely Transcendent, the Divine Source and Cause of all things. In Him all Goodness and all Beauty meet; He is Fair and Wise, the Eternal Beloved; He is Mind and Word and Power; in Him Salvation and Righteousness and Sanctification are to be

[1] *Epis.* XCV., *Paulino et Therasiæ*, 2.

found. He is the Essential Radiance, illuminating unto contemplation; He is Sun and Morning Star; He is Fire and Wind and the Water of Life; He is Spirit, Dew and Cloud, as He is also the Rock of Ages.[1] This Universal Cause, says Dionysius, "is neither affirmation nor negation, since It transcends all affirmation, by being the perfect and unique Cause of all things, and transcends all negation, by the pre-eminence of its simple and absolute nature . . . free from every limitation and beyond them all."[2]

This Ultimate Godhead is One and Perfect, and in its simple and undifferentiated Unity is beyond all limitation, and is not contained or comprehended in anything, but in order to be manifested It must overflow into multiplicity, and therefore It has issued forth into the world of Beings, and has penetrated all things in Its unceasing activities. The sublimely Transcendent in Its manifestation therefore becomes immanent, and there is nothing in the world "without some participation in the One, the Which in Its all-embracing Unity contains beforehand all things."[3] There is, then, a relation between the Absolute Godhead and the world of Being, for the former exists both as Ultimate Reality and as Manifested Appearance. God, in His activity, is the Manifestation of the Godhead, to Whom is due Creation and Revelation, and the Trinity is the eternally Manifested Godhead. All existent things form part of the Divine Life and Love, which is always purifying, enlightening and making perfect, and so for ever draws all back to Itself, the Source. "That Good which is above all light is called a Spiritual Light, because it is an Originating Beam and an Overflowing Radiance, illuminating with its fullness every Mind above the world around it or within it, and renewing all their spiritual powers."[4] Again Dionysius writes, "Goodness draweth all things to Itself and is the great Attractive Power which unites things that are sundered—unto the Good all things are turned—and after the Good all things do yearn."[5] This Good, which is also the All-beautiful, is the Goal of all things, and their Beloved, for all things do and must desire the Beautiful and the Good.

[1] *Divine Names*, Sect. vi. [2] *Mystical Theology*, v. (tr. C. E. Rolt).
[3] *Divine Names*, xiii. 2. [4] *Ibid.*, vi. [5] *Ibid.*, iv.

The soul of man is potentially divine, and therefore it is the image of God that is defiled by sin, but by purification it can once again shew its true nature. It is by the Via Negativa that the soul must render itself fit to return to its home in God. In the intent practice of mystic contemplation, it must leave behind the senses and the activities of the intellect, and all things that the senses or the intellect can perceive, and all things which are, and, with all the human powers quiescent, strive upwards towards union with Him Who is above all being and knowledge. So by unceasing and absolute renunciation of itself and all things, the soul will be borne upwards to the Ray of the divine Darkness, which is beyond all being. Unto this Darkness which is beyond Light, the mystic must seek to come, and through loss of sight and knowledge, pass beyond to the vision of That which transcends sight and knowledge.[1] This Divine Darkness is in truth the unapproachable Light in which God is said to dwell, and into it must all enter who would see and know Him. To those who have entered into that Holy of Holies, for whom the veil has been lifted, that they may look upon God face to face, is given the joy of abiding union with the Beloved. "They who are free and untrammelled enter into the true Mystical Darkness of Unknowing, whence all perception of understanding is excluded, and abide in that which is intangible and invisible, being wholly absorbed in Him Who is beyond all, and are united in their higher part to Him Who is wholly unknowable and Whom, by understanding nothing, they understand above all intelligence."[2] Perfect union implies deification, and Dionysius does not hesitate to use the word. "God deigned Himself to come to us with outstretched arms . . . and by union with Him, to assimilate, like as by fire, things that have been made one, in proportion to their aptitude for deification."[3] He says much the same thing elsewhere: "God bestows Deification itself by giving a faculty for it unto those that are deified," and again, "with understanding power He gives Himself for the Deification of those that turn to Him."[4]

[1] *Mystical Theology*, I., II.
[2] *Ibid.*, i. 3.
[3] *Eccles. Hierarchy*, p. 76.
[4] *Divine Names*, vii. 5, ix. 5.

Dionysius marks out clearly, in *The Heavenly Hierarchy* and *The Ecclesiastical Hierarchy*, the three stages of the mystic Way, through Purgation and Illumination to Perfection, the Unitive Life. Referring to the Illuminative Life, he says: " Every procession of illuminating light, proceeding from the Father, whilst visiting us as a gift of goodness, restores us again gradually as a unifying power and turns us to the oneness of our conducting Father and to a deifying simplicity."[1] Of the third stage, which is the aim of the mystic's striving, he says: " The purpose, then, of Hierarchy is the assimilation and union, as far as attainable, with God—by perfecting its own followers as Divine images, mirrors most luminous and without flaw, receptive of the primal light and the supremely Divine ray, and devoutly filled with the entrusted radiance, and again spreading this radiance ungrudgingly to those after it."[2]

Dionysius makes much of the imagery of fire, which he describes as passing through all things, unmingled, invincible, subduing all things to itself, unchangeable, penetrating, and therefore it has the qualities which fit it to be the image of the super-essential Divine Energy.[3]

The writings of Dionysius, through translations as well as in their original language, became widely known in both East and West, and formed the basis for much later mystical teaching. His debt to Plotinus and the Neo-Platonists is obvious in his conception of Ultimate Reality as the One, the Good, and the Beautiful, and also in his teaching on the ascent of the soul back to its divine Source. His teaching includes the idea of a mystic gnosis, beyond all human intelligence, which is the direct gift of God to those who seek Him in purity and all sincerity. His image of the Divine Darkness, the Cloud of Unknowing, became a favourite concept with later mystical writers, as representing the Veil, which to the true mystic revealed itself as being in reality only excess of Light, the Light Unapproachable. He taught to all who came after him the truth that God is All in All,

[1] *The Heavenly Hierarchy*, p. 1 (Parker's edition).

[2] *Ibid.*, p. 14.

[3] *Ibid.*, p. 56. For the use of Fire imagery by the mystics, *cf.* E. Underhill's *Mysticism*, pp. 500 *ff.*

but that His Essence is Love, and that the Divine Love is forever drawing back again to Itself those souls which are, indeed, a part of itself, sharers in the divine nature, which have for a brief while been parted from their Source, but must again return, to become one with Eternal Beauty and Eternal Love.

CHAPTER V

EARLY MYSTICISM IN THE MIDDLE EAST

The mystical writers whose teaching was considered in the last chapter wrote for the most part in Greek, for the members of the Greek-speaking Christian Church, but we find a similar development of mysticism and mystical doctrine in the Syriac-speaking Churches of the Middle East.

(*a*) Aphraates the Monk and Ephraim the Syrian

Aphraates the monk, whose ascetical teaching has been referred to above,[1] who was writing in the first half of the fourth century, has left us a little mystical teaching, in which he makes plain his faith that by a process of purification, to be attained by the most rigid asceticism, the seeker might become fit to look upon the Vision of God and to become the dwelling-place of the Holy Spirit. "Let us now awake from our sleep," he writes, "and lift up both our hearts and hands to God towards heaven ; lest suddenly the Lord of the house come. Let us make ready provision for our abiding-place, for the way that is narrow and strait. And let us be constant in prayer, that we may pass by the place where fear dwells. Let us cleanse our heart from iniquity, that we may see the Lofty One in His Honour. Let us be strangers to the world, even as Christ was not of it. Let us be unflagging in His service, that He may cause us to serve in the abode of the saints. Let us pray His prayer in purity, that it may have access to the Lord of Majesty. For fearful is the day in which He will come, and who is able to endure it ? Furious and hot is His wrath, and it will destroy all the wicked. Let us be poor in the world, and let us enrich many by the doctrine of our Lord. But let us forsake the world which is not ours that we may arrive at the place to which we have been invited. Let us raise up our eyes on high, that

[1] See pp. 27 *ff.*, 44, 45.

we may see the Splendour which shall be revealed. Whosoever loves fields and merchandise shall be shut out of the city of the Saints. Whosoever takes upon him the yoke of the saints, let him remove from him getting and spending. Whosoever desires to gain himself, let him remove from him the gain of the world. Whosoever cleanses his heart from deceits, his eyes shall behold the King in His Beauty. Whosoever is called the temple of God, let him purify his body from all uncleanness."[1] The " children of the Good " are those who have so purified themselves that they become the temple of God and live the life of union with Him. Though He be One, yet is He the One in all. " Every man," says Aphraates, " knows that the sun is fixed in the heavens, yet its rays are spread out in the earth and light from it enters by many doors and windows, and wherever the sunshine falls, it is called the sun. And though it fall in many places, it is thus called, but the real sun itself is in Heaven. Also the water of the sea is vast, and when thou takest one cup from it, that is called water. And though thou shouldest divide it into a thousand vessels, yet it is called water by its name. Thus also God, though He is One, yet dwells in many, and is diminished in nothing when He dwells in many ; as the sun is not a whit diminished in heaven, when its power is poured out in the earth. How much greater then is the power of God, since by the power of God the very sun itself subsists !"[2] So Aphraates teaches that God does in very truth dwell in the soul that is pure enough to be His shrine, and henceforth the mystic lives in and through God.

Among the chief of these mystical teachers of the Syriac-speaking Church was Ephraim the Syrian, already mentioned,[3] who spent the last years of his life at Edessa, living there the life of a solitary, devoted to asceticism and contemplation, and he was, perhaps, the most influential of all the Syriac writers.

He conceives of God as the One Reality, Who is infinitely beyond all that the finite mind of man can picture. " Praise to the One Being," he writes, " that is to us unsearchable ! His aspect cannot be discerned, that it should be portrayed

[1] *Of Monks*, par. 1. [2] *Ibid.*, par. 11.

[3] See pp. 29, 30.

by our understanding. He hears without ears; He speaks without mouth; He works without hands, and He sees without eyes; our soul ceases not nor desists, in Him Who is such."[1] Since to Ephraim God is the One Being, Source of all being, his conception of God is pantheistic. God is the Only Reality, the Hidden, Infinite Being, the Divine Essence, Beauty and Light, yet though He is transcendent, an unknowable, incomprehensible Entity, He is also immanent. "In His Majesty dwell powers, natures and Angels, and everything plungeth into it and welleth forth in it and yet is unable to search Him out. On one Breath all depend; It beareth all without weariness; in His fulness they all dwell, and as in an empty space they abide. He is too great to be hidden in anything. Lo! He is covered, though not hidden, for with Himself He veileth Himself. For He is near us and far off; though He is in us, He is not; and though the creation is in Him, it is as though it were not in Him; though no one is able to veil himself in Him, yet He covereth him in Himself."[2] The Absolute Godhead has been manifested forth in His Creation, but chiefly by the Incarnate Word. In one of his hymns Ephraim writes:

"Glory to the Silence that spake by His (the First-Born's) voice,
Glory to the One on high, Who was seen by His Day-spring,
Glory to the Spiritual, to the Hidden One, to that Living One,
Glory to that Hidden One, Who even with the Mind cannot be felt at all by them that pry into Him; but by His graciousness was felt by the hand of men."[3]

Man is made in the image of God and is meant to be His dwelling-place. "Blessed is He that sealed our soul," says Ephraim, "and adorned it and espoused it to Himself. Blessed He Who made our body a tabernacle for His unseen Nature. Glory to the Beautiful, Who conformed us to His image! Glory to Him, Who sowed His light in the dark-

[1] *Nisibene Hymns*, No. III., 2.
[2] *Adv. Scrutatores*, Rhythm V., 5, 6 (tr. J. B. Morris).
[3] *On the Nativity*, Rhythm II.

ness. Glory be to Him on high, Who mixed His salt in our minds, His leaven in our souls."[1] There is therefore a close and loving relationship between God and the soul, and to those who seek Him out with earnest striving and adoring love, He will reveal Himself; for He is not hard to approach in His high places, that He cannot be tracked out: to His true servants He is easy to find, and visible, while withdrawn and hidden from His creatures generally.[2] He is outside of, pre-eminent above, all things, and yet He is within everything. He has clothed Himself in all forms that we may behold Him, and He has clad Himself also in all voices that He may have intercourse with us.

By penitence, self-discipline and purification, the soul can find the Way to God. "Seek thou not here repose," Ephraim admonishes the seeker after God, "for this is a world of toil. And if thou canst wisely discern, change thou not time for time, that which abides for that which abides not, that which ceases not for that which ceases, nor truth for lying, nor body for shadow, nor watching for slumber, nor that which is in season for that which is out of season, nor the Time for the times. Collect thy mind, let it not wander among vanities which profit not.

"No one in creation is rich, but he that fears God; no one is truly poor, but he that lacks the truth. Flee and live in poverty; as a mother she pities her beloved. Seek thou refuge in indigence, who nourishes her children with choice things; her yoke is light and pleasant, and sweet to palate, her memory. The sick in conscience alone abhors the draught of poverty; the faint-hearted dreads the yoke of indigence that is honourable. Be not thou, through desires, needy and looking to others. Sufficient for thee is thy daily bread, that comes of the sweat of thy face. Praise and give thanks when thou art satisfied, that therein thou provoke not the Giver to anger. In purity strengthen thyself, that thou mayest gain from it profit."[3] Only by purification, that which is symbolised by the water of baptism, and by self-stripping, can the pearl of great price be obtained, and

[1] *On the Nativity*, Rhythm II.

[2] *Contra Scrutatores*, Rhythm I., 16.

[3] *On Admonition and Repentance*, pp. 20, 21.

Ephraim uses the image of the pearl and the diver, which became a favourite with both Christian and Muslim mystics. "The diver brings up, out of the sea, the pearl . . . bring up from the water, the purity that therein is hidden . . . the pearl that is set as a jewel, in the crown of the Godhead. . . . O gift that camest up without price with the diver! Thou laidest hold upon this visible light, that without price rises for the children of men, a parable of the hidden One, that without price gives the hidden Dayspring! Men stripped their clothes off and dived and drew thee out, O pearl! It was not kings that put thee before men, but those naked ones who were a type of the poor, and the fishers and the Galileans. For clothed bodies were not able to come to thee; they came that were stript as children."[1] By such self-stripping, purification is achieved, and Ephraim compares the soul to a mirror, a simile which was also used frequently afterwards by the Muslim mystics. "Herein is a mirror to be blamed," he says, "if its clearness is darkened, because there are spots on its substance; for the foulness that is on it becomes a covering before them that look on it. If our mirror be darkness, it is altogether joy to the hateful; because their blemishes are not reproved; but if polished and shining, it is our freedom that is adorned. Blessed be He Who polished our mirror!"[2] He writes elsewhere of the soul that is fit to look upon God, and to reflect His image in itself, "Thy mirror is clear and all of it turneth towards Thee. Thy brightness inciteth the filthy to cleanse themselves thereon, since no impurity can be joined unto Thee, unless it hath wiped from it its stains."[3]

The mystic's preoccupation along the Way must be vigils and prayer, the prayer of Quiet, in which the mind gathers itself up that it may not wander. "A virgin of the bride-chamber" is this mental prayer, and like a virgin it should not wander beyond the door of the mouth, for Truth is its chamber and Love its crown, while stillness and silence are as the watchers at the gate.[4] In prayer, Love and sincere

[1] *Hymn for the Epiphany*, vii. 18; *On the Faith*, v. 1, 3.
[2] *Nisibene Hymns*, xvi. 1, 4.
[3] *Adv. Scrut.*, xii. 5.
[4] *Ibid.*, xx. 2.

faith join together, as wings that cannot be separated, for Truth cannot fly without Love, nor Love ascend without Truth. To the one who thus communes in prayer with God and has this intercourse in love with Him, the Way reveals itself, and the very gates of Heaven are opened, and there is none to hinder the soul from entering therein.

But the kingdom of God in truth is found within the soul, when its eyes are opened to see and know. " His kingdom," writes Ephraim, " dwelleth in thee ; lo ! the riches of heaven are within thy soul, if thou be willing ! Enter in, leaving the wandering of pleasures and the corruption of lusts, the errors of the love of money, and the business that harmeth thee. Enter thou in and dwell in thine own self in the cleared ground of thine own mind and seek there the Kingdom. Enter thou in and dwell within thine heart, for lo ! there is God ; for it is not He that goeth forth from Thee, but thou that goest forth from Him."[1] Now can the soul look upon God as He is, for the darkness that was formerly upon the mind and veiled it from Him departs, and the soul beholds Him in His Beauty. With the eye of the soul, the mystic sees the Vision of God, revealed by the radiance of the Divine Light. " Praise thou the hidden light by means of the gleaming from Him: hard is it for the eye of the soul to look at the secret Light. By means of the shining from Him it is able to go to meet Him. He sent forth a brightness from Himself to them that sit in darkness. He turned away their eyes from the beauty of worthless things to the Beauty of God Himself."[2] By that Vision the soul is flooded with the Divine Radiance and by its means the soul goes up to Heaven, that " in one love " it may be mingled with the God it loves, and so pass into the unitive life. " Let each one of us, then," says Ephraim, " be a dwelling-place for Him Who loves us. Let us come unto Him and make our abode with Him. This is the Godhead Whom, though all the creation cannot contain, yet a lowly and humble soul suffices to receive Him."[3] Now is the soul deified, made one with God as God is one with it. " The Lord is blended with His creatures far and near, lo ! they

[1] *Adv. Scrut.*, 4, note c. [2] *Ibid.*, v. 9.
[3] *Hom. on Our Lord*, p. 57.

seek Him and He is carrying them. Everything is in Him and He is also in them all. He is the Life of our soul which dwelleth in us."[1]

On this wise, Ephraim the Syrian, one of the earliest of Christian mystics, led his disciples along the mystic Way, which he himself had trodden, through purification, by love and prayer, to the goal, the Vision of the Divine Beauty, and the life lived henceforth in God.

(*b*) John of Lycopolis

A writer who may be fittingly included among the mystical teachers of the Syriac-speaking community is John of Lycopolis,[2] already mentioned as one of the Egyptian fathers.[3] Though he lived in the Thebaïd and wrote in Greek, his works have come down to us only in Syriac translations, and since these have survived, while the Greek originals have been lost, it is evident that his influence was at least as great in the Syriac branch of the Church as in his own immediate sphere. In his treatise on *The Spiritual State of the Soul*,[4] he lays great stress on the ascetic preparation of the soul that seeks perfection. The fear of the Lord is the beginning of the Way; it stands as guardian at the door of the senses, that the soul's enemies may not enter in and make it forget God, and become unfit to be His dwelling-place.[5] Fasting must be not only of the body, from food for the body, but of the soul, from all corrupt affections and impure desires which dwell in it secretly.[6] Then, the soul begins to hunger for those things which are above the bodily senses, and being freed from the attractions of this world, seeks only to serve the Lord of Divine love. Now it is at rest, no longer troubled by conflicting thoughts, but concentrating all its power or thought on God, as it did when in its primitive state of purity.[7] It is cleansed of earthly affections and passions and is filled with the passion for God alone, and in this it rejoices as if it were already in the kingdom of God.

[1] *Adv. Scrut.*, lxx. 4, xix. 1.
[2] Ob. *c.* A.D. 394.
[3] See above, pp. 69, 70.
[4] *Cod. Sachau*, 203. Ed. A. Wensinck.
[5] *Ibid.*, sect. i., fol. 111*b*.
[6] *Ibid.*, xiv., fol. 115*a*.
[7] *Ibid.*, xvi., xvii., fol. 115*a*.

The soul has passed by the Purgative way and is now walking in the light. " As one who is sound in sight disports himself in the rays of the sun and no darkness comes upon his perfect sight, so also the soul, when it becomes sound and pure and attains to the pure sight which it had before it transgressed the commandment, then verily stands in that primitive and unspeakable purity which it had at the first. It is fearful lest it should fall ; it rejoices again in seeing what it has attained to by the help of Our Lord." The soul has now reached that state in which it is fit to look upon the Vision of God. It has been purified from human passions, and so made serene, as it once was, and now it beholds and experiences unspeakable things, while no passion arising from this world can hurt or disturb it, as it gazes in tranquillity upon the perfect serenity of Him before Whom it stands, and as it gazes upon God, the soul, in utter humility before that perfect Holiness, bows its head and weeps.[1] John describes the Vision thus, and it is evident that he describes what he himself has experienced : " When the soul is purified and made serene, and the knowledge of Christ the Lord dawns upon it, its mind ascends and beholds the Majesty of God, and sees Him to be Incomprehensible and Infinite. When it looks on high, it sees Him as at first, and when it looks within itself, it sees Him there. When the mind floats on the sea of the Majesty of God and His incomprehensibility, it is amazed and lost in wonder at the serene Majesty of God. And forthwith the soul becomes humble, so that if it were possible, when the effulgence of God's Majesty envelops it, it would take its place below the whole creation, because of its awe and wondering amazement at the Majesty of God, ineffable, incomprehensible as it is, beyond the penetration and seeking out of His servants."[2] The sight of God and the contemplation of the spiritual mysteries is the food of the soul, which sustains it and causes it to rejoice, as the material food sustains and rejoices the body.

The soul now lives the unitive life, abiding in God, in spiritual purity and serenity, even as a child rests in its

[1] *Cod. Sachau*, iv., fol. 112*a* ; xix., fol. 115*a*.
[2] *Ibid.*, vi., fol. 112*b*.

mother's bosom and rejoices with tears in the fervour of its love towards her. So the soul, too, in the ardour of its exceeding love towards Him and from the sweetness of rejoicing which it experiences in beholding its Bridegroom Christ, rejoices and weeps, and renounces this visible world and all that it contains. It renounces even itself, if only it be not deprived of the love of its heavenly Spouse.[1] Now the soul and God are bound together in closest union, for the soul has been absorbed and taken captive by Divine Love, and has renounced all that was its own, both external possessions and the inner possessions of its will and feeling, and it knows nothing now save His love. " For just as when the sun rises above the horizon, the shroud of darkness vanishes from the face of the earth, so that it reveals itself in all its beauty, so likewise when the love of Christ shines forth in the soul, and the veil of the former man is taken away, the hidden things which were not seen by it before become visible. As, when iron is placed in the fire, and the fire passes into it and becomes one substance with it, the iron partakes of the fire, and assumes its likeness and colour, and no longer appears as it formerly did, but takes on the aspect of the fire, because it has become absorbed in the fire and the fire in it, and so they have become one,[2] so when the love of Christ comes into the soul as a living fire which consumes the weeds of sin from the soul, it becomes one substance with Him and He with it. That which was old has become new, and that which was dead is now alive, and from the likeness of its own nature, it is changed into the likeness of God. Now everything which it sees appears to it as the likeness of God, for it is granted to the creatures to see the works of God spiritually, and it is absorbed in its love for all men. For if it were possible, it would perish itself, that

[1] *Cod. Sachau*, xi., fol. 114*a*.

[2] This simile of the iron and the fire was a favourite one with the mystics. *Cf.* above Macarius, p. 64; also St. Bernard on *The Love of God*, p. 45, and Richard of St. Victor: " When the soul is plunged in the fire of Divine love, like iron, it first loses its blackness, and then growing to white heat, it becomes like unto the fire itself. And lastly it grows liquid, and losing its nature is transmuted into an utterly different quality of being."

all might live, thereby becoming like to God, Whose life is immortal, not like the life of men."[1]

John sums up his own teaching in this little mystical treatise. "The gist of my words," he says, "is this: that everything which is of this world is opposed to that which belongs to the Way of Christ. . . . As long as the mind is a captive to, and dominated by, the things of this world, whether they be great or small, so long will the light of the truth of the Way of Christ be hidden from it. . . . When the creature is reborn from the material world into the spiritual world, it begins to see with the spiritual eye, while it increases in spiritual knowledge, according to its degree of purity and holiness."[2] John laments his own neglect of God, of intercourse with Him and contemplation of Him, for the sake of intercourse with men, to whom he had given his love instead of to God his Father, and he concludes by saying: "Now I, who am weak, admonish everyone who seeks to become the disciple of Christ, that he be not in bondage to anything of this world, whether it be manifest or secret, nor care for anything, except to be pleasing to God.

"But this I will say, that if a man does not, as far as is possible, keep his soul apart from the world, and renounce all that is in the world, both manifest and hidden, he cannot attain to the perfection of Christ Our Lord, to Whom be glory, and on us His mercy, for ever and ever. Amen."[3]

John's chief emphasis, therefore, is on asceticism, and especially on renunciation of the world, and the embracing of the solitary life, as the way to perfection for the soul. But to the soul that has trodden the Way unflinchingly, the end is assured, the Vision Blest will be granted to it, and it will have the joy of experiencing the life lived in conscious union with its Lord. John's mysticism, we note, is Christocentric, it is the "light of Christ" which dawns in the soul, the "love of Christ" which cleanses it from sin, and the Path is "the way of Christ." It is through Christ, as the Way, the Truth and the Life, that the soul of the mystic comes to look upon the very Essence of God, to be changed into His likeness and itself made Godlike.

[1] *Spiritual State of the Soul*, xii., fol. 114*b*.
[2] *Ibid.*, fol. 115*b*. [3] *Ibid.*, fol. 116*a*.

(c) The Book of the Holy Hierotheos

This mystical treatise has commonly been ascribed to Stephen Bar Sudayli, a monk who was living in Jerusalem at the end of the fifth century. The book was reputed to be his in the eighth and ninth centuries, and there is considerable internal evidence that part of it, at any rate, was his work. He was certainly influenced by Neo-Platonism and Alexandrian Christian theosophy, and though the book claims Dionysius the pseudo-Areopagite as a disciple of the author, it is probable that Stephen wrote after the appearance of the writings of Dionysius. The preface to the book states that "the holy Hierotheus" became the perfect Priest and Hierarch and Master-of-Revelations and Shewer-of-Fair-Things, and being inspired through his own purity, he was moved to write this mystical treatise to teach the Way of Perfection which leads to Heaven.[1]

The book deals chiefly with the Union of the soul with God, and the ascent thereto. God is the First Good, Who brought all things into existence and seeks to regain all who have fallen from their first estate, and to respond to their yearning for Himself. The First Good is also the Universal Essence, the Self-Existent, with Which all separate existences seek to unite themselves again, and Which is the fulfilment of their natural yearning. The mind of the mystic, therefore, seeks the way of ascent ; the fulfilment of the service of Minds and the completion of their labours is their glorious ascent, and God does not leave the Mind to fall, but calls and brings it back and presents and receives it . . . and they leave the labour in which they were, and purely and holily run the glorious race to be united, so far as is possible, with the Supreme Good, which was from of old, and press forward eagerly without hindrance to be with it and in it."[2]

Those who ascend require a purification as of fire ; they must be willing to endure the crucifixion of the old man, which means the slaying of the body of sin—" then the

[1] *Book of the Holy Hierotheos* (ed. Marsh), p. 149.
[2] *Ibid.*, Second Discourse, c. 12.

Mind (of the Mystic) draws near, nakedly, without soul and without body—and surrenders itself in holiness and humility to the Cross."[1] Love is the motive which incites the mystic to seek unification, but it belongs to a stage which is still far from the goal. " Love," says the author, " is the pure and holy communion which binds divinely, and wondrously encircles that which loves unification ; but those in this condition are also very far from unification. For, lo, the very name of Love is a sign of distinction, for Love is not established by one but by two, by the lover and by that which he loves . . . and on this side of Unification will be given to us the glorious title of Love."[2] Through purification and sanctification—the passive and the active sides of the preparation, whereby the soul is first cleansed from all defilement and then adorned with all virtues—the seeker passes to unification. And now the writer approaches that which he feels must be spoken of without words, for it is beyond speech, and must be perceived without the understanding, for it is above the intellect, being indeed the hidden Silence and the mystic Quiet, which does away with the senses and has no use for outward forms, which seeks in mystical stillness that perfect and original unification with the primeval Goodness, and that adherence thereto which is perfect and holy, for where One is, distinction prevails no more.[3] " I do not know," he writes, " how to put into words what things belong to the Mind at that time of Commingling, since all the glorious and holy Secrets of which the Mind is accounted worthy at the time when it becomes ' without appearance ' are, perhaps, beyond the power of speech."[4]

" Unification " is to this writer something less than complete union, which is expressed by this final " commingling." In unification there is still some distinction,[5] but in those who have been " commingled," no distinction and no difference can be found. Those who have been merely joined together in unification may be separated again, but those who have been truly united in " commingling " can no

[1] *Book of the Holy Hierotheos*, Second Discourse, c. 12.
[2] *Ibid.*, iv. 20. [3] *Ibid.*, ii. 3. [4] *Ibid.*, iv. 21.
[5] *Cf.* my *Rābi'a the Mystic and her Fellow-Saints in Islām*, pp. 78-80.

more be torn asunder.[1] The spiritual marriage of the soul and God has been consummated, and henceforth the mystic lives the unitive life and abides therein. The Essence of Water is one, though it may be divided into many portions; so also is the Essence of the Sun one, though its rays are many, but the ray commingled with the Essence ceases to be a ray. It is likewise with Fire, the Essence of which is one, though manifested in many flames, which are absorbed again into the Fire. So the Mind (of the mystic) made perfect, returns to its own Essence and is commingled with the Good and is no longer the Mind. " For when the Mind is commingled in the Good, that distinction which it formerly possessed is no longer known or seen ; and, further, when there is in it One, no longer are there counted with it Two : for the time is appointed and destined to be when the number Two (*i.e.*, duality) shall be no more ; for it is evident that whatsoever is divided, is divided from One, but if division be removed, of necessity All will become One."[2] Such a commingling means deification, for it is the identification of God with the soul of the mystic. The Mind, now made divine, becomes one with Christ and is itself the Son of God.[3] It goes even beyond that state ; " when the Minds have reached the fulness of divine growth and holy perfection, they then acquire the designation of the Godhead—nay, to speak mystically, they become the Essence of God."[4]

This writer's mystical doctrine is obviously derived from the Neo-Platonists and especially Plotinus, in respect of the soul's ascent back to its source, and in his view that the perfected soul becomes the divine Mind and is then commingled with Ultimate Reality, the Essence of the Godhead Itself. His mysticism is theocentric rather than Christocentric, but he doubtless owed much to the earlier mystical teaching of the Christian Church, and it is more than probable that certain sections of his book were based upon the " Areopagite " writings. Though Hierotheos wrote in Syriac and Dionysius in Greek, there is a great similarity in the phrases used, and by both writers it is the " via nega-

[1] *Book of the Holy Hierotheos*, iv. 21. [2] *Ibid.*, iv. 21.
[3] *Cf.* St. Paul, Gal. ii. 20 ; Rom. viii. 14.
[4] *Book of the Holy Hierotheos*, iii. 1.

tiva" that is pointed out as the only way to perfection and to union. Hierotheos teaches a thoroughgoing pantheism: God is All in all, and unto Him must all return. His is an esoteric doctrine also; there is need for the concealment of these holy mysteries, because all minds are not pure enough or bright enough to receive them.

The book was widely read among Eastern Christians, and there is little doubt that it had a direct influence upon the belief and conduct of the members of the Syriac Church. It was in use as a guide to mystical doctrine and practice for more than thirteen centuries,[1] and may be regarded as the main source of western Syriac Mysticism, while the next writer to be considered, Isaac of Nineveh, is the chief representative of eastern Syriac Mysticism.

(*d*) Isaac of Nineveh

Isaac of Nineveh, living in the seventh century A.D., was ordained Bishop of Nineveh by the Catholicos Mār George. After holding this office for only five months, he resigned it and went away to live in the mountains with the solitaries. There he made a study of Mysticism, and penetrated deeply into its doctrines and practice. His *Mystical Treatises*, intended for the guidance of solitaries who were seeking to tread the mystic Way, were written in the second half of the seventh century A.D. He mentions several of his sources, such as the Life of Anthony, Evagrius, St. Basil and Dionysius, and it seems probable that he was acquainted with the *Book of Hierotheos*.[2]

He is concerned more with the Way, and the first two stages of it—*i.e.*, Purification and Illumination—than with speculation concerning the nature of the Godhead and Its relation to the soul, or with the final goal of the mystic, the union with God. God is the only real Being; He is therefore the Creator and Final Cause of all things, and to Him all things must seek to return. He is perfect Goodness, and therefore the Way must mean purification from all defilement for those who would look upon Him as He is. Isaac's

[1] *Cf.* Marsh, *op. cit.*, pp. 248, 249.
[2] *Ibid.*, pp. 251-255.

admonition not to venture to look at the Sun until the apple of the soul's eye has been purified, recalls the words of Plotinus, "Never did the eye see the sun unless it had first become sun-like, and never can the soul have vision of the First Beauty unless itself be beautiful."[1] Asceticism is the only means of purification, "the mother of saintliness," and to Isaac withdrawal from the world seemed a necessary means to the practice of effective asceticism. No one could come near to God except by being far from the world; by fleeing from the delights of this world, the mind would be free to behold the world to come; only those who had ceased to long after this world's goods were dead to the world in truth, and it is only the heart which is really dead to the world which is wholly astir in God.[2] The seeker, writes Isaac, "considers this world as a place of transition for those who enter into it. They have entered it as an inn for the night and left it as travellers—without thinking of return—this world will be in his eyes as a prison, and its first sweetness will be more bitter than any bitter thing and the love of his life and its desirable beauty will seem the type of Hell."[3]

When the ties of the material have been dissolved, then are forged the bonds with God. Death in life will save the soul from life in death. Hardships must be welcomed for the sake of the good, the love of God cannot be kindled in a heart that loves comfort. "Until the outward man becomes dead to the ways of the world, not only to sin, but also to the whole bodily service—until the natural impulse is brought low—so that the sweetness of sin has no more mastery over the heart, the spirit of God does not spread its sweetness, and man's limbs are not unveiled to life, and divine impulses do not show themselves in the soul."[4] Naked the swimmer dives into the sea to find a pearl, and naked the solitary should live in this world in order that he may find the pearl of great price.[5] The servant of God who thus strips himself, and, renouncing the world, betakes himself to the solitary life, and gives himself up night and day to the works of God, need have no anxiety as to his own re-

[1] *Ennead*, i. 9. (S. Mackenna's translation.)
[2] *Mystical Treatises* (tr. A. Wensinck), pp. 1, 29, 292.
[3] *Ibid.*, pp. 154, 155. [4] *Ibid.*, p. 41. [5] *Ibid.*, p. 218.

quirements in the way of dress and food and shelter. God will care for him and give him all he needs in due season. Such confidence in God is beautiful and fitting, and the servant who practises it is strengthened against all fear and, having entrusted his life to God, can dwell in mental peace.[1] The mystic, free from anxiety, now follows the Way to perfection, and is encouraged by the evidence given to him, that he is making progress and ever drawing nearer to his goal. " Every station which on the morrow thou attainest to in the way of excellence and knowledge of the truth," Isaac tells the seeker, " will be found by thee more glorious and excellent than that in which thou hast spent the night before. Thou departest, wondering at the beauty of the station which thou hast entered today. But its beauty vanishes by the beauty of that which thou wilt reach to-morrow."[2]

From labour and vigils in solitude—for solitude is the beginning of the purification of the soul, bringing about the liberation of the true man and giving fresh life to the soul—springs purity of mind, which consists in being held captive by the attraction of Divine things, and from purity of mind arises inward light. This spiritual attraction comes from love in the heart, for the lover counts his own life as nothing in comparison with his Friend; in all that he does, he is inflamed with this consuming passion of love for God; the soul that loves God can find its rest in Him alone. Love of one's neighbour is a thing excellent and commendable, but only if the thought of it does not turn us from the love of God, which is the highest and the only abiding type of love.[3] " Love which is maintained by things," says Isaac, " is to be compared with a small flame whose light subsists by oil, and a stream subsisting through rain, whose flow ceases as soon as the supply which maintains it becomes deficient. Love of which God is the cause, is as a source welling from the depth, whose current will never cease. For He alone is the source of love whose supply does not fail."[4] Love, he says, is the wine which gladdens the heart of man, and blessed is that man who has drunk thereof. Again he says that re-

[1] *Mystical Treatises*, pp. 46, 67.
[2] *Ibid.*, p. 122.
[3] *Ibid.*, p. 221.
[4] *Ibid.*, p. 256.

pentance is the ship, fear her governor, and love the Divine port. When we have reached Love, we have reached God.[1]

It is by prayer that love is maintained, for prayer is intercourse with God, by which the mind is enlightened and the soul exalted, and the spirit brought to concentrate on that which is Divine, and at the time of prayer, the spirit is rapt away and beholds things unspeakable. "What time is so holy and fit for sanctification and receiving of gifts," asks Isaac, "as the time of prayer, in which man speaks with God? At this time . . . of God alone he thinks, and Him alone he supplicates; his whole thought is absorbed in discourse with Him and His heart is full of Him. It is in this state, therefore, that the Holy Spirit joins with the things, which the man prays, some unattainable insights which it stirs in him, so that by these insights . . . the mind is absorbed in ecstasy."[2] The highest form of prayer is mental prayer, which is pure prayer, for all prayer that can be prayed, Isaac considers to lie on this side of spirituality. The words uttered by the tongue and the petitions of the heart in prayer are but keys; "What comes after them is the entering into the treasury. Here, then, all mouths and tongues are silent, and the heart, the treasurer of the thoughts, the mind, the governor of the senses, the daring spirit, that swift bird, and all their means and powers . . . have to stand still there; for the Master of the house has come."[3] There is no prayer beyond pure prayer, because beyond this limit prayer passes into ecstasy; the spirit no longer sees, but it beholds. Prayer was the seed, contemplation is the harvest, and the reaper stands amazed to see how from the poor, bare grains he sowed, a harvest of glorious ears has sprung up before him.[4]

The soul of the mystic has passed through the stages of purification and illumination, from bodily knowledge to psychic knowledge, and at last it has reached the stage of perfection, of the spiritual gnosis, that light which dawns in the soul and reveals to it the hidden mysteries and the secret riches of the Godhead. By this the soul is kindled to the faith of certainty and rapt away from this visible world, and

[1] *Mystical Treatises*, pp. 211, 212. [2] *Ibid.*, p. 117.
[3] *Ibid.*, p. 112. [4] *Ibid.*, pp. 112, 113.

as one intoxicated with that wine of the love of God, it remains continually in ecstatic contemplation of Him, and by "insight without sight," it is able to look upon the Divine Essence.[1] Having that Vision before it, the soul cannot be drawn aside to concern itself with any lower being. "When the beauty of all which exists in that order of things is inferior to His Beauties, how should it be possible for the mind not to fix its gaze exclusively on Him?"[2] So, in this world, here and now, the veil is sometimes drawn aside from before the eyes of the spirit, so that the mind is rapt away in ecstasy and gazes upon the Divine glory; but such glimpses of the Invisible are of short duration in this life, lest the soul should be unwilling ever to return to earth. But in the next life the soul will dwell forever in the Presence of God and gaze unceasingly upon that wondrous Vision.[3]

Yet it is not necessary to search heaven and earth to attain to that Vision of God. The soul is His image, and when the soul is purified, the mystic will find God within himself; "the ladder to the Kingdom is hidden within thee," says Isaac, "and within thy soul."[4] Again he says: "Grace makes manifest all the glory which God has hidden in the nature of the soul, showing the soul this glory and making it glad because of its own beauty. So that when it sees the great and unspeakable treasures which God has laid in it and which were hidden from it, by the defiled mantle of affections and ignorance, but which, now that it has torn asunder the garment of affections, He has shown to it—it is captured on account of its gladness by His love and turns its back on earthly things.

"Moreover, it does not remember the body which hid its own beauties from its sight. Then it sees heavenly beauties in itself, as the exact mirror which by its great purity shows the beauty of faces."[5]

The soul now knows itself to be one with God, it has become the image of the Godhead, "through unification with the Incomprehensible," and it now lives the unitive life. Blessed is that one to whom this fountain has been opened and who drinks therefrom at all times; his end is

[1] *Mystical Treatises*, pp. 248 *ff.* [2] *Ibid.*, p. 203.
[3] *Ibid.*, pp. 203, 204. [4] *Ibid.*, p. 8. [5] *Ibid.*, p. 349.

attained, he has reached the Goal, and now he lives the perfect life in God.

Isaac's eschatological teaching is simple and spiritual. To be saved from hell *is* the Kingdom, and to be shut out from the Kingdom *is* hell, and again he says: " Scourgings for love's sake, namely, of those who perceive that they have sinned against love, are more hard and bitter than tortures through fear. . . . In hell, the hard tortures are grief for love. The inhabitants of heaven, however, make drunk their soul with the delight of love."[1]

To sum up the mystical teaching of Isaac of Nineveh: he holds that God is the only real Being; that man is made in the Divine image, and by purification can cleanse the soul from the defilements of sin, so that the image of God within it will once more be revealed. The soul, thus purified, can look upon God in all His Beauty, and once again be joined to That from Which it first came forth. He was plainly influenced by the teachings of the Alexandrian Hellenists and the Stoics—who taught that God was with man and within him—and to some extent by Philo, who also regarded man as the reflection of the Divine, and whose description of the soul rapt away from consciousness of itself when it has penetrated into the Holy of Holies, is very like Isaac's description of the Vision. From Plato, no doubt through the writings of Plotinus, he has taken the idea of the ascent of the soul.[2]

Isaac is thoroughly representative of the mysticism of his time and of the Middle East, and, as we shall see, his teaching had an influence which was not limited to the members of the Christian Church, but had also a considerable effect on the mysticism of Islām.

[1] *Mystical Treatises*, p. 136.

[2] *Cf.* the teachings of a much later mystic, Walter Hilton (*ob.* 1396), whose *Scale of Perfection* gives a similar idea of the soul and its relation to God.

PART II

CHAPTER VI

CHRISTIANITY AND ISLĀM AT THE BEGINNING OF THE ISLAMIC ERA

It was in such an environment that Islām had its rise and the Arabs made themselves predominant, in the first place, as a political power, and in the second, as the preachers of a new faith. They found, both in their own native country and in those countries which they invaded and conquered, Christians living and practising their faith, in some cases as a minority among pagans, in others as the representatives of the prevailing religion of the country.

In Arabia itself, Christianity had been established from an early period, probably as the result of the efforts of missionaries from Syria or ʻIrāq, since South Arabia was on the regular route from Syria to ʻIrāq. Legend attributed the first preaching of Christianity in this region to a Syrian named Phemion, a pious ascetic, who wandered from village to village, working for his own maintenance, "whose prayers were answered." He was captured by Arabs, who sold him as a slave in Najrān. His master saw him one night praying, while the whole house in which he was seemed to be filled with light, a well-known sign of sanctity. He was said to have destroyed the sacred palm-tree worshipped by the inhabitants of Najrān, and to have converted them to Christianity.[1] About the middle of the fourth century, the Emperor Constantius II. sent an embassy under the Indian monk and bishop Theophilus to South Arabia, to seek an alliance with the Ḥimyarites and to attract the people of Yaman to Christianity. Theophilus was successful to a considerable extent; permission was given to build churches, and it is said that the king became a Christian.[2] The Nestorian chroniclers tell also of a travelling merchant

[1] Ṭabarī I., ii. 919 *ff.*

[2] Philostorgius, *H.E.*, Bk. II.

named Ḥannān, who lived in the days of Yazdigird I. (A.D. 399-420), and visited Ḥīra, and there made acquaintance with Christians and learnt their doctrine. He took his new faith back to his native land, and converted not only his own family, but others, who combined with him in the work of winning Ḥimyar and the neighbouring districts to Christianity. Whatever may have been the means whereby, or the exact date at which, Christianity came into Arabia, it was certainly in existence there from the fourth century onwards, and a modern traveller states that "literature, monuments and oral tradition concur to show that Christianity was pretty widely diffused throughout the Najrān of Yaman and Ḥaḍramaut, and no less that this country was then far more populous and enjoying a higher degree of prosperity and civilization than since."[1]

In the sixth century, probably about 523 A.D., the Christians of Najrān were subject to severe persecution by Dhū-Nuwās, the Ḥimyarite King of al-Yaman, who put many of them to death. The Christians sought help from the Emperor at Constantinople, and he urged the Christian King of Abyssinia to avenge this persecution by the invasion of al-Yaman.[2] An Abyssinian overlordship was thus established in South Arabia, and Abraha al-Ashram was appointed governor there and built a great cathedral at Ṣan'ā. In A.D. 597 Yaman became a Persian province and Nestorianism was introduced there, a fact not without importance in regard to the impression made by Christianity upon the mind of Muḥammad when he came to formulate the doctrines of his new faith. At this period Christianity was spread among all the tribes belonging to the old Roman province of Arabia, especially among the Qudā'a, and there were Christians in Wādī al-Qurā, east of the Ḥijāz, where there were hermitages to be found, in Ayla, at the head of the Gulf of Acaba, and in Taimā; these Christians were probably Melkites. Ayla probably became Christian at an early date, owing to its proximity to Syria and Palestine, and its ruler was a Christian when Muḥammad made his

[1] W. G. Palgrave, *A Year's Journey through Central and Eastern Arabia*, i. 88.

[2] *Cf.* Assem., *B.O.*, i. 359, 361.

appearance. Dūma al-Jandal, a fortified place on the way from Damascus to Medīna, was also entirely Christian at the beginning of the Islamic era, and was ruled by a Christian king, with a bishop under the jurisdiction of Damascus.[1] There seems to be no evidence of a pre-Muslim translation of the Bible into Arabic, or of a Christian Church at that period using an Arabic service. It is probable that the Christian Bible in use in Arabia at this time was in Syriac, and the Christians there would be familiar at least with the Gospels and the Psalms.

While Christians at this time were but a small minority in Arabia, in Egypt their religion was practically that of the state. Alexandria was the headquarters of the school of the Christian Hellenists, and Christians were to be found everywhere in the towns and villages of Egypt. Most of North Africa, thanks, in part at least, to the labours of St. Augustine, was also Christian. South of Egypt was the strong Christian kingdom of Nubia. In Asia Minor, Christianity had penetrated into all departments of life; Armenia had become officially a Christian country by the end of the third century, and Cappadocia was entirely Christian by A.D. 325. Pontus and Phrygia were early Christianised and, as we have seen, monasticism and the cult of the spiritual life, organised and developed by the labours of St. Basil, had taken a great hold on the country.

Syria and Palestine had been the first home of Christianity, and from its first foundation in Jerusalem, Damascus and Antioch, the Church had extended itself as far as the Arabian desert. Bishoprics were established beyond the Jordan, and in Palmyra and the district east of Jordan were to be found many Christian hermits, who influenced many of the desert Arabs, and won numbers of them to Christianity; St. Nilus is mentioned as one who evangelised these savage tribes.[2] When certain of these Arabs, whom the historians call "Saracens," about A.D. 376 revolted against the Roman Empire under their Christian queen Maria, "who, notwithstanding her sex, possessed masculine intrepidity," she offered to make peace if the Arab monk Moses, one of these

[1] Mas'ūdī, viii. 248, 249.

[2] Montalembert, *The Monks of the West*, p. 249.

solitaries, was constituted bishop. This was done, and Maria made peace with Rome, and Moses was able to do good work among her subjects.[1] The chief of these Christian desert tribes were the Benī Ghassān, who in A.D. 548 sent to Byzantium, asking for a Monophysite bishop for the Arab tribes, and Theodora the Empress, in response, arranged for the consecration of Bishop Theodore to Baṣra, for the Arabs. The Benī Ghassān were held responsible to the Roman Government for the good behaviour of all the Arab tribes of Palestine, Arabia, Phœnicia, and North Syria. They acted as frontier guards, and at the time when Muḥammad appeared, they were regarded as the leaders of Arab Christianity. Other Syrian Bedouin tribes who were Christians at this period were the Benī Tanūkh, living near Aleppo, the Benī Salīḥ, the Jurājima, living near Antioch, and the tribes of Bahrā, Lakhm and Judhām.

Farther East, Christianity had established itself in Mesopotamia and Persia. As early as the third century the Christian Church was widely spread and covered an area extending from the mountains of Kurdistān to the Persian Gulf, and was governed by more than twenty bishops.[2] The Emperor Constantine, in a letter to Sapor, King of Persia, speaks of his joy in the multitudes of Persians who had become Christians, and the fact that the finest provinces of Persia were honoured with their residence.[3] Edessa was the metropolis of the Syriac-speaking Church, and from there Christianity spread down the Euphrates and across the Tigris. There were churches to be found at Nisibis, Arbela, Jundê-Shāpūr, Kashkar and Seleucia-Ctesiphon, which became the seat of the Nestorian patriarch, and in the fifth century there were bishoprics established at Rayy, Herāt, Merv, Teherān, and Ispahān. The Christian converts in 'Irāq and Persia worked hard as missionaries among all their neighbours, and Christian merchants did their part as they travelled up and down the country on their business. By the end of the sixth century there was hardly a town

[1] Socrates, *Hist. Eccles.*, IV. xxxvi.; Theodoret, *Hist. Eccles.*, III. xix.

[2] W. A. Wigram, *History of the Assyrian Church*, pp. 24 *ff*.

[3] Theodoret *op. cit.*, I. xxv.

without its church and bishop. Missions were sent to evangelise the Huns and the Turks, and in the seventh century large communities of Turks were converted by the Metropolitan Elijah of Merv. At this time Christianity had penetrated into Eastern and Western Turkistan, Mongolia, Manchuria, North China and South-Eastern Siberia, while there were bishoprics, in addition to those already mentioned, at Gīlān, Sijistān and Ṭūs.[1]

A number of the Christians in these regions belonged to Arab tribes, including the Benī 'Abd al-Qays in Baḥrayn, and the famous tribe of the Benī Taghlib in central Mesopotamia. At the time when Islām arose, they were a numerous tribe, entirely Christian and very powerful.[2] Ḥīra, where some of the Taghlibites established themselves, became the headquarters of the Christian Arabs in 'Irāq territory, and they were known there as *'Ibād* (*i.e.*, servants of God). Ḥīra was the seat of the Lakhmide dynasty, which was responsible to the Persian Government for the Arabs within the Persian Empire, in the same way that the Ghassānides were responsible to the Roman Government for those in Syria and Arabia, though the Lakhmide rulers, unlike the Ghassānides, were non-Christian.

We find, then, that at the time when Muḥammad appeared Christianity was a living force in Arabia, Egypt, North Africa, Nubia, Syria, and Asia Minor, in Mesopotamia and Persia, on the shores of the Persian Gulf, in Turkestān, and still farther East, so that at the time when he was evolving his new creed and endeavouring to formulate its doctrine and practice, he was in close contact with Christians and the Christian Church, and that later, when his armies and those of his successors sought to secure political power for Islām, and to enforce its acceptance, it was into countries mainly Christian that they penetrated, it was peoples strongly influenced by Christianity whom they conquered, and it was in the midst of populations permeated by Christian teaching and Christian culture that they established themselves.

The contact between Muslims and Christians in the first

[1] *Cf.* A. Mingana, *Early Spread of Christianity in Central Asia and the Far East*, pp. 7 *ff*.

[2] Balādhurī, i. 110, 248, 249.

centuries after the conquest was of necessity close, and we find it operating in various spheres of life—political, social, professional, cultural and religious. Not only were many of those conquered by the Arabs, Christian at the time of the conquest, but large numbers of them retained their faith on the terms granted by the conquerors, which generally involved the payment of a tribute in return for the right to retain and practise their faith without hindrance. Muḥammad himself made terms with the Christians of Najrān, who sent a deputation consisting of forty ecclesiastics, led by the bishop, and twenty laymen. He granted them protection for their religion and their churches and for monastic institutions, as well as for their bishops, priests, monks and hermits, none of whom was to be moved from his abode.[1] 'Umar, wishing to carry out the injunction of the Prophet to allow only one faith in Arabia, expelled the Christians from Najd, almost as soon as he assumed office, and transported them to Syria, east of Jordan and 'Irāq, where they were granted lands in compensation for those of which they had been deprived. Yet Christian influence was not altogether at an end in Arabia, for towards the end of the eighth century the Catholicos Timothy consecrated a bishop named Peter for Yaman and Ṣan'ā, and the Catholicos John V. wrote a letter in A.D. 901 to a priest named Ḥasan, who lived in Yaman, answering certain questions which Ḥasan had addressed to him.[2]

At the conquest of Damascus in A.D. 634, Khālid, who had been sent by the Caliph Abū Bakr to subdue Syria, made an agreement with the Christian bishop that he would give security for the lives of Christians and their goods and churches. At first the great basilica of St. John appears to have been used for worship by both Christians and Muslims, but later the Christians were obliged to accept churches in the suburbs in the place of the Church of St. John, which became a mosque. But evidently amicable relations existed between conquerors and conquered at this early stage. Similar terms were made for other places in Palestine and Syria, including Jerusalem, which was taken in A.D. 628. 'Umar made the following agreement, which applied also to

[1] Ibn Sa'd, i. 2, 35 *ff*.

[2] L. Cheikko, *al-Naṣrāniyya*, i. 67.

the villages: "In the Name of God the Merciful, the Compassionate! This is the security granted to the people of Aelya by 'Umar, the Commander of the Faithful. He grants them security for their lives and their property, their churches and their crosses, and everything else which concerns their religion. Their churches shall not become dwelling-houses nor be demolished; there shall be no diminution of what belongs to them or is included in their property, nor any (destruction) of the crosses of the people nor of any part of their possessions, nor shall they be coerced in the matter of their faith, nor shall any one of them be harmed."[1] We have a witness to the respect inspired by the life led by the Christian ascetics in the instruction given by Abū Bakr to the soldiers who were going into Syria, "You will find people who have secluded themselves in cells; let them alone, for they have secluded themselves for the sake of God." In A.D. 670 Arculfus, a Frankish bishop who made a pilgrimage to the Holy Land, and afterwards wrote a detailed account of his travels, saw the great churches in Jerusalem, and reported that they were treated tolerantly by the Muslims.[2] While the Benī Ghassān abjured their faith and became Muslims, many of the Christian Bedouins adhered to their religion. The Jurājima made peace on condition of helping the Muslims in time of war, but they themselves remained Christian. The same was the case with the Benī Tanūkh, who remained Christian up to the reign of the Caliph al-Mahdī (A.D. 775-786). The Bishop of Ayla, on the borders of Syria (*cf.* p. 104 above), whose name was John b. Rūba, made peace with the Prophet on payment of a *jizya* amounting to three hundred dinars.[3] 'Umar, when he visited Syria in A.D. 639, stayed with the Bishop of Ayla, and he showed friendliness towards the Christians of the town. Elsewhere, many of those forming the agricultural population of Syria, while remaining Christian, settled down peacefully under Muslim rule.

Islām was introduced into Africa by the invasion of Egypt in A.D. 640, and 'Amr b. al-'Āṣ was entrusted with the com-

[1] Ṭabarī I., v. 2405.
[2] *Cf.* A. J. Butler, *The Arab Conquest of Egypt*, p. 497.
[3] *Cf.* L. Cheikko, *al-Naṣrāniyya*, p. 108; Mas'ūdī, viii. 272.

mand. When he had defeated the Copts, he left them in possession of their churches and allowed them autonomy in all ecclesiastical affairs. Abū Ṣāliḥ, in his "Akhbār min nawāhi miṣr wa aqtā'iha," composed at the beginning of the thirteenth century, shows how friendly had been the relations existing between Copts and Muslims in the early centuries of Islām, and he gives a tradition according to which Muḥammad said, "The Copts are the most noble of foreigners, the gentlest of them in action, the best in qualities and the nearest in kinship to the Arabs generally, and to the Quraysh in particular,"[1] and so the Prophet definitely commended the Copts to the care of the Muslims. In addition to the Copts of Egypt, who have lived side by side with the Muslims from the seventh century up to the present day, in North Africa also, where Idrīs of Morocco, in A.D. 789, compelled many Christians to accept Islām, small numbers of Christians survived for several centuries.

In the Middle East, Christianity survived to a considerable extent, after the Muslim conquest. Ishō-yahbh, the Nestorian patriarch, negotiated with the Arabs on behalf of his church, and both Nestorians and Jacobites secured recognition of their status as a "*milla*" (religious sect) by payment of a tribute, and were accorded the right to keep their churches, but not to build new ones.[2] This agreement was renewed and confirmed by 'Umar b. al-Khaṭṭāb. In Edessa the Christians were allowed to keep the cathedral and its surroundings as their property, with the same proviso that they were not to build any new churches beyond what they already had. The same was the case in Raqqa. While many of the Nestorian Christians living in the district round about the Tigris became Muslims, others remained faithful to their religion, and this was true also of those who had been converted to Christianity in Turkistān. The existence of a considerable Christian community in Russian Turkistān as late as the ninth century has been proved by the recent discovery of two cemeteries containing Christian tombstones going back to that period, and a Syriac document, written probably in the latter part of the eighth century, by a Jacobite writer

[1] *Op. cit.*, fol. 28*b*.

[2] *Cf.* W. A. Wigram, *History of the Assyrian Church*, p. 309.

who lived in or near Baghdād, gives an account of a mission from the Christian Turks to Ctesiphon, to ask for the consecration of a bishop by the Nestorian Catholicos. These Christian Turks were at this time under four kings, each of whom ruled over four hundred thousand families : they had priests, deacons, and monks, possessed many places of worship, and they read the Scriptures in the Syriac language.[1]

In the Euphrates district a number of the nomad tribes remained Christian, including the Benī Taghlib, who refused to abjure their faith and imposed conditions, insisting on the free exercise of their faith, and on being excepted from the *jizya*, in lieu of which they paid a double alms. 'Umar would not bring pressure to bear upon them, but forbade them to teach Christianity to their children, a prohibition which they ignored. We hear of George, Bishop of the Arab tribes (*ob. c.* 724), whose diocese included the Arabs of al-Kūfa, Tanūkh, the Tha'labites, the Taghlibites, and other nomad Arabs of Mesopotamia.[2] Christianity remained the religion of the Benī Taghlib under the rule of the Ummayads and the 'Abbāsides. As for Ḥīra, when Khālid attacked it in A.D. 633, he first seized some Christian convents on the outskirts, and the inmates, being expelled thence, urged the defenders of Ḥīra to capitulate. They did so, making terms with Khālid, by which they were left free to remain Christians on payment of tribute, and several centuries later many of the inhabitants of the neighbourhood were still Christians. Many of the town dwellers retained their Christian faith, and also the agricultural population, for the time being, though later on large numbers of them apostatised. Yet there are still to be found members of the Nestorian Church and Jacobites, even at the present day, in the regions of 'Irāq now predominantly Muslim.

In A.D. 711 the Arabs penetrated into Spain, and so brought the new faith into Europe. While many of the Christian inhabitants Islamised, a considerable number remained true to their faith, and these were allowed the free exercise of their religion, and their religious buildings, including the convents and monasteries, were left undisturbed.

[1] A. Mingana, *op. cit.*, pp. 40, 70-71.

[2] W. Wright, *History of Syriac Literature*, p. 156.

It is plain, then, that the political triumph of Islām did not mean the extermination of Christianity or of its adherents, who continued to live side by side with the Arabs. It would appear, too, that the relations of Christians and Muslims, the conquered and the conquerors, were friendly enough on the whole, in the years immediately succeeding the conquest, in most of the countries concerned.

In the matter of social relationships also, the Muslims came into close contact with their Christian subjects, chiefly by means of marriage with Christian women. In too many cases these were forced marriages with captives carried off against their will to the ḥarīms of the conquerors, but in time some at least of these women may have become reconciled to their fate, and it is probable that their Arab husbands felt some respect for wives who, in many instances, must have been their superiors in culture and upbringing. The story of Hind the younger, known as the builder of a convent at Ḥīra, who was the daughter of Nuʿmān b. al-Mundhir, king of Ḥīra, suggests that Christian women were able to secure the respect of the Muslim conquerors. When Khālid took possession of Ḥīra, he invited Ḥind to Islamise and offered her a Muslim husband, but she refused to desert her own faith. She also declined the gifts he offered her and asked only for protection for the Christians, which she obtained.[1] It is possible that, as time went on, women would intermarry more willingly with Muslims, since the Prophet had laid it down that Christian wives could not be compelled to renounce their faith. The Muslims who married such women would be brought into the relation of kinship with the fathers and brothers and other relatives of such Christian wives. In Spain such intermarriages between Muslims and Spanish Christians seem to have been quite common. This practice of intermarriage was of great importance, not only for the promotion of friendly social relations between Christians and Muslims, but much more for the opportunity which it gave to Christian mothers of influencing the next generation of Muslims, who were their children, and entrusted to their care in their early years. It is true that all the children of such marriages would be brought up as

[1] Yāqūt, ii. 708.

Muslims, but as the offspring of Christian mothers they could hardly fail to be affected by Christianising influences, and, in not a few cases, they must have imbibed Christian teaching and ideas from their mothers. The definitely Christian tone of some Muslim writers, and especially of the Ṣūfīs, may with great probability be traced back, in part at least, to this heritage from Christian mothers.

In professional matters, the Muslims were not only brought into close contact with Christians, but were obliged to depend upon them to a large extent, because of the superior knowledge of their Christian subjects in science and the arts, of which the Arabs themselves knew little or nothing at the time of the conquest. In many places the civil administration was left practically unaltered, and as the Muslim conquerors had no knowledge of the methods employed and the business details involved in the systems of administration which they found in existence, they were perforce obliged to fall back upon Christian officials to carry on the business of the State. In Egypt, the Copts were allowed to take a large share in the affairs of the Government, as secretaries and clerks, and up to the present day this holds good. Under the Ummayad caliphs, Syrian Christians frequently held high office at Court and, in the reign of Mu'āwiya, the governor of Medīna employed Christians from Ayla, to police the sacred city. The father of the Christian theologian John of Damascus was counsellor to the Caliph 'Abd al-Malik (A.D. 685-705), and John himself held a similar official position till he withdrew to a life of seclusion in the monastery of Saba. Christians were frequently entrusted with the finances—*e.g.*, the Copts were appointed to deal with the land tax in Egypt—and in Persia the Christians were found to be the most reliable among the Government officials. 'Abd al-'Azīz, governor of Egypt (A.D. 677-686), had Christian chamberlains, Melkites, who are known to us because of a church they built at Helouan, and Christian chamberlains were employed also by al-Ma'mūn (A.D. 813-833), and a church at al-Kantara, dedicated to the Pure Virgin, which they restored, was known as the "Church of the Christian chamberlains."[1] This Caliph displayed a very

[1] Abū Ṣāliḥ, *op. cit.*, fols. 52*a*, 53*a*.

liberal spirit towards non-Muslims, and entrusted the greater part of the work of government to Greek and Latin Christians.[1] The Caliph al-Mu'taṣim (A.D. 833-842) employed two Christian brothers, one of whom, Salmāya, acted as a kind of Secretary of State, who countersigned the royal decrees, while the other, Ibrāhīm, had the care of the privy seal, and the oversight of the Treasury. Under the Caliph al-Mu'tadid (A.D. 892-902) a Christian, 'Umar b. Yūsuf, was appointed as governor of Anbār; twice we hear of a Christian as Secretary of State for War during the reign of al-Mu'tamid (A.D. 870-892) and again in the reign of al-Muqtadir (A.D. 908-932).[2]

Christians were also much respected as doctors, since in their knowledge and practice of medicine they were far superior to the untutored Arabs, and as physicians they frequently rose to positions of power and dignity under Muslim rulers. A Christian physician was employed by Mu'āwiya, who appointed him to collect religious imposts in Ḥoms. The 'Abbaside Caliphs regularly employed Christian doctors, and Hārūn al-Rashīd had two in his service. Farther East also, Christian doctors were held in high esteem, and in Persia it was considered that there were no physicians like the Christians. It is interesting in this connection to note that a traveller, passing through Muslim lands so recently as the nineteenth century, speaks of a Christian tribe to be found between Syria and Arabia, the members of which were practising as doctors, and he reports that the Muslims whom he met told him that medical science was the offspring and heritage of the Christians.[3] The relations of trust and respect which most naturally prevail between doctor and patient, must have contributed to some extent towards keeping Muslims and Christians on terms of friendliness, where the former had to depend on the latter for professional services and attention in time of illness.

Christians, too, were to the fore as architects and builders.

[1] For other examples of Christians employed in the Muslim Government services *cf.* A. S. Tritton, *The Caliphs and their non-Muslim Subjects*, pp. 18 *ff*.

[2] T. W. Arnold, *The Preaching of Islām*, pp. 63, 64.

[3] W. G. Palgrave, *op. cit.*, p. 150.

They were mainly responsible for the building of modern Cairo, and at Damascus it was Syrian and Greek architects who were responsible for the erection of the buildings for which the Muslims were famed; from the beginning it would seem that the builder's craft has been recognised by the Muslims to be one in which their Christian subjects were especially proficient, and this recognition prevails even at the present time. When the great mosque of St. John in Damascus was seriously damaged by fire in recent years, Christians were employed in the work of rebuilding, and only Christian craftsmen were found capable of replacing the beautiful carvings in white marble with which the interior is adorned.

In their education and culture generally, the Christians were far ahead of the Arab conquerors, and if the Muslims wished to bring themselves up to the level which their Christian subjects had attained, centuries before the Muslim conquest, they had perforce to learn from the Christians and exchange the rôle of ruler for that of pupil, and be content to let their subjects become their teachers. Alexandria, Damascus, Baghdād, and Edessa were all centres of intellectual life at the time when the Arabs took possession of them, and it was by the Christian Church that this intellectual life, which owed so much to the influence of Hellenism, had been fostered and developed. Under the 'Ummayads the Syrians exercised a great influence upon Islām, and even those of them who became Muslims retained their own customs and mentality. In Damascus most of the Greek and Latin authors, including, of course, those of the Christian Church, were known and read in the original, as well as in Syriac translations. So the Christians were in a position to initiate their rulers into a knowledge of the philosophy, astronomy, physics and medicine of the Greeks, and this higher culture, permeated by Christian ideas, had a great influence upon the intellectual development of Islām, bringing Muslim thinkers, whether consciously or unconsciously, into contact with Christian thought. Christian scholars had done much work in the translation of Greek writings on theology, philosophy and science, into Syriac, one of the most notable being Jacob of Edessa (*c.* A.D. 640-708), who was appointed Bishop of Edessa in 679, a theologian and a philosopher, who gave his time chiefly to the translation of Greek theological writings, but also occupied himself with philosophy, and wrote a number of epistles. After the Muslim conquest these Christian scholars continued the good work by translating both Greek and Syriac works into Arabic. While their translations had been faithful in the main, much that was pagan and especially repugnant to Christian ideas had been replaced by Christian material, and it would be in this Christianised form that it appeared in the Arabic translations.[1] The 'Abbāside caliphs, especially, encouraged Christians to translate Greek philosophy and other literature into Arabic. It was not only as translators that the Christians proved themselves conspicuous in literary achievement; as original writers their work also commended itself to their Muslim neighbours, *e.g.*, the discourses of Abraham of Nephtar, who lived in the sixth and seventh centuries, were translated into both Arabic and Persian, and in poetry also there were Christians whose verses were very acceptable to Muslims and Christians alike. The court of the kings of Ḥīra, a Christian centre, and of the Ghassānides, were the resort of the most famous poets of the day, and some of these were Christians, such as 'Adī b. Zayd, an 'Ibādī poet. A Christian of the Benī Taghlib, al-Akhtal, was court poet in the reign of the Caliph Mu'āwiya, and was a great favourite also with the Caliph 'Abd al-Malik. He made no concealment of his faith and did not suffer any lack of esteem because of it.[2]

The chief educational establishments which the Muslim conquerors found in existence were naturally Christian, and while great schools were to be found in Egypt at Alexandria, and in Syria and Asia Minor, notably at Damascus and Antioch, it was the Nestorian and Jacobite Churches of the Middle East which especially emphasised education and the establishment of schools as an essential part of their church work, and the sixth century saw the rise of a large number of educational centres in Persia. We read of colleges for

[1] *Cf.* de Boer, *History of Philosophy in Islām*, p. 15.

[2] H. Lammens, J. A., ix. 1894, p. 107; *cf.* also A. S. Tritton, *op. cit.*, pp. 164 *ff.*

Tartars at Merv and for Arabs at Khirta and Prat d'Maishan.[1] The greatest and best-known school of the Nestorian Church was the University of Nisibis, to which many of the staff and students of the famous "School of the Persians," said to have been founded by St. Ephraim at Edessa, had betaken themselves, when their own school was closed by the Emperor Zeno in A.D. 489. This University of Nisibis was located in a monastery, the tutors being monks, and the students underwent a three years' course, mainly theological, though Greek philosophy was studied as the foundation of Christian theology. It produced patriarchs and bishops for the Nestorian Church, and spread its culture throughout the country. Another famous Christian school was that of Jundê-Shāpūr (Bēth Lapat) in Persia, established on the model of the school of Antioch, and founded originally by Chosroes Anūshīrwān (A.D. 531-597), for philosophical and medical studies, but its teachers were mainly Nestorian Christians. This school was flourishing in the time of the 'Abbāsides and their private physicians had been educated there.[2] At Harrān or Charræ (near Edessa), which was largely a heathen city, but a good deal affected by Christian influences, there was a school of philosophy and science which continued to flourish after the Arab conquest. The professors of this school were active as translators and authors, and kept in contact with Persian and Arab scholars from the eighth to the tenth centuries. Baghdād, at the period when it was the centre of the Muslim world, was distinguished for its literary brilliance and its schools of learning, and these also were the work of Christian scholars. al-Ma'mūn surrounded himself with the best of the Greek, Syrian, Persian and Coptic savants, and following his visit in A.D. 823 to Ḥarrān, large numbers of valuable manuscripts in Greek and Syriac were transported to Baghdād and were there entrusted to Christian translators, including Ibn Na'-īma of Ḥoms, Qusta b. Lūqa, Ḥunayn b. Isḥāq, and Ḥubaysh b. al-Ḥasan al'Asam, who made Baghdād their headquarters, and who were also original writers. al-Ma'mūn

[1] *Cf.* Wigram, *History of the Assyrian Church*, p. 238, and Assem., *B.O.*, iv. 932.

[2] *Cf.* L. Labourt, *Le Christianisme dans l'Empire perse*, pp. 131 *ff*.

especially collected the works of the School of Alexandria, and had them translated into Arabic and distributed.[1] It was in the Christian schools that a knowledge of Syriac and Greek was taught and preserved.

Obviously, therefore, the Muslims had to turn to Christian teachers for the scholarship and knowledge in which they themselves were so lacking, and they did not hesitate to employ Christian tutors for the instruction of their children. Greek, Syrian and Persian scholars were called upon to give instruction to the Arabs, who proved themselves to be diligent pupils. The Caliph ʻAbd al-Malik appointed a Christian, Athanasius of Edessa, as tutor to his brother ʻAbd al-ʻAzīz. Jacob of Edessa, already mentioned, when asked by Christian teachers whether Christians ought to teach Muslim pupils, pronounced it lawful for Christian ecclesiastics to give higher instruction to the children of Muslim parents,[2] and the question would not have arisen unless there had been a demand for such instruction on the part of Muslims. Khālid, son of the Caliph Yazīd (*ob.* 704), studied alchemy under the guidance of a Christian monk, and it would appear that some of the earliest Muslim theologians had Christian teachers. al-Ma'mūn even founded a school for girls, at which the professors were women from Athens and Constantinople. It seems certain, therefore, that the Muslims chose to benefit both by regular school instruction and by private tuition at the hands of Christian teachers, and this gave to the latter a considerable opportunity of influencing their pupils.

We find, then, that the Muslims were brought into close contact, over a wide area, with a culture that was not their own or of Arab origin, but rather Hellenistic and Christian, and that this Christian-Hellenistic culture was transmitted to them by Christian scholars, writers, and teachers, and their dependence upon such Christian instructors for the knowledge and culture which they saw to be so desirable, must have made for friendly intercourse, and must have

[1] L. Massignon, *Recueil de Textes inédits*, p. 175; *cf.* also R. A. Nicholson, *Literary History of the Arabs*, p. 359, and Wright, *op. cit.*, p. 211.

[2] de Boer, *op. cit.*, p. 15.

meant that Christians who stood in such a relation to Muslims were held in honour and esteem, and there is no lack of evidence that this was the case in all the countries where such contact took place.

Most important of all, perhaps, was the relationship between Muslims and Christians in religious matters. We have already seen that the Christians were left free to practise their faith and were allowed to retain their religious buildings, while their priests and monks were to be free from interference. This meant that the Muslims were living in the midst of Christian observances and could not fail to become familiar with the characteristics of Christian worship. The monastic life and the practices of the hermits and other solitaries seem especially to have struck the imagination of the Muslim conquerors. Everywhere, these devout followers of the religious life were to be found at this period, as we have seen.[1] In Egypt and Syria such hermits and monks abounded: in the province of the Fayyūm alone there were thirty-three monasteries in the eighth century, and we are told of great numbers of monasteries in Mesopotamia in the reign of Heraclius. Between A.D. 610 and 630 the Northern provinces of Persia were peopled with hermits and cœnobites, and at the time of the Muslim invasion there were about sixty monasteries to be found there. As late as the fifteenth century Maqrīzī speaks of eighty-one monasteries for men which were known to him and five convents of women, in Egypt. There is mention to be found even in pre-Islamic poetry of the Christian hermits dwelling in their cells, with their lamps serving as a guide to the lonely traveller. One poet writes:

"O Friend, see the lightning there! it flickered and now is gone.
As though flashed a pair of hands in the pillar of crowned cloud.
Nay, was it its blaze, or the lamps of a hermit that dwells alone,
And pours o'er the twisted wicks the oil from his slender cruse?"[2]

[1] *Cf.* Chaps. II. and III. above. [2] Imr al-Qays, Lyall, p. 103.

This was a sight with which the Muslims must have become increasingly familiar as their conquests were extended. Again of the Christian character we read:

"A nature is theirs, God gives the like to no other men—
a wisdom that never sleeps, a bounty that never fails.
Their home is in God's own land, His chosen of old; their
faith is steadfast; their hope is set on nought but the
world to come;
Their sandals are soft and fine and girded with chastity;
they welcome with garlands sweet the dawn of the
Feast of Palms."[1]

These were poems preserved by the Muslims, and their increasing contact with Christians does not seem to have inspired them with any desire to deny them these qualities. They knew of the Easter lamp in the chapel of the monks,[2] of the prayer-life of the monks,[3] of their copying of the Scriptures. All these things were a source of interest to the Muslims, and inspired them to imitation, so far as they could be introduced into Islām. As a result of this interest and of the admiration which the Muslims could hardly deny to the lives and character of those Christians who were unfeignedly sincere and devout in the practice of their faith, we find that in several cases there were friendly relations between Muslim rulers and Christian ecclesiastics. A Nestorian bishop wrote in A.D. 649: "These Arabs fight not against the Christian religion; nay, rather they defend our faith, they revere our priests and Saints, and they make gifts to our churches and monasteries."[4] The Muslims did, in fact, accord privileges to the Nestorians. 'Abd Allah b. Ismā'īl, in a letter to al-Kindī, says: "Among all the Christians, they are the most sympathetic to the Muslims and the most closely allied to them in their beliefs. The Prophet has praised them and is bound to them by solemn agreements. He wished to recognise in that way the help which the Nestorian religious leaders gave him in predicting the high mission to which

[1] al-Nābigha, *ibid.*, p. 96.
[2] *Cf.* L. Cheikko, *al-Naṣrāniyya*, p. 216.
[3] *Ibid.*, p. 392.
[4] *Cf.* A. J. Butler, *op. cit.*, p. 159.

he was called. Therefore Muḥammad felt a most sincere affection for them and loved to have intercourse with them."[1] These were the Nestorians whom the Prophet had met in Arabia, but favour seems to have been accorded to them also at the headquarters of their Church in 'Irāq and Persia. Athanasius of Edessa was allowed to build many new churches and monasteries in the reign of 'Abd al-Malik. There was indeed an expansion of the Nestorian Church under Muslim rule, and the Nestorians were able to do extensive missionary work, after the conquest, in Central Asia, South India and China, and it was under the rule of the 'Abbāsides that this Church attained to its greatest development, when it included about one hundred dioceses, grouped into twenty-five metropolitan districts.[2]

In Egypt, when a great deputation of monks from Wādī Naṭrūn offered allegiance to 'Amr b. al-'Ās, the governor under Mu'āwiya, he not only gave them security, but summoned Benjamin, the Coptic patriarch, from the retreat to which he had been driven by his enemies, and reinstated him in his office. We read of friendly relations between several of the caliphs and the Coptic abbots, and Matthias, the founder of the great monastery of Esneh, used to be taken into consultation by the Muslim governor, who also sent him presents as a mark of favour.[3] This friendly sympathy on the part of the Muslim rulers showed itself in practical help of a kind that might have been least expected, but which proves the respect which they felt for the Christian Church. 'Amr, in Egypt, took pains to preserve the Christian churches, and in the earliest period of Muslim rule, the Copts were even allowed to erect new churches. There are several instances of Muslim governors both authorising and assisting in the restoration of churches and monasteries. The Muslim rulers seem often to have visited Christian monasteries. Khamārawayh (A.D. 884-895), son of Ibn Ṭūlūn, built an upper room in the Melkite monastery of al-Qusayr, and he used to go there frequently to admire the Byzantine glass mosaics in the church attached to the monastery.[4] The monastery of Nahyā was famous among the

[1] al-Kindī, *Risāla*, p. 6.
[2] *Cf.* Labourt, *op. cit.*, p. 349.
[3] Abū Ṣāliḥ, *op. cit.*, fol. 79*a*.
[4] *Ibid.*, fols. 49*a*, 50*b*.

Muslims; al-Mu'izz encamped beneath the walls of this monastery and laid out a garden, containing a well, and water-wheel there.[1]

In some places it would appear that Muslims performed minor religious duties for the Christian community, and were allowed to be present at Christian services, including even the celebration of the Eucharist, and in some cases Muslims and Christians combined in observing the feasts of the latter. For instance, the Festival of the Baptism of Christ, kept on January 6, was observed by both Muslims and Christians at the Church of St. John the Baptist in Cairo.[2] At Esneh the Muslims and Christians used to fraternise on the Feast of the Nativity, and the former burned candles and lighted lamps and burned logs of fragrant wood, in celebration of the feast.[3] A parallel to this can be found in the modern observance of the feast of Shamm al-Nessīm (the Coptic Easter Monday), which is celebrated with equal zest by both Muslims and Copts, and is one of the most popular festivals of the Muḥammadan year.

It appears that in these early days Muslims were by no means averse to discussing theological matters with Christians. The Qur'ān itself authorises such discussions,[4] and Christian writers make provision for such discussions in their books. In Damascus, before the Arab conquest, the Christian theologians had been accustomed to enter into controversy on the most subtle points of religious metaphysics, and they were prepared to carry on discussions with the votaries of the new faith, which at first was generally regarded as a form of heresy. John of Damascus in his book on *Heresies* gives a section to Islām; he also includes a dialogue with a Saracen, given as a guide to Christians in their arguments with Muslims.[5] His pupil, Theodore Abū Qurra, wrote several controversial dialogues discussing the Muslim and Christian points of view. We read also of the Nestorian patriarch Timothy holding discussions on religious matters in the presence of the Caliph Hārūn al-Rashīd. The author of the *Risāla*, written *c.* A.D. 813-833 to contro-

[1] Abū Ṣāliḥ, fol. 61*b*.
[2] *Ibid.*, *op. cit.*, fols. 40*b*, 41*a*.
[3] *Ibid.*, fol. 102*b*.
[4] Sūra x. 94; v. 18.
[5] *De Hæresibus Liber*, par. 101.

vert the arguments of the Christian ʿAbd al-Messīḥ al-Kindī, says that he has studied the various Christian sects and also the New Testament, and goes on to state : " I have met with many monks, well known for their extreme asceticism and their great knowledge, and I have visited many monasteries and their churches, and I have been present at their prayers, those seven lengthy ones which they call the Offices, and I observed their wonderful diligence therein and how they bent low, worshipping with their faces bowed down to the ground, especially on Sunday and Saturday nights and on their festivals, when they keep watch, standing on their feet, praising and glorifying God, and confessing Him all through the night, and they spend the whole day standing in prayer, and in their prayers make constant mention of the Father, the Son and the Holy Spirit, and in the days of their retreats, when they stand bare-footed, in sackcloth and ashes, with much weeping and shedding of tears continually. And I saw how they offered the Eucharist, how they kept the purest of the bread for it, and offered long prayers in great humility as they elevated it upon the Altar in that place called the Sanctuary, together with the chalices filled with wine. I have observed also the meditations of the monks in their cells during their fasts. Also I have visited their Metropolitans and Bishops, well known for their knowledge of spiritual things, and their great learning, famed for their profound knowledge of Christianity, and displaying great asceticism with regard to the world. And I have discussed with them impartially, seeking for the truth."[1] All these instances go to prove that arguments and controversial discussions were frequent between Christians and Muslims, and the latter could hardly fail to become well acquainted with Christian views of theology and philosophy and to know what Christian doctrine and the Christian system of ethics really represented.

In conclusion, it is evident that Islām, during the first centuries of its existence, at a time when its theological doctrines were being formulated, and, which is more important for our purpose, at a time when its mystical doctrines were developing, found itself almost everywhere in a Chris-

[1] al-Kindī, *Risala*, p. 6.

tian environment, in close contact with Christian forms of worship and Christian culture. It is clear that the dependence of the Muslims upon Christians for practically all that made for progress and civilisation brought them into close touch with Christian ideals and Christian habits of thought, a fact which could not fail to have an effect upon the religious development of Islām, both in its orthodox form, and in that most unorthodox form which we know as Islamic mysticism or Ṣūfīsm. But this Christian influence made itself felt, not only directly in the ways we have indicated, where it was exercised by those who remained Christian and who maintained their Christianity openly, but perhaps even more effectively, by indirect means, by the secret pressure exerted by those Christians who had become Muslim in name, but not in fact, who were secretly imposing Christian ideals of thought and conduct upon those Muslims who were, nominally at least, their co-religionists. We read that the Syrians, who formed an important part of the Ummayyad armies, cared little for Islām, and were described as "Arabs like strangers and Muslims with the characteristics of Christians." We can hardly measure the effect of this vast undercurrent of Christian belief existing within Islām itself, and gradually leavening the mass of orthodoxy with the germs of that which was to become the most vital element in the religion of Islām, sowing the seeds of that which was to blossom into a fair flower springing from soil apparently barren—Ṣūfīsm, with its strange unlikeness to that faith in which it had its origin, and its still stranger likeness to the faith which Islām sought to supersede and to destroy.

CHAPTER VII

ASCETICISM AND MYSTICISM IN ORTHODOX ISLĀM

As we have seen in the last chapter, it was inevitable that Christianity should have its effect upon the religious development of Islām, and Christian elements were to be found even in the time of Muḥammad, and in the Qur'ān itself, as well as in the Traditions, and in the rules for religious observances accepted by the orthodox as having the authority, or being in accordance with the precepts, of the founder of their faith. We are concerned mainly with this Christian influence, as it affected ascetical practices and doctrines and the rise of mystical tendencies within orthodox Islām.

Muḥammad himself is said to have led a very ascetic life in the earliest stage of his ministry ; he was reputed to have fasted and prayed much, and to have spent lonely vigils in a cave on Mount Ḥirā. This pursuit of ascetic practices seems to have been due to a sense of sin which led him to seek peace of conscience in the same way as the Christian solitaries. A tradition states that Abū Bakr once asked Muḥammad for a prayer for his own private use, and the Prophet gave him this form : " O God, I have wronged my own soul with grievous sin, and Thou alone dost forgive sins ; forgive me with Thy forgiveness and have compassion upon me, for in truth Thou art the Forgiving, the Merciful."[1] It was at this period, when the impulse to introspection was most active in Muḥammad's case, that he showed also a tendency to self-mortification, and attached great importance to severe exercises of penance. He instituted the fast of Ramaḍān and the custom of seclusion in his own *masjid* during the fast-month. In this he seems to have followed the example of the Christian hermits, who secluded themselves in cells in the desert, and the Christian custom of going into retreat, for a period of solitude consecrated to prayer, penance and meditation, a custom practised in the

[1] Bukhārī.

Christian Church from the beginning of its existence. In addition to the Fast, the Prophet enforced the five daily prayers, the pilgrimage to Mecca, and abstinence from wine, all of which were forms of self-discipline, imposed with the aim of subordinating the desires of the body to the spiritual welfare of the soul. The poverty of the Prophet and his household is often noted by Muslim writers, and we find that, in accordance with the example he set, asceticism and puritanism were characteristic of the earliest believers, and simplicity of life was regarded as the mark of the strict Muslim.

Not only in his personal practice, but also in his religious teaching, Muḥammad gave a definite place to asceticism, the motive for which is shown to be an intense fear of God and His Judgment, inspired by man's consciousness of his own sins. Muḥammad proclaimed insistently the Judgments of God against transgressors and the punishments of Hell for the godless. His eschatological teaching is almost identical with that of the Syrian Christian Church of his time and before it. This type of theology, with its emphasis on fear, so characteristic of the Syrian Church, was due to its adherence to ascetic ideals, in which it was strongly influenced by Egyptian monasticism. We find that the Qur'ānic teaching on Eternity and Judgment had been forestalled in Syrian literature, a fact not to be accounted for by any universal religious tendency, for there appears to be the self-same homiletic scheme as the foundation of both. It is not only the choice and method of the eschatological teaching of Muḥammad, which, in addition, reveals a close acquaintance with the apocalyptic literature of Eastern monasticism, especially the apocalypses of St. Paul and St. John, but above all the application and religious construction of the eschatological texts. The relation between the two is shown not only in regard to religious thought, but in the use of homiletic forms and well-established phrases. This, of course, was derived not from any direct study of Christian literature, but from what Muḥammad had heard of Christianity through his personal intercourse with Christians, or at second-hand from others.[1] Tradition relates that the Prophet once at the

[1] *Cf.* Tor Andrae, *Der Ursprung des Islams und das Christentum*, p. 139.

fair of 'Uqāz heard a Yamanite preacher, who was probably a Nestorian Christian, and it was no doubt to the strong Nestorian mission in Yaman that he owed what knowledge he had of Syrian Christianity.

As a consequence of the eschatological teaching of the Qur'ān, and its emphasis on fear, there is the enjoinment to various forms of self-discipline and asceticism, as a means of avoiding sin and so escaping judgment. Penitence was the first step in the right direction. Sinners must suffer the due punishment of their sins, " save those who shall repent and believe, and do righteous works . . . for them God will change their evil things into good things, for God is Gracious, Merciful. And whoso turneth to God and doeth what is right, He verily will convert with a true conversion."[1] For the transgressor, there were forms of penance allotted in early Islām. Having turned to God, it was incumbent on the believer to keep Him in remembrance and to beware of negligence and heedlessness. " Remember thy Lord within thyself, in humility and fear, with low-spoken words in the morning and at evening, and be not one of the heedless."[2] Frequent warnings against indifference and neglect of what is due to God are also characteristic of the Syrian Christian writers.

Fasting is definitely enjoined in the Qur'ān as a form of self-discipline. The fast of Ramaḍān, demanding complete abstinence from sunrise to sunset, for a whole month, may be connected with the fact that the month was especially sacred even in pre-Islamic times, but it seems more probable that it was instituted in imitation of the Christian season of Lent, while making more severe demands than the Lenten fast, upon those who observed it. The principle of penitential fasting was recognised by Muḥammad's ordinances, in which he enjoins fasting as a penance for homicide, perjury and hasty divorce.[3] It was imposed for three days during the Pilgrimage and for seven on returning.[4] Also the thirteenth, fourteenth and fifteenth of each month were gener-

[1] Sūra xxv. 70, 71.
[2] Sūra vii. 204. *Cf.* also Sūras xxi. 1, xix. 4.
[3] Sūras iv. 94; v. 91; lviii. 5.
[4] Sūra ii. 192.

ally observed as days of fast, and the tenth day of the month of Muḥarram, while strict Muslims fasted on Mondays and Thursdays. Voluntary fasting was regarded as a meritorious act. A temporary vow of chastity was also imposed during the Pilgrimage.[1]

Prayer is enjoined in the Qur'ān as a duty never to be neglected, for it turned the thoughts of the believer away from what was evil to what was good, and made him oblivious of the claims of the creatures and attentive only to the claims of the Creator. "Recite the portions of the book which have been revealed to thee and continue to pray, for prayer restraineth from what is shameful and blameworthy. And the greatest duty is the remembrance of God; and God knoweth what ye do."[2] "Observe strictly the prayers," Muḥammad says elsewhere, "and stand up full of devotion to God. And if you have any alarm, then pray . . . but when you are safe, then remember God, how He hath made you to know what you knew not."[3] Much stress was laid on the duty of night-prayers and, as we have seen, the Prophet himself set an example in this respect. He adjures the believer thus: "Make mention of the name of thy Lord at morn, at even and at night. Adore Him and give glory to Him the livelong night."[4] Set prayer three times a day seems to have been his first rule: "Observe prayer at early morning, at the close of the day, and at the approach of night; surely good deeds drive away evil deeds."[5] There is a definite recommendation not only to night-prayers but to vigils. "Observe prayer from the setting of the sun," the Prophet directs, "until the first darkening of the night and the daybreak-reading—and watch unto it in the night."[6] In a fine passage the Prophet describes the practice of the truly devout: "The God of Mercy . . . is He Who hath ordained the night and the day to succeed one another for those who desire to be mindful of God or seek to be thankful. And the servants of the God of Mercy are . . . they who pass the night prostrating themselves in the worship of their Lord, and

[1] Sūra ii. 193.
[2] Sūra xxix. 44.
[3] Sūra ii. 239, 240.
[4] Sūra lxxvi. 25.
[5] Sūra xi. 116.
[6] Sūra xvii. 81.

standing."[1] Humility before the power of God is fitting for the believer. " Hath not the time yet come for those who believe, to humble their hearts in remembering God and the truth which He hath sent down, and that they be not like those to whom the Scriptures were given heretofore, whose lifetime was prolonged, so their hearts were hardened and many of them transgressed ?"[2] At the same time, the Muslim believers are pointed to the Christian priests and monks as an example, because they are free from pride.

Unworldliness is constantly set before the believer as a virtue to be aimed at, since the goods of this world are but vanity, and the believer must seek to detach his heart from all else save God alone. " Know that this world's life is only a sport and pastime and outward show and a cause of vain-glory among you ! And a vying in the multiplication of riches and children is like the plants which spring up after rain . . . whose growth rejoiceth the husbandman ; then they wither away and thou seest them all yellow ; then they become stubble. And in the hereafter is a severe chastisement or else forgiveness from God and His satisfaction ; and this world's life is but a passing enjoyment."[3] Over against the transience of this life is set the everlastingness of the life to come. " O my people ! the life of this world is only a passing joy, but the life to come is an everlasting abode."[4] In all early Muslim writings we find the strong contrast drawn between this world (*al-dunyā*) and the world to come (*al-ākhir*), between the transient, the worthless, the unreal, and the abiding, the good, and the truly existent. " The life of this world," Muḥammad says again, " is but a pastime and a play, but the abode of the world to come is life indeed ; did they but know !"[5] Therefore all who have wealth should treat it only as a trust and should be generous in giving to the poor and needy, while those who suffer affliction should bear it patiently ; the believer should be concerned neither with prosperity nor adversity, but only with the will of his Lord. " He is righteous who believeth in God and in the

[1] Sūra xxv. 63-65. *Cf.* also Sūra lxxiii. 20.
[2] Sūra lvii. 14.
[3] Sūra lvii. 19. *Cf.* also Sūra viii. 68.
[4] Sūra xl. 42. [5] Sūra xxix. 64.

Last Day . . . who for the love of God distributeth his wealth to his kindred, and to the orphans and the needy and the wayfarer, and those who ask for help, and to ransom the captives; he who observeth prayer and payeth the legal alms, and who is of those who fulfil the promises they have made, who are patient in distress and hardships and in time of trouble: these are they who are sincere and these are they who fear the Lord."[1] Again the Prophet says, "Your God is the One God. To Him, therefore, should you surrender yourselves; and carry thou good tidings to the humble, whose hearts, when mention is made of God, thrill with awe; and to those who are patient under all that befalleth them, and who observe prayer and give alms of that with which we have supplied them."[2] Only those who have purified themselves by these means will be enabled to devote themselves to their Lord with entire devotion.

This emphasis on asceticism and the need for self-discipline we find chiefly in the earlier Sūras of the Qur'ān, for increasing success and prosperity, together with the fact that the tendency to asceticism, especially in the form of monasticism, was recognised to be Christian, led Muḥammad to lay little stress upon it after the Hijra.[3] But the practice itself had taken root among the early Muslims, and therefore we find a large number of Traditions advocating asceticism, and in order that they might carry the more weight, many of these recommendations to otherworldliness and self-mortification are attributed to Muḥammad himself; among these are included the words and deeds of Jesus, falsely attributed to the Prophet, but in addition we find many Logia ascribed to Jesus Himself by the Muslim writers, which were evidently accepted by the Christian traditions of the Oriental Churches of the seventh century. For the orthodox, therefore, in addition to the teaching of the Qur'ān, there was ample justification in the Traditions for the practice of asceticism.

On the subject of Repentance as the first step on the way to God there are a number of Traditions. The Prophet is

[1] Sūra ii. 172. *Cf.* Sūras lxxvi. 8; xc. 10.
[2] Sūra xxii. 35-36.
[3] *Cf.* Sūras ix. 31; lvii. 27.

related, on the authority of 'Ā'isha, to have said, " Verily, when a servant confesses his faults and repents and turns to the court of God, God approves of his repentance."[1] A tradition ascribed to Abū Hurayra states that God has said, " I am near the thought of My servant, who is thinking of Me ; that is, I pardon his sins, when he asks for it, and approve his repentance, when he repents and turns away from sin ; and I accept, when he supplicates, and I am with him when he remembers Me ; and when he remembers Me within himself, I am mindful of him within Myself, and if he remembers Me among others, I am still more mindful of him among others."[2] Abū Hurayra is responsible for another Tradition stating that God accepts the repentance of him who repents before the sun arises from its setting ; and another Tradition says, " God is verily glad at the repentance of His servants, when they repent and turn to Him."[3] There is a curious tradition showing how great a part fear played as a motive for Muslim asceticism, a tradition for which there is no evidence that it belongs to the earliest period of Islām, though from its content it seems most probable. " Of Jesus it is related that He came across about forty thousand women whose colour had changed (*i.e.*, they were wan and pale), and who were wearing garments of haircloth and wool, and He said to them, ' What has changed your colour, O ye crowds of women ?' They replied, ' The remembrance of Hell-fire has changed our colour, O Son of Mary, for whoever enters the Fire shall taste neither rest nor drink.' "[4]

On the subject of Fasting there is a good deal to be found in the Traditions, and amongst the sayings relating to it is one that states, " God hears the prayers of those that fast."[5] There is also a Tradition ascribed to Abū Hurayra, according to which, " Fasting is a shield against the devil's wickedness in the world and from hell-fire in the world to come."[6] Again, Abū Mālik al-Ash'arī gives a Tradition, which says, " Verily there are houses in Paradise, and God has prepared

[1] *Mishkāt al-Maṣābīḥ*, X. iii. 1.
[2] *Op. cit.*, IX. ii. 1.
[3] *Op. cit.*, X. iii. 1.
[4] *Logia et Agrapha*, No. 84 (3).
[5] *Mishkāt al-Maṣābīḥ*, IX. i. 2.
[6] *Ibid.*, VII. i. 1.

them for persons who follow up fasting and say prayers at night when others are sleeping."[1]

The Traditions deal at length with Prayer (*ṣalāt*), which is regarded as having power to cleanse from sin. One Tradition says, "Prayer is like a stream of sweet water which flows past the door of each one of you, into which he plunges five times a day ; do you suppose that anything remains of his uncleanness after that ?"[2] The Traditions also emphasise the importance of being free from all distractions during Prayer, because it is a time of intimate intercourse with God. "When one of you performs the *ṣalāt* he is in confidential converse with his Lord."[3] We have already seen that Muḥammad was accustomed to pray in the night, and that in the Qur'ān he advocated the observance of night-prayers, and there is equal emphasis upon this duty in the Traditions. There is a night-prayer attributed to the Prophet, in which he prayed, "Pardon my faults, of which I have been guilty, and which I may commit henceforward, and forgive the sins I have concealed and the sins I have disclosed, and those which Thou knowest better than I."[4] Again the Prophet is reputed to have said that there was not a Muslim who went to sleep on the remembrance of God, and who, on awakening in the night, asked for some good thing from God, but would have it granted to him.[5] The night-prayers are especially effective, not only in obtaining what may be asked for, but in ensuring the protection of God against the wiles of the devil, who is naturally most active in the watches of the night and most dangerous when men are asleep. The devil tempts men to sleep, says the Prophet, and ties knots upon the neck of God's servant, and if the servant awakes and remembers God and says his prayers, the knots are untied, and he rises in the morning in gladness and purity.[6] Abū Umāyma gives a Tradition containing the same teaching, which exhorts the believer, saying, "Rise for the night-prayers, because such was the occupation of the righteous who have preceded you ; and it is a

[1] *Mishkāt al-Maṣābīḥ*, VII. i. 1.
[2] *Cf.* Bukhārī, i. 143.
[3] Aḥmad b. Ḥanbal, ii. 36 ; *cf.* also ii. 460.
[4] *Mishkāt al-Maṣābīḥ*, IV. xxxiii. 1.
[5] *Ibid.*, IV. xxxiii. 2.
[6] *Ibid.*, IV. xxxiv. 1.

means whereby you come near to your God ; and thereby your faults are hidden and sins are prevented."[1] Closely connected with Prayer is *dhikr*, which with the tongue is "mention" and with the mind is "remembrance," but which, both in the Qur'ān and the Traditions, is used to mean the worship or glorification of God (*cf.* p. 137). There is a Tradition which says, "There sits not a company remembering God, but angels surround them and the (divine) mercy covers them, and God Most High remembers them among those who are with Him."[2]

The Traditions are full of exhortations to silence, devotion, humility and otherworldliness. A saying is attributed both to the Messiah and to Muḥammad, according to which, "There are four (good) things which can be attained only by effort : silence, which is the beginning of the life of devotion and humility, and frequent remembrance of God and fewness of possessions."[3] Much speaking was not commended by those who advocated an ascetic life, for it was conducive to the uttering of vain words and boasting, while humility, on the other hand, was best displayed in silence. Mālik b. Anas was responsible for a Tradition which ascribed to Jesus the saying, "Do not speak much . . . except in the mention of God, for you will harden your hearts, and a hard heart is far from God Most High, but you do not realise it."[4] Poverty and the simple life were enjoined in the Traditions as a means of attaining the joys of Paradise hereafter. 'Ubayd b. 'Umayr, one of the contemporaries of the Prophet, pointed to the example of Christ, the Son of Mary, Who used to dress in haircloth and eat the fruit of trees, Who had no posterity who might die, nor house to be destroyed, nor did He lay up for the morrow, and when night overtook Him, He slept where He happened to be.[5] There is a saying attributed by Mālik b. Dīnār to the Messiah, urging man to live the life of discipline, in order to escape

[1] *Mishkāt al-Maṣābīḥ*, IV. xxxiv. 2.

[2] *Cf. Mishkāt al-Maṣābīḥ*, IX. ii. 1. This seems to be a re-echo of Luke xii. 8 : "Whosoever shall confess Me before men, him shall the Son of man also confess before the angels of God."

[3] *Logia et Agrapha*, No. 76.

[4] *Ibid.*, No. 142.

[5] *Ibid.*, No. 77.

from the consequences of sin and attain to the rewards of righteousness, "The fear of God and love of Paradise produce patience in affliction and remove a man far from the things of this world. Verily I say unto you that to eat barley-bread and to sleep on the refuse-heaps with the dogs is a little thing to do in the search for Paradise."[1] That poverty, for the sake of God, is one of the surest recommendations for admission to Paradise is made clear in more than one of the Traditions. The Prophet is said to have declared that he would stand at the door of Paradise and that most of those who would enter would be poor.[2] Another statement ascribed to him was to the effect that the poor would enter Paradise five hundred days before the rich, and these five hundred days were half of one of God's days.[3] The true believer had no need of this world's riches, because his provision (*rizq*) came from God, and faith was shown by complete dependence upon God for all his requirements. One of the sayings regarding this, attributed to the Prophet, is a re-echo of the Christian gospel; 'Umar b. al-Khaṭṭāb related that he said, "If you put your whole trust in God, as you should do, He most certainly will give you sustenance, as He gives it to the birds; they come out hungry in the morning, but return full to their nests."[4]

The same warnings against the delusions of this world that were given in the Qur'ān appear again in full force in the Traditions. "The world is sweet in the heart and green to the eye," the Prophet is reported to have said; "then look to your actions, and abstain from the world and its wickedness."[5] Separation from the world and its snares was enjoined in the Tradition according to which an Arab asked Muḥammad which was the best of actions, and the one which would receive the greatest reward, and the Prophet replied, "The best of actions is this, that you separate from the world and die whilst your tongue is moist in repeating the name of God."[6] There is a well-known saying ascribed to Jesus according to which He said, "This world is a

[1] *Logia et Agrapha*, No. 70. [2] *Mishkāt al-Maṣābīḥ*, XXII. xxiv. 1.
[3] *Ibid.*, XXII. xxiv. 2. [4] *Ibid.*, XXII. xxvii. 1.
[5] *Ibid.*, XIII. i. 1. *Cf.* the teaching of Isaac of Nineveh, p. 98 above.
[6] *Ibid.*, IX. ii. 2.

bridge: cross by it and do not linger on it."[1] In the same sense is the tradition according to which the Prophet said to Ibn 'Umar, "Be in the world as a stranger or a sojourner who passes on, and count yourself to be as one of the dead."[2] Two early Traditions ascribe to Jesus a solemn warning to those who falsely pretend to seek the things of the next world, while in reality they are secretly attached to the goods of this world and corrupted by them. "How shall it be," asked Jesus, "with a man reputed to be wise, who, after he has set his face towards the next world, turns aside to the life of this world, and how will it be with a wise man who seeks the Word (of God) in order to teach it, but not in order to practise it?"[3]

Again, "Jesus, Son of Mary, said: 'O wise but evil men, ye have fasted, prayed and given alms, but those things which ye commanded (to others), ye have not fulfilled, and those things which ye taught, ye have not done. How evil is your course of life, for ye have repented in word and by assertion of faith, but have done according to your sinful desires. What avails it to you to purify yourselves outwardly while your hearts remain defiled? Verily I say unto you, Be not like unto sieves, through which the good flour falls to the ground, while the chaff remains therein. So ye also utter wisdom by your mouths, while hatred remains in your hearts. O ye who are in bondage to this world, how shall the next world be attained, by one whose lust for this world is not satisfied, and whose craving for it is not at an end? Verily I say unto you, that your hearts shall mourn for your deeds. For ye have done lip-service to this world and have trodden good deeds underfoot. Verily I say unto you, Ye have corrupted your future life, and the good things of the next world. What man is viler than one of you, since ye were not ignorant (of what ye did)? Woe unto you, how long will ye point out the way to those who grope in darkness, while ye yourselves know not the road? Thus you exhort those attracted by this world, in order that they may

[1] *Logia et Agrapha*, No. 46.

[2] *Mishkāt al-Maṣābīḥ*, XXII. xxv. 1. *Cf.* Isaac of Nineveh, p. 98 above.

[3] *Logia et Agrapha*, No. 6.

relinquish it little by little to you. Woe unto you, for of what profit is it to a darkened house, if the lamp is placed upon its roof, while within it is deserted and in darkness? So likewise, what shall it profit you that the light of knowledge is in your mouths, while within your souls are barren and untended? O ye who are in bondage to this world! Ye are neither like slaves who show reverence, nor like free men who give liberally of what they possess.'" Soon, He continues, shall this world prove to be the destruction of its bondslaves, who shall be torn from all upon which they had depended, and be led unto everlasting punishment.[1] The derivation of this passage from the Christian gospel is obvious in every line of it,[2] but the fact that it finds a place among the early traditions of Islām proves that its teachings, with their emphasis upon the evil of this world and its power for destruction, found ready acceptance among those who wished to advocate asceticism and the unworldly life among the Muslims of the early centuries of Islām.

It is not difficult to trace the connection between these teachings on asceticism and self-discipline, which appear in both the Qur'ān and the Traditions, and the doctrines of Christianity with which, as we have seen in the last chapter, the Muslims had every opportunity to become acquainted in the first centuries of the Islāmic era. The very language used to express the theological and ascetical conceptions of Islām is borrowed from that of the Christian Church; especially we find words derived from the Aramaic, which evidently came through the Syrian Church of Ḥīra and the Nestorian teachers who were to be found in Arabia itself. From Yaman Muḥammad took the name "Raḥmān" (the Merciful), "Raḥmānān" being the title given to God the Father by the Christians of South Arabia. From Yaman, too, he took the name of "Mu'minīn" (believers). The presence in the Qur'ān of such words as "ṣalāt" (prayer), which does not seem to occur in pre-Qur'ānic literature, which was not Arabic, but Aramaic in origin (Aram. *Ṣelōtā*), and used by the Eastern Christians; "Subḥān" (glory be to God), which is frequently used in the Qur'ān,[3] with its derivatives "sab-

[1] *Logia et Agrapha*, No. 53. [2] *Cf.* Matt. xxiii. 13 *ff.*
[3] *Cf.* Sūras v. 116; x. 10; ii. 30; xxvii. 8.

baḥ" (to glorify God) and "tasbīḥ" (invocation, glorification), which is a loan-word from the Aramaic, from the root "shebaḥ" (to praise), and was possibly an imitation of the Christian Gloria[1]; "tazakka" (to purify), used especially in connection with a return to God,[2] taken from the Syriac "dakā," which, with its derivatives, is used frequently in the Peshitta[3]; "furqān" (illumination), employed in the Qur'ān, sometimes to mean "revelation," which is the Arabic sense of the word,[4] and also with the meaning of "salvation"[5] from the Syriac "pūrqānā" (salvation, redemption); "'abd" (servant of God), with its derivative "'ubudīya" (service, adoration), also used in this sense in the Peshitta;[6] "dhikr" (remembrance), used constantly in the Qur'ān in the sense of remembrance or mention of God, and so with the meaning of "worship,"[7] corresponding to the Syriac "dukrānā," in common use with the same signification—all these, and others, reveal a Christian influence, while there are to be found, in addition to these, expressions used in the Qur'ān or the Traditions which had a definitely Christian association for Muḥammad and his followers. Among those to be found in the Qur'ān are "tawba" (repentance, from the Aramaic *tethūba*) literally, a coming back to God, for which the same word, used with the same meaning, is found in the Syriac gospels; "rabb" (Lord), with its derivatives "rabbānī" (Divine, godly), and "rubūbīya" (Divinity, deity), applied in the Qur'ān only to God, had been used in the Gospels, and was used throughout the Christian Church to designate both God the Father and God the Son; "ṣawm" (abstinence), originally meaning "to stand still, without occupation," was probably used with the meaning of "fasting," by Muḥammad, because he knew it to be used in this sense by Christians and Jews. These examples go to prove that for the elements in the new faith which had little or no connection with Arab paganism, Muḥammad for his terminology was obliged to have recourse

[1] *Cf.* p. 139. [2] *Cf.* Sūra xci. 9; lxxxvii. 14.
[3] *Cf.* Matt. viii. 3; John xiii. 10; 1 Cor. v. 8.
[4] *Cf.* Sūras xxi. 49; iii. 2; xxv. 1. [5] Sūra viii. 29, 42.
[6] Rom. i. 1; 2 Tim. ii. 24.
[7] *Cf.* Sūras ii. 196; xxxiii. 35; lviii. 20.

to the Christian Church, and to make use of its language to express religious doctrines and ideas which were, like the language in which they were clothed, definitely borrowed from, or based upon, similar Christian doctrines.

In considering the ascetical elements in orthodox Islām, we find that the motive for repentance, as already pointed out, was primarily the fear of Divine punishment, and the same fear was to be found among the Eastern Christians with whom Muḥammad was in contact. His conception of the Day of Judgment and a Second Return,[1] and his descriptions of Hell-fire as contrasted with the joys of Heaven, all find their parallels in the New Testament, and it was this fear of Judgment, which had had so great an influence in sending the early Christians of Egypt and Syria out into the deserts in order to expiate their sins and to avoid further temptation, which influenced Muḥammad and his followers, in the first place, to seek safety in asceticism. Of these ascetic practices, fasting, as we have noted, was definitely enjoined in the Qur'ān and elsewhere, not only in the form of total abstinence fron sunrise to sunset during Ramaḍān, but as a work of supererogation and as a means of penance for various offences. Here, again, the obvious source was Christianity, for the Christian Lent, and the fasts of the Christian year, together with the frugal habits of the solitaries, were customs with which the pagan Arabs were familiar in their intercourse with their Christian neighbours.

Muḥammad's regulations and injunctions with regard to prayer also suggest a Christian origin. As we have seen, in the earlier Sūras he recommended prayer three times a day, but later increased these times of prayer to five, which in some measure corresponded to the Christian Office. As he took the word " ṣalāt " (prayer) from the Arabian Christians, so also apparently he took the ceremony ; the standing, bowing down and prostrations, together with the praises of God and repetitions of formulæ, were undoubtedly intended to imitate the ritual prayer of the Christians, while the traditional references to forms for personal and informal prayer given by the Prophet to his companions point to a knowledge of the part played by personal intercession in the lives

[1] *Cf.* Sūras lii. 7-14 ; lxxviii. 18, 19 ; xxvii. 9.

of Christians. From Christianity he probably derived the whole idea of the efficacy of prayer to accomplish its aim in this life. The night-prayers were, without doubt, an imitation of the nocturnal offices in use in Christian monasteries. The mention of vigils and readings must have been inspired by the habits of the Syrian monks and anchorites, of whom Thomas of Margā relates that many read the psalter twice between the evening and the morning, while the observance of vigils was generally regarded in the Oriental Christian Church as a work of devotion well-pleasing to God. The word " tahajjud " (to awake from sleep), used in the Qur'ān (Sūra xvii. 80), suggests a connection with the custom of keeping awake at night, so much practised by the ascetics and mystics of West Asia. In Syriac ascetical literature, keeping awake is commended as a work of great merit, combined with the reading of Scripture, meditation and ritual prayer. Ephraim the Syrian strongly commends it. " Ye then watch as lights in this night of starry light. For though so dark be its colour yet in virtue it is clear. For whoever is like this clear One, wakeful and prayerful in darkness, him in this darkness visible a light unseen surrounds !"[1] Elsewhere he writes :

" Let us become in our vigils diligent watchers,
And present continually our holy prayers ;
That with those virgins who displayed wisdom
We may meet the Bridegroom in the day of His appearing."[2]

The brief ejaculatory prayers given for use by Muslims in the night correspond to the form of the night-prayers used by the Egyptian monks and the use of the " tasbīḥ " (praise to God), the " subḥān " (glory be to God) and the doxology " allah akbar " (God is most great), increases the resemblance.[3]

The Christian Church placed good works, and especially almsgiving, on a level above fasting and vigils, and we have

[1] *On the Nativity*, i.
[2] *Renunciation of the World* (tr. H. Burgess).
[3] *Cf.* Tor Andrae, *op. cit.*, pp. 191 *ff.*

noted the stress that Muḥammad, in the Qur'ān, laid upon giving the legal alms, upon generosity towards the poor and needy, those near of kin and orphans, and upon the duty of ransoming captives, and this latter duty of the manumission of slaves was accounted a meritorious action in the Syrian Church.

The influence of the New Testament and of Christian asceticism upon the otherworldliness of the Qur'ān and its doctrine of constant insistence upon the vanity of this world and its riches, together with the call to live for the other world alone, is too obvious to require proof. Again and again Muḥammad urges men not to lay up for themselves treasures in this world, where moth and rust do corrupt and where thieves break through and steal, but to lay up for themselves treasures in heaven, which none could wrest from them. Equally strongly does he insist, with St. Paul, that the things which are seen are temporal, and it is the things which are not seen which are eternal. It was not only what he had heard of the teachings of Christianity in this respect, but what he saw all around him of the practice of the life of unworldliness, poverty and renunciation, by the monks and the solitaries, which could not fail to impress him. The Christian origin of this unworldly teaching is frankly acknowledged in the Traditions, as we have seen above, for many of the parables and sayings relating to the ascetic life are put into the mouth of Jesus. The Qur'ānic teaching on the renunciation of the world also bears a close resemblance to that given by Ephraim the Syrian, who writes in one of his hymns :

" Alas for thee, O world, how much art thou loved,
Thy beauties are many, but they are not permanent,
For thou art but a dream, without real existence ;
I renounce thee henceforth, O wicked world !

Woe be to whoever shall love thee, O world !
For he will be caught in thy snares, and in the nets
thou layest for him,
He shall lose his soul and yet not possess thee ;
I renounce thee henceforth, O wicked world !

Omnipotent and merciful is God towards those
Who reject this world, which is passing away,
And meditate continually, upon that which remaineth,
I renounce thee henceforth, O transitory world !

Glory be to the Good, to Whom appertain
Both these worlds and all that is in them ;
Both that which passeth away and that which remaineth,
I renounce thee henceforth, O transitory world !"[1]

There is one respect in which Muḥammad makes a notable omission in his teaching on asceticism, and that is in his refusal to advocate celibacy ; yet this goes rather to prove that his ascetical teaching was derived from Christianity than otherwise, for the Nestorians made no such ideal of celibacy as the other Eastern Churches ; they had, on the contrary, a high esteem for marriage and the procreation of children. Nestorian Christians did not uphold the idea of virginity as the best and highest type of life for the Christian, hence if Muḥammad heard the Gospel, and learnt what little he did learn of Christian doctrine, mainly from Nestorian sources, he would not hear the praise of virginity and the celibate that he would undoubtedly have done had he derived his knowledge of Christianity from the Greek-speaking Church. But as regards this particular feature of asceticism, we realise that Muḥammad, in any case, would have been loath to advocate what was not only contrary to his own personal inclinations and practice, but also foreign to Semitic ideas, since the Semitic races have always set a high value on marriage and the production of offspring, as a duty incumbent on every man.

We have already drawn attention to the intimate association, especially in the Orient, of asceticism with Mysticism,[2] and since we have a definitely ascetical doctrine set forth in orthodox Islām, which we have seen to be derived largely from Christian sources, it is perhaps not surprising that we

[1] *Renunciation of the World.* In reference to the last verse, it is interesting to note that the Muslims constantly spoke of the " Lord of the two worlds " (*rabb al-ʿālamayn*).

[2] See above, pp. 10, 45.

should find certain elements of mystical doctrine in the Qur'ān and the Traditions, most probably of a similar origin. There is little evidence that Muḥammad himself was naturally disposed towards asceticism ; he accepted it as a means towards an end, in the earliest stage of his career, but later showed a disposition to repudiate it. So also we should judge that he was not a mystic by temperament, any more than he was an ascetic ; but in spite of this, we find certain indications of a mystical doctrine in the Qur'ān, which, by those who were of the truly mystical temperament, were incorporated into the fully-developed system of Islamic Mysticism which we find in existence at a later period.

Muḥammad's vocation was to make known the Unity of God, and this was developed into a doctrine of God as the Sole Reality, which is at the basis of all systems of Mysticism. He taught not only the negation of all plurality in the person and nature of the One Being, but regarded Him as Self-Existent, the Sole Agent, and the Sole Cause of all existence and all action. " He is God alone : God the Eternal ! He begets not, nor is He begotten ; and there is none like unto Him."[1] " Truly your God is but One, Lord of the Heavens and of the Earth and of all that lies between them and Lord of the horizons. . . . His, whatsoever is in the heavens and whatsoever is in the earth and whatsoever is between the two, and whatsoever lies beneath the moist earth ! It needs not to raise thy voice, for He knoweth the secrets of men's hearts and what is yet more hidden. God ! There is no God but He ! Most excellent are His Names !"[2] He is the Creator, and all the creatures, of whatever grade, material or spiritual, instinctive or intelligent, are passive before Him ; He is their absolute Ruler, and all that comes to pass is in accordance with His sole and absolute Will.

" He causeth the dawn to break and hath ordained the night for rest and the sun and the moon for reckoning time ! This is the ordinance of the Mighty, the Wise !

" And it is He Who hath made the stars for you that ye may be guided thereby in the darknesses of the land and of the sea !

" And it is He Who sendeth down rain from Heaven ; and

[1] Sūra cxii. [2] Sūras xxxvii. 4, 5 ; xx. 5, 6, 7.

we bring forth by it the buds of all the plants, and from it we bring forth the green foliage, and the grain in the ear, and from the sheaths of the palm-trees clustering dates within reach, and gardens of grapes and olives and pomegranates, alike and unlike.

"Sole Maker of the Heavens and the Earth! He hath created everything and He knoweth all things! This is God your Lord. There is no God but He, the Creator of all things; therefore worship Him; for He watcheth over all things. No vision comprehends Him, but He comprehendeth all vision, and He is the Subtile, the All-Informed. . . . The words of thy Lord are perfect in truth and in justice; none can change His words; He is the Hearer, the Knower."[1] God is Omnipotent, Omniscient, Present everywhere, All-Seeing yet unseen, the First and the Last, the Mighty and the Wise, the Gracious, the Merciful, the Forgiving. He is also the Primal Light: "God is the Light of the Heavens and of the Earth. His Light is like a niche in which is a lamp . . . the lamp within a glass . . . the glass like unto a brightly-shining star. It is lit from a blessed olive-tree belonging neither to the East nor to the West, the oil whereof would almost give light, even though fire toucheth it not! It is light upon light. God guideth to His light whom He will and God setteth forth parables to men, for God knoweth all things."[2]

The conception of God found in the Qur'ān, particularly the aspects of this conception most acceptable to the mystics, is shown again in the Traditions. A prayer said to have been given by the Prophet to Abū Bakr runs, "O God! the Knower of the hidden and the open, the present and the absent, the Creator of all regions and the worlds; Thou Who dost cherish all things: the Lord and King of all: I witness that there is no God but Thee."[3] Abū Hurayra relates that the Prophet used to say: "O Lord of everything, O Sender down of the Law, the Gospels and the Qur'ān . . . Thou art the First and there was nothing before Thee; and Thou art the Last, and there is nothing after Thee; and Thou dost hide Thyself and there is nothing beyond Thee."[4]

[1] Sūra vi. 96 *ff.*
[2] Sūra xxiv. 35.
[3] *Mishkāt al-Maṣābīḥ*, X. ii. 2.
[4] *Ibid.*, X. v. 2.

Muḥammad was reputed to have said that God was veiled in seventy veils of light and among the invocations attributed to him was this: " O Light of light, Thou art veiled to Thy creature and it does not attain to Thy light. O Light of light, Thy light illuminates the people of heaven and enlightens the people of earth. O Light of all light, Thy light is praised by all light." Among the traditional invocations is also this, " I invoke Thee by the light of Thy countenance, which has filled the foundations of Thy tabernacle."[1]

Orthodox Islām, therefore, depicts a God transcendent, incomprehensible, infinitely above and beyond that which He has brought into being, and the Qur'ān emphasises the gulf between the human creature and the Divine Essence, yet man is set apart from the other creatures in being capable of receiving the Divine revelation, and the Qur'ān does give some indication of the possibility of a mystical union. There are some among mankind " who have near access to God."[2] " God will guide to Himself the one Who turneth to Him, those who believe and whose hearts rest securely on the thought of God."[3] The possibility of communication between God and man, as distinct from the remainder of creation, rests, of course, on the fact that he consists not only of body but of soul, the " ẓāhir " (outward) and the " bāṭin " (inward). The essence of man, according to the Qur'ānic psychology, is the heart, containing the secret and hidden shrine of the conscience (*sirr*), by which God can speak to man, and the secrets of which lie bare to Him.[4] Within him also is the " nafs " (self), which is the " I," regarded by the mystics as the carnal soul, which is led astray by evil desires, but which can be purified by faith, so that the believer realises anew the primeval covenant made between his soul and God, and remembers that he was created for the adoration and the service of his Lord.[5] Man was created originally in purity, and within him is a Divine spark, for God breathed into him of His own Spirit, and man in this primal state of purity was exalted even above the angels, who were bidden

[1] *Cf.* Carra de Vaux, *Journal Asiatique*, 1902, xix. 84.
[2] Sūra iii. 40.
[3] Sūra xiii. 27, 28.
[4] Sūras vi. 3; xx. 6; ix. 79.
[5] Sūras vii. 171; li. 56.

to worship him because of the Divinity within.[1] "Blessed is that man who hath kept his soul pure, and undone is he who hath corrupted it."[2]

So, because of this real affinity between God and the soul of man, there is a means by which the gulf between the Creator and the creature can be bridged, and the soul can break the fetters of earth and ascend again unto its home in God; orthodox Islām always teaches the immortality of the soul.[3] Those who seek God in truth will find that He comes to meet them on the way and to guide them to the goal. "God is the guardian of those who believe; He shall bring them out of darkness into light."[4] Again, there is the promise, "To such of them as believed gave we their reward. . . . O ye who believe! fear God and believe in His apostle; two portions of His mercy will He bestow on you. He will give unto you light to walk in and He will forgive you."[5] In the Traditions there is a saying, ascribed to the Prophet, which runs, "God has said: 'I am present when My servant thinks of Me: I am with him when he remembers Me . . . whosoever seeks to approach Me by a span, I will seek to approach him by a cubit; and he who seeks to approach Me by one cubit, I will seek to approach him by two fathoms; and whoever walks towards Me, I will run towards him.'"[6]

There are indications in the Qur'ān of the Way that must be trodden by the seeker who desired to draw near to God, to attain to knowledge of Him, and finally to become His dwelling-place. "We sent unto you an apostle from among yourselves to recite our communications unto you, and to purify you, and to instruct you in the Book and in the Wisdom, and to teach you that which ye knew not."[7] Here is an indication of a doctrine of esoteric knowledge, which afterwards developed with the Ṣūfīs into that of mystic gnosis (*maʿrifa*). To attain that "wisdom," purification is needed, and in spite of Muḥammad's deep sense of the absolute sovereignty of God, he had at the same time a

[1] Sūras xv. 29; xxxii. 8; xxxviii. 72.
[2] Sūra xci. 9, 10.
[3] *Cf.* Sūra xliv. 56.
[4] Sūra ii. 258.
[5] Sūra lvii. 27, 28.
[6] *Cf. Mishkāt al-Maṣābīḥ*, IX. ii. 1.
[7] Sūra ii. 146.

sense that man must be held to be responsible for his sins, and that his punishment is just if he does not repent and seek to make amends. That original purity in which man was created must be regained if he is to be fit to be reunited with God. To this end were given all the ascetical regulations already mentioned, that the believer might be prepared for his high destiny; sin, and above all, the sin of idolatry, is impurity (*najas*); righteousness, summed up in unswerving faith in God, is purity. "It is not righteousness to turn your faces towards the East and the West, but righteousness is to believe in God."[1] Again it is written, "Happy is he who is purified and who remembereth the name of his Lord and prayeth."[2] This faith can be marred by neglect and unbelief and waywardness of will, and hence the many warnings against heedlessness (*ghafla*) and disobedience. The pure heart is that which is perfect in faith and free from stain (*salīm*), and none can be saved "except the one who comes to God with a pure heart."[3] Purity of intention and motive is needed as well as abstention from the actual commission of sin, for not only the body, but the mind, must be cleansed of all that is contrary to the Will of God.

Vice can be conquered by virtue; that which is stained can be cleansed by what is pure. The idea of the soul as a mirror, reflecting the image of God in proportion to its own brightness, had been used before Islām by Ephraim the Syrian and other Christian mystics,[4] and we find the same conception in the Traditions. There is one attributed to Abū Hurayra which runs thus: "Verily, when a true believer commits a fault, a black spot is created in his heart, and if his sins are increased, the black spot increases, so that it takes possession of the whole heart. For this spot is a rust which God has mentioned in the revelation, "their hearts became rusty from their works" (Sūra, lxxxiii. 14).[5] On the same subject 'Abdallah b. 'Umar gives a tradition

[1] Sūra ii. 172. [2] Sūra lxxxvii. 14, 15. [3] Sūra xxvi. 89.

[4] *Cf.* above, pp. 32, 88. *Cf.* also Evagrius: "As man is not able to behold his likeness in water set unto motion, so the mind cannot behold Our Lord in itself as in a mirror, if it does not purify the inner soul from the affections caused by the things of the world."

[5] *Mishkāt al-Maṣābīḥ*, X. iii. 2.

of the Prophet, relating that he used to say, "There is a polish for everything that becomes rusty, and the polish for the heart is the remembrance of God."[1] This idea of the rusty mirror and the need for polishing it was a favourite one with the later Ṣūfīs. The feeling that it was the "heart" which required cleansing, and the thoughts which must be purified, and that the performance of an outward ritual of worship, and of good works, was not enough, must have led the early Muslims to "interiorisation," and the practice of meditation, which in its turn led to contemplation. It was this sense of the spiritual as the real which led to the contrast between the transient and the abiding, and the feeling of the unreality of this earthly life as compared with the everlasting life in God. The true believers are those whose eyes are fixed not upon the things which are seen, which are temporal, but upon the unseen things, which are eternal: they are "the God-fearing, who believe in the Unseen."[2]

The conception of access to God and union with Him, strange as it may seem in connection with orthodox Islām, was not unknown to Muḥammad; in a verse which evidently alludes to the Christian cult of the saints and the belief in their intercession, he says, "Those whom ye call on, themselves desire a means of access to their Lord, striving which of them shall be nearest to Him."[3] Communication between God and man is shown in the Qur'ān to be by means of revelation, the Word. Muḥammad, like others before him, was faced by the difficulty of establishing any contact between the transcendent and Infinite Godhead and His finite creatures, and therefore sought some mediating agency as a link, and in the Christian adaptation of the Logos doctrine he found what seemed a solution of the problem. Since, as we have seen, he recognised that the soul, by its affinity with the Divine, had a capacity for receiving revelation, it was by this means that the link was forged. God sent His revelation, the Divine Word, and the soul that had been cleansed from its earthly impurities and was restored to its primal purity could receive and apprehend that Word, and becoming thus in very truth the dwelling-place of the Divine,

[1] *Mishkāt al-Maṣābīḥ*, IX. ii. 2.

[2] Sūra ii. 2.

[3] Sūra xviii. 59.

could be enabled to interpret that Word to others. That Muḥammad derived this doctrine from Christianity is proved by the fact that he speaks of Jesus as Himself the very Word of God, Who perfectly interpreted God to man. "Remember when the angel said, 'O Mary! verily God announceth to thee the Word from Him; His name shall be Christ Jesus, the Son of Mary, illustrious in this world and the next, and one of those who have near access to God.'"[1] Again Muḥammad states, "Jesus, Son of Mary, is an apostle of God, and His Word which is conveyed into Mary, and a spirit proceeding from Himself."[2] Only those whose faith is secure and whose hearts are pure can accept this Revelation which brings them near to God, and enables them to live the unitive life in Him. "They who believe and work righteousness; blessedness awaiteth them,"[3] and it is interesting to note that the word employed for "blessedness" (*ṭūbā*) is that used for the Beatitudes in the Christian gospel.

It is by the help of the Holy Spirit that the elect are enabled thus to apprehend the Divine Word and to arrive at union. "With His own Spirit He strengthened them,"[4] that Spirit which proceedeth at the command of God. So they attain to knowledge of the Divine myṣtery,[5] and to the state of perfect satisfaction (*riḍā'*)—which means that they are satisfied with God, completely acquiescent in His Will, and He is satisfied with them, His true servants—and to the state of perfect tranquillity (*ṭumā'nīna*), the peace of God which passeth all understanding, in which they abide in God and enjoy Him for ever. "None either in the Heavens or in the Earth knoweth the Unseen but God . . . yet they have attained to some knowledge of the life to come."[6] These are they who enjoy that perfect repose of the blessed, "Surely Guidance shall come to you from Me, and whosoever shall follow My guidance, on them shall come no fear, neither shall they grieve."[7] "God is well-pleased with them and they with Him. This is the true salvation."[8] The pure in heart "shall be within the mercy of God; therein shall they abide for ever."[9] The experience of the unitive life enjoyed

[1] Sūra iii. 40. [2] Sūra iv. 169. [3] Sūra xiii. 28.
[4] Sūra lviii. 22. [5] Sūra lxxii. 27. [6] Sūra xxvii. 66.
[7] Sūra ii. 36. [8] Sūra v. 119. [9] Sūra iii. 103.

in this world is a foretaste of the joy to come, when the blessed shall live for ever in the Presence of God; to the one who has lived in, and for, God will come the call, "Soul at rest, return to thy Lord, satisfied with Him, giving satisfaction to Him. So enter among My servants and come into My Paradise."[1]

In the Traditions also there are references to the state of "satisfaction" and the unitive life. It is related in a Tradition by an unknown author, and therefore of uncertain date, that Jesus was asked which was the best of all works, and He replied, "Satisfaction with God Most High and love towards Him."[2] Another Tradition attributes to Jesus the saying, "Verily if, when I come into the innermost shrine of My servant, I find therein no love of this world or the next, then I fill him with love to Me and hold him safely, as My friend."[3] There is a very comprehensive description of the unitive state, when the soul which has received the Divine Word is enabled to interpret it to others, because it is itself one with God, in a Tradition ascribed to Abū Hurayra. "God said, 'My servant is always seeking to approach Me, so that I love him. And when I love him, I am his hearing by which he hears, and I am his sight by which he sees, and I am his hands by which he grasps, and I am his feet by which he walks."[4]

When we come to consider the origin of these mystical doctrines found in Orthodox Islām, it seems evident that they must, to a considerable extent, be derived from similar doctrines in Christianity, where, as we have seen in previous chapters, Mysticism had early taken root and had reached a considerable development at the beginning of the Islāmic era, especially in those Eastern Churches with which Muḥammad and his immediate successors were brought into such close contact.

The doctrine of One God he must have derived from the Jews and Christians, for he found no such doctrine among

[1] Sūra xxxix. 27-30. *Cf.* Matt. xxv. 21. For the mystical teaching of the Qur'ān *cf.* also L. Massignon, *La Passion d'al-Hallāj*, ii. 498-504.

[2] *Logia et Agrapha*, No. 91.

[3] *Ibid.*, No. 90. *Cf.* John xiv. 23; xv. 14.

[4] *Mishkāt al-Maṣābīḥ*, IX. ii. 1. *Cf.* for other examples Goldziher, *Muhammedanische Studien*, ii. 393.

his fellow-pagans. In some of the Qur'ānic verses quoted above there is a strong resemblance to the New Testament conception of God: "By Him were all things created, that are in heaven and that are in earth, visible and invisible, whether they be thrones or dominions or principalities or powers, all things were created by Him and for Him. And He is before all things and by Him all things consist." Again St. Paul writes, "Of Him and through Him and to Him are all things: to Whom be glory for ever,"[1] and he urges his hearers to turn from the vanities of this passing life unto "the living God, which made heaven and earth and the sea and all things that are therein . . . He did good and gave us rain from heaven and fruitful seasons, filling our hearts with food and gladness."[2] The conception of God as Creator and Sole Cause and Predestinator is set forth in the sermon at Athens: "God that madeth the world and all things therein, seeing that He is Lord of heaven and earth . . . giveth to all life and breath and all things . . . and hath made all nations of men for to dwell on all the face of the earth, and hath determined the times before appointed, and the bounds of their habitation."[3] God is the One Who "seeth in secret": it is He "Who searcheth the hearts." In Christianity, too, was found the conception of God as Light, both in the Gospel[4] and in such early mystical writers as Ephraim the Syrian[5] and John of Lycopolis, while to St. Augustine also He was the "Light Unchangeable." It may have been from the Creed itself, from the "Light of light," that Muḥammad derived this mystical conception.[6] The doctrine of the abiding nature of God, Who was from everlasting and shall be unto eternity, emphasised in the Tradition given above, which actually mentions the Gospels,[7] may well have been derived from hearing the verse, "I am Alpha and Omega, the beginning and the ending, saith the Lord, which is and which was and which is to come, the Almighty."[8]

The idea that the "heart" represents the spiritual essence

[1] Col. i. 15-17, ii. 9.
[2] Acts xiv. 15-17.
[3] Acts xvii. 24-26. *Cf.* also p. 86 above.
[4] *Cf.* John i. 4-10.
[5] See above, p. 89.
[6] See above, pp. 143, 144.
[7] *Ibid.*
[8] Rev. i. 8.

of man is set forth again and again in the New Testament: "With the heart man believeth unto righteousness," says St. Paul.[1] "Sanctify the Lord God in your hearts," writes St. Peter.[2] So also Isaac of Nineveh says, "The heart is the central organ of the inward senses. . . . It is purified through great trouble and by being deprived of all association with the world, together with a complete mortification in every point."[3] The Qur'ānic idea of man as created in purity, having something of the Divine within him, because God breathed into him of His Spirit, might indeed be taken direct from the Jewish account of the Creation in Genesis, but it is possible that Muḥammad knew something of the stress laid by Christian writers on the fact that man was made in the image of God and ought therefore to strive to become fit to recognise the Divine element within himself and to receive the gift of the Word. The Qur'ānic promise that illumination will be given to those who walk in the Path of God recalls the Pauline exhortation, "For ye were sometimes darkness, but now are ye light in the Lord; walk as children of the light."[4]

The teaching of orthodox Islām regarding the need for purification and the cleansing of the heart from all defilement, for those who are to hear and receive the Word of God, is all to be found in the New Testament. "Let us cleanse ourselves from all filthiness of the flesh and spirit," says St. Paul, "perfecting holiness in the fear of God."[5] "To be carnally-minded," that is, to give way to the carnal soul, the *nafs*, he says elsewhere, "is death, but to be spiritually-minded is life and peace—and peace is what Muḥammad describes as the state of the spiritually perfect—"for if ye live after the flesh, ye shall die, but if ye through the Spirit do mortify the deeds of the body, ye shall live."[6] We have seen again and again, both in the Qur'ān and in the Traditions, how the life of the world to come is set over against the life of this world, and the believer is bidden to cast aside what is transient for the sake of that which abides for ever, and how the very words of the Gospel are used to emphasise this doctrine, so that its origin can hardly be in

[1] Rom. x. 10. [2] 1 Pet. iii. 15. [3] *Mystical Treatises*, p. 20.
[4] Ephes. v. 8. [5] 2 Cor. vii. 1. [6] Rom. viii. 6, 13.

doubt. "He that loveth his life shall lose it, and he that loseth his life in this world shall keep it unto life eternal" was taught by Muḥammad as insistently as by St. John.

The transformation of the soul, by which, when purified from sin, and emptied of self and inspired by faith, it should be prepared to receive and to be the interpreter of the Divine Word, was to be accomplished, as we have seen, with the help of the Holy Spirit, and from no other source than Christianity could Muḥammad have derived this essentially Christian doctrine. The Divine mystery, the Wisdom of God, have been revealed to man by the Spirit: "God hath revealed them unto us by His Spirit; for the Spirit searcheth all things, yea, the deep things of God . . . the things of God knoweth no man, but the Spirit of God. Now we have received, not the spirit of the world, but the Spirit which is of God; that we might know the things that are freely given to us of God."[1] So also St. John wrote, "It is the Spirit that quickeneth"—that is, which brings the soul to rebirth in God. Those who have been transformed and have received and apprehended the Divine revelation are living the life of God and abide in it for ever; He is well-pleased with them and they with Him. Such is the teaching of orthodox Islām and such is also the Christian doctrine of those who have attained salvation through the Word of God. "Ye have purified your souls in obeying the truth through the Spirit . . . being born again, not of corruptible seed, but of incorruptible, by the Word of God, which liveth and abideth for ever. For all flesh is as grass and all the glory of man as the flower of grass. The grass withereth and the flower thereof falleth away. But the Word of the Lord endureth for ever."[2]

It would appear, then, that Muḥammad, from what he saw and heard around him of Christian asceticism, and from the fragments of Christian mystical teaching which came to his knowledge, laid the foundation, perhaps all unwittingly, of a doctrine of mysticism, based on asceticism, which was further developed by the early Traditionists, and later became that fully-developed system of Islamic Mysticism which we know as Ṣūfism.

[1] 1 Cor. ii. 10-12. [2] 1 Pet. i. 22-25.

CHAPTER VIII

THE RISE OF ṢŪFISM AND THE EARLY ASCETIC IDEAL

As indicated in the last chapter, orthodox Islām included a considerable amount of teaching on asceticism, and in the earliest years of Islām, and even in the pre-Islamic period, there were individuals definitely practising the ascetic life. Such were the Ḥanīfs, a group of Arab ascetics who had a considerable influence upon Muḥammad. Among them was Zayd b. 'Amr b. Nufayl, who died before the Prophet's mission, who is described as withdrawing from the worship of idols and abstaining from that which had died of itself or had been sacrificed to idols and from blood, who forbade the burying alive of infants, and proclaimed that he worshipped the God of Abraham, so that his asceticism seems to have been based on Jewish and Christian ideals. The rise of the Ḥanīfs was part of an ascetic movement in Arabia in the seventh century, which was undoubtedly inspired by the example of the Christian hermits who were to be found there. Among the companions of the Prophet were Abū Dharr and Ḥudayfa, both famed for their asceticism. Of the former, it was said that a friend brought him a gift of one hundred dirhams, and he returned it, saying, "We have a she-goat from which to obtain milk, and a riding-beast on whose back to ride swiftly, and we have no need of anything else."[1] Of Ḥudayfa b. Ḥusayl al-Yamān (*ob.* A.D. 657) we read that he admonished his contemporaries to spiritual revival by means of daily penitence, and he speaks of the heart of the true believer, "which is pure as a clear-burning torch." He uttered bitter predictions of imminent judgment on his generation, and his ascetical tendencies were shown by the tradition ascribed to him, saying that "When God loves a servant, He proves him by suffering."[2] al-Sarrāj gives a long list of companions of the Prophet who were conspicuous

[1] al-Sarrāj, *Kitāb al-Luma'*, p. 135.

[2] For traditions ascribed to Ḥudayfa *cf.* A. b. Ḥanbal, v. 383, 406 *ff.*

for their asceticism and quietism.[1] Among them was Ḥāritha, who is related to have said: "I have turned aside my soul from this world, and I have watched by night and I have longed by day, and so I seem to contemplate the very Throne of God."[2] In the earliest period of Islām there were also the "Ahl al-Ṣuffa" (People of the Bench), devoted to the religious life, who sat on stone benches outside the mosques, hence their name, and received alms from the devout. They were said to exceed three hundred in number, and neither sowed seed nor kept flocks, nor engaged in merchandise. They ate their food in the mosque and slept there. The Prophet was on terms of intimacy with them and used to urge the people to honour them and become acquainted with their virtues. Among them was a certain Ibn Umm, whom the Prophet had been bidden by God to honour. These people lived a life of great asceticism and poverty, ill-clad and homeless, but devout in worship and given to much weeping for their sins.[3]

Celibacy, the characteristic ideal of the Christian ascetics of Syria and Egypt, though it found no acceptance with the Prophet himself, was not unknown among his followers even in his lifetime. al-Ṭabarī mentions the house of Sa'd b. Khaythama, "who was a celibate, without family," and says further, "there were celibates among the followers of the Apostle from among those who fled to him, and therefore this house of Sa'd b. Khaythama was called the house of the celibates."[4] Ibn Baṭṭūṭa also refers to such a house, not far from Medīna, a ruined dwelling, known as the abode of the celibates, of which it was said that 'Umar built it for the celibates of Islām.[5]

The first century of Islām was very favourable to the spread of asceticism, on account of the general disgust with the growth of materialism, in contrast to the simple ideals of life taught and practised by Muḥammad and his companions, and of dissatisfaction with the dissensions, both religious and political, with which the world of Islām was rent at this time. During the second half of the seventh century this

[1] *Op. cit.*, pp. 135-140. [2] al-Sarrāj, *op. cit.*, p. 13.
[3] *Ibid.*, pp. 132, 133. *Cf.* also Ibn al-Jawzi, *Talbīs Iblīs*, pp. 176, 177.
[4] *Annales*, i. 1243. [5] *Tuḥfatal-Nuẓẓār*, i. 289, 290.

ascetic movement remained orthodox and its leaders were of the Pietist type. At the basis of this asceticism, as of that taught by Muḥammad himself in the Qur'ān, was the fear of Judgment, resulting in a deep consciousness of sin and of human weakness, and a consequent desire for complete submission to the Will of God. As yet there were no organised religious orders, nor any definite type of monastic life in Islām, but the customs of going into retreat (*ī'tikāf*), and observing vows of silence, both customs probably of Christian origin, were practised by these early ascetics. In the time of the Caliph Abū Bakr, a woman of the tribe of Aḥmas, named Zaynab, was reported to him as having maintained complete silence during her sojourn at Mecca, having taken a vow to keep silence for the period of the pilgrimage.[1] We hear of an ascetic named 'Āmir b. 'Abd al-Qays, who was summoned before the Caliph in A.H. 33 on the charge of not eating meat, of expressing his disapproval of marriage, and of failing to attend the Friday service in the mosque.[2] In A.H. 82 the morality of these saintly ascetics (*adab al-Ṣāliḥīn*) was spoken of with approval.[3] Generally speaking, these ascetics of saintly life were held in great respect; we read of such persons being employed as messengers to subject kings, or as arbiters in cases of dispute, or as mounting the pulpit to dissuade Muslims from disputing among themselves.[4] Such men were usually distinguished by a costume of white wool, which they had adopted most probably in imitation of the Christian monks, who wore similar garments,[5] and some of these pious men followed the Christian example also in keeping out of the world altogether.

They were known by various names: ascetics (*zuhhād*), devout men (*nussāk*), those given to sacred reading (*qurrā'*), popular preachers (*qussās*), monks or hermits (*ruhbān*, identical with the name given to the Christian monks), and penitents or weepers (*bakkā'ūn*). Among the latter we know of one Ṣub'am b. Mālik, the devotee, who was God-fearing and a "weeper."[6] It was said of Sha'wāna, one of the ear-

[1] al-Bukhārī, iii. 17, No. 26. [2] Ṭabarī, i. 2924.
[3] *Ibid.*, ii. 1083. [4] *Ibid.*, ii. 1228, 1386, 1392.
[5] Evagrius had directed that monks should wear a sheepskin.
[6] Abū al-Maḥāsin, i. 396.

liest of the woman ascetics, that "her character bore witness that she feared God greatly, in that she wept continually," and she used to say, "I would that I might weep blood, and even so I should not be content." She said also, "Let him who cannot weep have compassion on those who weep, for he who weeps, weeps only out of knowledge of his sins and for that in which he has gone astray." She herself never heard the mention of the Name of God without weeping.[1] So also the Ṣūfī Aḥmad b. Abī al-Ḥawwārī (*ob.* A.D. 860) relates, "I went in to Abū Sulaymān (al-Darānī) one day, and he was weeping, and I said to him, 'What makes you weep?' and he said, 'O Aḥmad, why should I not weep, for when night comes and eyes are closed and every lover is alone with his beloved, and the people of love stand upon their feet, and tears flow over their cheeks, and sprinkle the places wherein they pray, then God Most Glorious looks down and cries aloud, "O Gabriel, dear unto Me are they who delight in My Word and find their rest in the remembrance of My Name. Verily, I am beholding them in their loneliness, I hear their lamentation and I look upon their tears. Why, O Gabriel, dost thou not cry out concerning them, 'What is this weeping? Did ye ever see a lover who tormented his lovers?' Or how should it befit Me to chastise those who, when night covers them, show their affection for Me? I swear by Myself that when they shall appear at the Resurrection, I will assuredly unveil to them My glorious Face, so that they may look upon Me and I may look upon them.'"[2] It was the same Abū Sulaymān who said, "When the heart weeps for what is lost, the spirit laughs for what it has found." Weeping as a sign of repentance was much approved among the early Christian ascetics, who may well have been the model for these early Muslim ascetics. Ephraim the Syrian was much admired for his constant weeping, "As with all men to breathe is a natural function unceasing in exercise, so with Ephraim was it natural to weep. There was no day, no night, no hour, no moment, however brief, in which his eyes were not wakeful and filled with tears, while he bewailed the faults and follies

[1] al-Munāwī, "Kawākib," fol. 58*b*.
[2] al-Qushayrī, *Risāla*, p. 20.

now of his own life, now of mankind."[1] In his writings, too, Ephraim laid stress on this meritorious custom of weeping as a sign of contrition.

> " The whole multitude of my responsibilities
> Together would make supplication
> Until they obtain acquittal ;
> And would utter sounds of weeping,
> And pour out tears like water :
> And our heart would break with sighing
> Until there is forgiveness."[2]

So in the Syrian Church we find that an early designation of the ascetic was the title of " Weeper." Isaac of Nineveh writes of the value of tears. " When (the seeker) begins to leave the bodiliness of this world and moves in that territory which lies beyond this visible nature, then at once he will reach the grace of tears . . . those tears will begin and they will conduct him to the complete love of God."[3] Again he says, " What is the meditation of the solitary in his cell but weeping ? . . . Who knows the profits of weeping, save those who have given themselves to it ? . . . If anyone weeps constantly, the affections (*i.e.*, the sensual desires) will not approach his heart."[4] In a similar strain the Muslim ascetic ʻAbd al-Wāḥid b. Zayd (*ob.* 793) exhorted his fellow-ascetics, " O brethren, will ye not weep in desire for God ? Shall he who weeps in longing for his Lord be denied the Vision of Him ?"[5] And later on, the " gift of tears " became a distinctive sign of the great Ṣūfīs.

This ascetic movement of the first two centuries of Islām, with its encouragement to renunciation and otherworldliness, was gradually combined with tendencies towards mysticism—al-Jāḥiẓ and Ibn al-Jawzī include the names of over forty well-known ascetics of this period whose practice of " interiorisation " showed that they knew what it was to live the mystic life. So there developed the earliest

[1] Life (*Nicene and Post-Nicene Fathers*), p. 126.
[2] *Exhortation to Repentance*, P. ii, lines 139-145. *Cf.* also St. Basil, p. 56 above.
[3] *Mystical Treatises*, p. 164. [4] *Ibid.*, pp. 169, 170.
[5] *Recueil*, p. 5.

form of Ṣūfism as we know it. al-Qushayrī writes of this development that " the elect among men, who were deeply concerned with matters of religion, were called ' ascetics ' and ' devotees.' Then heresies appeared and there arose disputes between the different sects, each one claiming to possess ' ascetics,' and the elect of the people of the Sunna, whose souls were set on God, and who kept their hearts from the misfortunes of heedlessness, became known by the name of Ṣūfīs, and this name became generally applied to these great souls a little before the end of the second century of the Hijra."[1] The historian Ibn Khaldūn gives a similar account of the rise of Ṣūfism. He says, " The Way of life adopted by the Ṣūfīs was in force from the beginnings of Islām and the most eminent of the Companions and their disciples considered it to be the way of Truth and Guidance. It was based upon devotion and separation to God and the renunciation of the pomps and vanities of this world, and the reckoning as nothing, pleasures and riches and fame, and (it included) retreat for purposes of devotion. Nothing was more common among the Companions and others of the Faithful in the earliest times, and when the love of the world was widespread in the second century (of the Islamic era), and later, and most men allowed themselves to be dragged into the whirlpool of the world, those consecrated to piety were called Ṣūfīs."[2]

Their name of " Ṣūfī " was taken from the garments of wool (*ṣūf*) which, as we have seen, they had most probably borrowed from the custom of their Christian neighbours, the monks. These early Ṣūfīs—unlike those of later times, who banded themselves into orders and lived a common life under a common roof, in a monastery (*khānaqāh* or *ribāṭ*)—lived in isolation, without any common ties or doctrine. They felt that they had found the way to salvation for themselves and were satisfied with that and with the task of showing the way to others who might come to consult them. They were still primarily ascetics, more concerned as yet with good works than with theosophical theories. Theirs was a life of mortification and self-discipline, devoted to poverty and prayer and meditation, the same type of life

[1] Jami, *Nafaḥāt al-Uns*, p. 31.

[2] Ibn Khaldūn, iii. 59, 60.

which they had seen to be lived by the monks and nuns with whom they came into contact. It was these early Ṣūfīs who drew from the New Testament the parables and sayings of Jesus, which lent authority to the pursuit of the ascetic ideal, and which were incorporated into the Ḥadīth, in order that orthodox Islām might be held responsible for the adoption of the ascetic life, by those who were still the devoted adherents of Muḥammad and his teachings. Among these sayings is one according to which Jesus said: "Verily the friends of God fear nothing and grieve for nothing. For they look upon the inner reality of this world, while other men look upon its outward appearance. Also they look forward to the end of this world, while others look to the immediate present here. They destroy in it what they fear may destroy them and abandon what they know will abandon them. They are hostile to those things with which other men make peace, and bless the things which other men hate. They show the greatest admiration for the good deeds of others, while they themselves possess goods worthy of the greatest admiration. Among them knowledge is guidance, by which they themselves gain knowledge. They do not put faith except in that for which they hope, nor fear anything except that which should be avoided."[1] Another saying from the same source states: "The Messiah said: 'The world is the devil's field and its people are his tillers.'"[2] We find a saying of Jesus quoted by the Ṣūfī writer Abū Ṭālib al-Makkī which runs, "The sweetness of this world is the bitterness of the next. Ostentation in dress is pride of heart, that is to say, vanity and boasting. A full belly means abundance of lusts, that is to say, it is their nourishment and stimulus. Verily I say unto you, that as the invalid does not delight in the goodness of food, so he who loves this world does not discover the sweetness of devotion."[3] From the same source we have another saying; "Jesus said: 'Truly the love of this world corrupts religion. But to Me, this world is the same as a stone or a clod.'"[4] Yet another Ṣūfī tradition relates that Jesus said: "Every word, which is not a mention of God, is vain. All silence, which is not medita-

[1] *Logia et Agrapha*, No. 115. [2] *Ibid.*, No. 117.
[3] *Qūt al-Qulūb*, i. 256. [4] *Ibid.*, i. 263.

tion, is negligence; all contemplation, which is not accompanied by tears, is make-believe. Blessed is he whose speech is the mention of God, whose silence is meditation, and whose contemplation consists of tears."[1]

al-Sarrāj gives a tradition to the effect that the name of Ṣūfī was attached to men of exceptional piety before Islām,[2] but in fact this is most improbable. The Ṣūfīs seem to have been known as such first in Kūfa. Abū Hāshim, a native of that place, who died in A.D. 777-8, is usually mentioned as the one to whom this title was first given.[3] Another resident of Kūfa, contemporary with Abū Hāshim, to whom the name of "al-Ṣūfī" was also applied, was Jābir b. Ḥayyān, a Shiʿite alchemist. That Ṣūfism should have had its rise and earliest development in Kūfa and the neighbourhood is a fact of some significance in our consideration of the sources of Ṣūfism, and the main influences by which its development was affected, for Kūfa at this time was one of the chief centres of Shiʿite doctrine, and of Christian-Hellenistic ideas. It is not to be wondered at, then, that the ideals of these very early Ṣūfīs should have been mainly ascetic. We are told by an early writer on Ṣūfism that the Ṣūfīs "are those who for the sake of God have turned aside from all that might distract them from Him and have preferred Him above all else. . . . For His sake they have deserted their native lands and forsaken their brethren and abandoned their kindred, and for Him have cut themselves off from all ties and fled from the face of mankind, seeking intimacy with Him and alienation from all else."[4] The same writer tells us of the austerity and simplicity of the lives led by the Ṣūfīs. "They are content with little in the way of worldly goods and are satisfied with the very minimum of food to keep them alive, and limit themselves to the least that is necessary in the way of clothing and bedding. They choose poverty rather than riches, embracing want and avoiding plenty, preferring hunger to satisfaction and little to much. They renounce dignity and honour and rank, and show

[1] *Logia et Agrapha*, No. 136.
[2] *Kitāb al-Lumaʿ*, p. 22. *Cf.* also Ibn al-Jawzi, *Talbīs Iblīs*, p. 171.
[3] *Cf.* Jāmī, *Nafaḥāt al-Uns*, p. 34.
[4] al-Sarrāj, *Kitāb al-Lumaʿ*, p. 3.

compassion upon mankind, and humility towards small and great. . . . They remain constant when God tries them and are content with His decrees, enduring with patience their continual struggles in opposition to the fleshly lusts, while they abstain from the pleasures of the carnal self, and fight against it, since God has described it as being headstrong to do evil, and has said that the chief of a man's enemies is within himself."[1]

The first line of development of Ṣūfī asceticism was that of supererogation, going beyond what was required by the religious law, and what was considered sufficient for others; their renunciation was to be not only of the unlawful, the common kind, but further, of the lawful, a more special type, and finally, of all, whatever it might be, save God Himself.[2] These ascetic ideals showed themselves in the usual external forms. The white woollen robe worn by the earliest Ṣūfīs as a sign of simplicity was later replaced by the patched frock (*khirqa*) which became their characteristic attire, and with which the novice was invested by his Shaykh when admitted into the circle of his disciples. Fasting and abstinence were practised: the Ṣūfīs ate only from "lawful" food—that is, food earned by the labours of their own hands, or provided by a fellow-Ṣūfī, who had earned it. All food the origin of which was unknown was unlawful, and there are stories told of how eminent Ṣūfīs were warned that the food they were about to eat was unlawful, and they refrained in time. Of Ḥārith al-Muḥāsibī it was related that a vein in his finger throbbed if he attempted to eat anything dubious, and of Bishr al-Ḥāfī (the Barefooted), that when he tried to stretch out his hand to take such unlawful food, his hand refused to move, and so he was saved from a sinful act.[3]

Fasting was carried to much greater lengths than was required by the Islāmic law. In addition to Ramaḍān and the other orthodox fasts, voluntary fasts of varying lengths and severity were undertaken, in order that the flesh might be mortified and the spirit gain illumination. Some Ṣūfīs fasted every other day, some one day in three or two days out of three.[4] Some abstained from eating special kinds of food.

[1] al-Sarrāj, *op. cit.*, pp. 11, 12.
[2] al-Qushayrī, *Risāla*, pp. 74, 75.
[3] al-Sarrāj, *op. cit.*, p. 45.
[4] *Ibid.*, p. 163.

There is a story which tells how Rābi'a al-'Adawiyya of Baṣra, one of the best-known of the early Ṣūfīs, at a time when she was laid aside by illness was asked by Sufyān al-Thawrī, one of her friends, "O Rābi'a, what do you desire?" and she replied, "O Sufyān, how can you ask me such a question as 'What do I desire?' I swear by the glory of God that for twelve years I have desired fresh dates, and you know that in Baṣra dates are plentiful, and I have not yet tasted them. I am a servant (of God), and what has a servant to do with desire?"[1] The Persian Ṣūfī Abū Yazīd al-Bisṭāmi (*ob.* A.D. 875) declared, "I have not found the true knowledge of God, except in a hungry stomach and a naked body."[2] al-Ghazālī, writing much later, but basing what he had to say of Ṣūfism on the teaching and practice of the earliest of the Ṣūfīs, says that hunger produces the following beneficial results: (*a*) Purification of the soul and illumination of the mind; (*b*) the capacity to enjoy spiritual pleasures; (*c*) humility; (*d*) remembrance of the poor; (*e*) freedom from all sinful desires; (*f*) resistance to the temptation to sleep, and a stimulus to vigils; (*g*) the affording of opportunity for the ritual of worship; (*h*) physical health; (*i*) the reduction of expenses; and (*j*) the provision of means to feed the poor.[3] The Ṣūfīs held, however, that the true fast was abstention from desire, and that the fasting of the heart was more important than the fasting of the body. They maintained that fasting was of three kinds—the common sort, abstention from food; the special kind, of those devotees who abstained not only from food but from sinful emotion; and the most special kind, that of the "elect of the elect," the perfect Ṣūfīs who abstained from every sinful thought.[4]

These early Ṣūfī ascetics gave much time to prayer, and had a regular service of prayers and devotional exercises, accompanied by the reading of the Qur'ān, which corresponded to the litanies and offices recited by the Christian monks. The purpose of these prayers was the frequent remembrance of God, and a special form was that known as

[1] 'Aṭṭār, *Tadhkirat al-Awliyā*, i. 70, 71.
[2] al-Munāwī, "Kawākib," fol. 123*b*.
[3] *Iḥyā*, iii. 72 *ff*.
[4] al-Hujwīrī, *Kashf al-Maḥjūb*, pp. 413 *ff*.

the *dhikr* (see p. 137 above), which often consisted simply of the repetition of the Divine Name and meditation upon it, and later became the accompaniment of the rhythmic dances of the Dervishes and was an inducement to the production of a state of ecstasy. Prayer, to these early Ṣūfīs, was a means of drawing near to God, and of excluding all the outward distractions which might be a cause of separation between the servant and his Lord. One of the early Ṣūfī shaykhs said of this : " For him who prays four things are needful : the annihilation of the carnal soul, the passing away of the natural qualities, the purification of the inmost self, and perfect contemplation. By him who is intent on prayer, annihilation can only be obtained by concentration of thought, by which he secures control of the lower soul : the passing away of human nature is attained only by the affirmation of the Divine Majesty, for the Divine Majesty is eternal ; purity of the inmost self is obtained only by love ; and perfect contemplation only by purity of the inmost self."[1] Isaac of Nineveh had also written of the need of inward peace in prayer, " By much beseeching the heart becomes humble. . . . Until the heart becomes humble it will not rest from distraction."[2] We have an account by an early Ṣūfī writer of the right way in which to approach God in prayer, which bears a close resemblance to the teaching of some modern mystics on Mental Prayer. He says, " Before the time of prayer comes, the servant must be in a state of preparation, and his attitude must be that which is essential for prayer, namely, a state of meditation and recollection, free from wandering thoughts, and consideration or remembrance of aught save God alone. Those who enter thus upon prayer, with heart intent only upon God, will proceed from prayer to prayer, in that same state of recollection, and will remain therein after they have ceased to pray."[3] So the Christian Evagrius had said, " Strive to set up your mind at

[1] Hujwīrī, *op. cit.*, p. 390.

[2] *Mystical Treatises*, p. 71.

[3] al-Sarrāj, *op. cit.*, p. 154. *Cf.* Fr. Andrew : " Let your body be utterly still, your mind attentive but silent, your will obedient but patient, hushing every desire and just waiting in stillness upon God " (*The Adventure of Prayer*, p. 2).

the time of prayer, deaf, without speech ; so you will be able to pray. . . . Pure prayer is the glorification of the heart, the contemplation of God and ecstasy in Him."[1] And Isaac of Nineveh writes : "During prayer, prayer itself is cut off and the mind is absorbed in ecstasy and the desire of what the mystic prayed for is forgotten. He is no longer in this world. Further, there is no discrimination of the body, nor of the soul, nor remembrance of anything."[2] Abū Ṭālib al-Makkī includes in his writings prayers of a very Christian form,[3] and since the best of the Ṣūfīs professed themselves to be indifferent to the attractions of either this world or the next, their prayers took the form of confession of their sins to God, or expressions of their joy in the sense of His Presence, rather than of petitions or formal intercessions.

The ascetic practices of these early Ṣūfīs, as we have already noted, included renunciation of the world, the acceptance of poverty, self-abnegation and self-discipline. al-Ghazali writes that "the doctrine which has for its aim this state (*zuhd*=renunciation) consists in knowing that what is renounced is of little value in comparison with what is received. It is like the knowledge of the merchant who knows that what he receives in exchange for his merchandise is worth more than what he sells, and so he desires the sale. Whoever has not this knowledge cannot detach himself from the merchandise. So he who has understood that what belongs to God is abiding and that the other life is better and more lasting than this (*i.e.*, that its joys are better in themselves and more lasting), as jewels are better and more durable than snow, desires to exchange this life for that other. No one who is possessed of snow would find any hardship in exchanging it for jewels and pearls. For this world is like snow exposed to the sun, which continues to melt until it disappears altogether, while the next life is like a precious stone which never passes away."[4] Here the motive is the advantage to the Ṣūfī in exchanging the transient for the eternal, and al-Sarrāj writes in the same strain.

[1] *Cf.* Wensinck, *Book of the Dove*, p. xxxiv.
[2] *Mystical Treatises*, p. 117.
[3] *Qūt al-Qulūb*, i. 8.
[4] *Iḥyā*, iv. 187.

"Renunciation is the basis of all spiritual progress, and is the first step on the way for those who set their faces towards God, who seek to consecrate themselves to His service alone, to carry out His Will and to trust completely in Him. That one who does not base his practice of religion on renunciation cannot hope to make progress therein, for the love of this world leads to all sin, and the renunciation thereof leads to all good deeds and to obedience to the Will of God."[1] This renunciation is to be spiritual as well as material. "The real meaning of detachment from the world (*tajrīd*), says an old Ṣūfī writer, "is to be separated outwardly from all possessions and inwardly from what is unreal. It is to take nothing from what belongs to this world, nor to seek anything in exchange for what has been renounced of things transitory, not even eternity itself. That renunciation has been made for the sake of the One True God, for no cause or reason save Him alone."[2] So Renunciation, carried to its farthest extent, meant not only the abandonment of all the temporary pleasures of this world, but of eternal bliss also. "The mark of the true Ṣūfī," says al-Qushayrī, "is that he should be indifferent to this world and the next."[3]

Poverty was practised in the literal sense of lack of worldly goods—the Ṣūfīs possessed little that they could call their own, and it was practised partly in order that the soul might not be distracted by worldly things from its quest for God, and partly as a means of self-discipline, because, as one writer wisely observes, the soul by nature hates poverty and loves wealth. But just as the true fast was not physical but spiritual, so the most spiritually-minded of the Ṣūfīs held that true Poverty consisted not in lack of worldly possessions, but in the exercise of patience and resignation to the will of God, and indifference to both wealth and poverty. It was well that the Ṣūfī should sacrifice all material goods, but he was not truly "poor" until he had stripped himself of "self," and this meant the infliction of mortifications and self-discipline and the abnegation of the personal, individual

[1] *Kitāb al-Luma'*, p. 46.
[2] al-Kalābādhī, "Kitāb al-Ta'arruf," fol. 31*a*.
[3] *Risāla*, p. 166.

will, in the Will of God. There are many stories of the self-discipline administered, and afflictions accepted in order that the individual will might be subdued to the Divine Will. One of the Ṣūfīs, Ibn Khafīf, who belonged to Shirāz, and died in A.D. 982, says, "I went out once from Baghdād to the river al-Nāshirīya, and when I had walked a little way, I heard a snorting and a trampling in the water, and I saw al-Nūrī (a fellow-Ṣūfī), who had cast himself into the water and mud, and he was stamping and inflicting on himself every kind of misery, and he said to me, 'Are you regarding what God is doing to me? He has slain me with many deaths.' Then he threw himself into the thicket, on to the roots of the cut reeds (for he wished to meet with a wild beast). He then said, 'When wild beasts were mentioned, I found that I was terrified, so I said to myself, "I will throw thee to that of which thou art terrified."' "[1]

We read of even more drastic self-discipline inflicted on himself by Abū Bakr Zaqqāq, a Ṣūfī who died at Cairo in A.D. 902, who related of himself, "I sought hospitality from an Arab tribe, and I saw there a beautiful maiden, and I looked upon her, and I plucked out the eye with which I had beheld her and I said (to it), 'It was thy like which looked upon God.'"[2] Here there seems to be an unmistakable reference to the Gospel recommendation, given in this very connection, to pluck out an offending member lest the whole body be cast into Hell.[3]

The feeling that affliction in this life may gladly be endured for the sake of attaining to the life with God in the world to come, is illustrated by a story of Abū Shu'ayb Ṣāliḥ al-Muqaffa' al-Miṣrī, a Ṣūfī ascetic who died about A.D. 902 and was therefore contemporary with the two mentioned above. A certain man said, "We had a guest-house and there came to us a poor man, wearing two patched robes, who was called Abū Sulaymān; he asked for hospitality, and I said to my son, 'Go with him to the house.' He stayed with us for nine days, and ate a meal once in three days, and I invited him to remain, but he said, 'Hospitality

[1] *Recueil*, p. 83. [2] *Ibid.*, p. 330.
[3] Matt. v. 28-30.

is for three days."[1] I said to him, 'Do not cut us off from news of you.' He remained away from us for twelve years, then he turned up again, and I said, 'Whence have you come?' and he replied, 'I came across a certain Shaykh, called Abū Shu'ayb al-Muqaffa', who was afflicted, and I stayed with him and served him for a year, and it occurred to me to ask him what was the cause of his affliction. When I approached him, he began to speak before I asked him and said, "Why should you ask about what does not concern you?" So I was patient until three years had passed, and he said to me in the third year, "You must certainly have your way," and so I told him that I had observed his affliction. Then he said, "Whilst I was praying at night, behold a light shone upon me from the *miḥrāb*,[2] and I said, 'Avaunt thee, accursed one, for my Lord, to Whom be glory and majesty, has no need to appear to a creature.' Three times I said this, then I heard a voice calling me from the *miḥrāb*, and I said, 'Here am I, Lord,' and He said, 'Dost thou desire that death come to thee forthwith, and we will requite thee for what has befallen thee, or that we should afflict thee with affliction, whereby we shall raise thee to the highest rank (among the saints)?' And I chose affliction, and I lost the use of my eyes and my hands and my feet." So he spoke, and I remained serving him for twelve years. Then one day he said, "Come near to me," and I approached him and I heard his limbs saying to one another, "Come forth," and his limbs all appeared before him, and he gave praise and glorified God, and then he died.' "[3]

It was from this ascetic and quietistic ideal of the early Ṣūfīs that some of the earliest definitions of Ṣūfism were derived. The first of which we know is that of Ma'rūf al-Karkhī, who died in A.D. 815, highly reputed as a saint, who defined Ṣūfism as "the apprehension of Divine realities and the re-

[1] The rule of Arab hospitality is to give it for three days to any stranger, even an enemy, who asks for it, but after three days he ceases to be a guest and can no longer claim the protection afforded to him by that position.

[2] A niche in the mosque indicating the direction of Mecca, towards which the Muslim worshipper turns for prayer.

[3] *Recueil*, pp. 43, 44.

nunciation of human possessions."[1] Another is that of Bishr al-Ḥāfī, the Bare-Footed, whose surname sufficiently indicated his manner of life, who said, "The Ṣūfī is that one whose heart is pure towards God," that is, whose heart is concerned with none but God. Dhū al-Nūn al-Miṣrī (*ob.* A.D. 859) describes the Ṣūfīs as "those who have preferred God to all else, and so He has preferred them to all else." Sahl Tustarī, an ascetic of Khuzistān, who died in exile at Baṣra in A.D. 896, defined the Ṣūfī as "that one who has become pure from defilement and is full of meditation, and has drawn so near to God that he is cut off from all mankind, and in his eyes dust and gold are all one." Definitions given by al-Nūrī (*ob.* A.D. 907), whose self-mortification has been mentioned above, include a definition of the Ṣūfīs as "those whose souls have been freed from the defilement of the flesh and have been purified from the sins of the carnal self, and have been delivered from sensual desire, and are at rest with God in the first rank and the most exalted degree, and having fled from all save Him, they are neither masters (*i.e.*, they possess nothing) nor slaves (*i.e.*, their desires do not possess them)." A parallel to the latter statement is found in Isaac of Nineveh's teaching on Asceticism, "He who is master of possessions is the slave of passions."[2] From al-Nūrī, too, comes the definition of Ṣūfism as the renunciation of all gain for the self, for the sake of winning God, and again, "Ṣūfism is enmity to the world and love to the Lord." From al-Junayd of Baghdād, one of the greatest and most revered of the early Ṣūfī teachers, who died in A.D. 910, come two definitions still based on the ascetic ideal. "Ṣūfism," he says, "means that God makes thee to die to thyself, and makes thee alive in Him." In a much more complete definition he says, "Ṣūfism is to purify the heart from the recurrence of creaturely temptations, to say farewell to all the natural inclinations, to subdue the qualities which belong to humanity, to keep far from the claims of the senses, to adhere to spiritual qualities, to ascend by means of Divine knowledge, to be occupied with that which is eternally the best, to give wise counsel to all people, faith-

[1] Qushayrī, *op. cit.*, p. 165. [2] *Mystical Treatises*, p. 29.

fully to observe the truth, and to follow the Prophet in respect of the religious Law."[1]

At this early stage, then, we find Ṣūfism still following along the lines of orthodox Islām, seeking for spiritual revival and for ultimate salvation by means of a loyal devotion to the religious practices prescribed by Islām, with the addition of works of supererogation, and an asceticism characterised especially by detachment from the world. As yet, though its followers sought for an ever-increasing knowledge of God, and an ever-closer communion with Him, they had not evolved the theosophic and mystical doctrines which, a little later, become a fully-developed system of mysticism, with strongly pantheistic tendencies. This primitive Ṣūfism was based on the assumption that devout practice would procure spiritual graces for the soul; it was therefore a Way of life, a journey to God, and all the asceticism of the Ṣūfīs was but a means to their end, the attainment of communion, nay, even of union, with Him. At first they were concerned with the Way and only that stage of it which corresponded to the Purgative life of the later Western mystics, that is to say, with the purification of the senses, attained by bodily discipline, but as time went on they concerned themselves also with the stage corresponding to the Illuminative life, the purification of the mind and the will, attained by mental discipline, which enabled them to receive the Divine guidance, and to merge the individual will in the Will of God; and finally they began to concern themselves, and made it their chief and all-absorbing concern, with the Unitive life, the Goal of the journey, for which spiritual discipline, in fact complete self-abnegation, was required, so that the individual personality might pass away in the soul's consciousness of the Divine.[2]

The real aim of all these ascetical exercises and practices was a direct spiritual experience, the mystic consciousness of

[1] For further definitions of Ṣūfism, both early and late, *cf.* R. A. Nicholson, *J.R.A.S.*, 1906, pp. 303 *ff.*

[2] So Isaac of Nineveh writes: "Bodily discipline in solitude purifies the body from the material elements in it. Mental discipline makes the soul humble. Spiritual discipline produces the nakedness of mind which is called immaterial contemplation" (*Mystical Treatises*, p. 202).

union with God. al-Ghazālī, in his "*Munqidh*," describing the Ṣūfī teaching, says, "The aim of their doctrine is to cut off the passions of the soul, and to purge it of its evil tendencies and bad qualities until one arrives thereby at disengaging the heart of all save God, and occupying it only with the remembrance of Him. I studied . . . until I had arrived at the real aim of their doctrine and had understood what was to be attained by studying and listening. Then it appeared to me that what belongs exclusively to them is that which cannot be attained by study but only by actual experience, by ecstasy and by the transformation of character. So then it was plain to me that the Ṣūfīs were men who had known the mystic experience, not merely men of words—I was convinced that there could be no hope of gaining the happiness of the next world except by complete devotion and the subjugation of the sensual desires arising in the carnal soul, and that the chief thing of all is to cut the heart off from attachment to this world and to turn aside from this transient abode, and to turn in penitence towards that which abides for ever, and to devote oneself entirely to God."[1]

The Ṣūfīs believed that the Goal could only be attained by those who faithfully and untiringly followed the "Path." The mystic Path (*ṭarīqa*), they held, was made up of a number of stages, and as the soul passed through these it acquired certain qualities, which enabled it to rise higher and higher, and to attain to yet more exalted stations, until at last, through its own unwearied efforts, and with the help of the Divine grace, it would triumph over all hindrances and find its true home in God. The first step on the Way was Repentance (*tawba*), which corresponded to "conversion" in Christian theology. It meant the abandonment of all that had hitherto attracted the soul, all worldly pleasures, all sensual joys, all human ties, and turning to God, the traveller setting his face steadfastly in the direction in which he meant to travel, and recognising the Goal towards which his steps were bent. The Ṣūfī al-Mu'ādh when questioned about repentance, said, "Are you asking me about the repentance of return (to God) or the repentance of shame?"

[1] Pp. 77 *ff*.

and when asked to explain the distinction, he said, "The repentance of return is that due to your fear of God, because of His power over you, but the repentance of shame is due to your shame before God because of His nearness to you."[1] Dhū al-Nūn al-Miṣrī declared that repentance was of three kinds: the common kind, repentance from sin; that of the elect, repentance from neglect; and that of the gnostics, the elect of the elect, repentance, that is, turning away, from all save God.[2] al-Junayd also took the view that Repentance meant not the remembrance of sins, but the forgetting of them. "The truly sincere," he says, "do not remember their sins, because their hearts are occupied with the Majesty of God and the continual remembrance of Him."[3] This is the Repentance which is the first stage of the Ṣūfī Path. Patience (*ṣabr*) and Gratitude (*shukr*) were early stages on the Way, of which little needs to be said here, except that they represented acceptance of affliction, which, as we have seen, was regarded by the Ṣūfīs, like the Christian ascetics, as a cause for satisfaction rather than complaint. Gratitude is the active form of the virtue of which Patience represents the passive form. All that comes from the hand of God, whether in the form of benefits or misfortunes, was to be accepted, not only without complaint, but with gratitude, yet not for its own sake, but because it was the gift of God. "Gratitude," says Qushayrī, "is the vision of the Giver, not of the gift."[4] Another Ṣūfī writer tells us, "The real meaning of gratitude is the vision of our failure to be grateful for the bounty of the All-Glorious."[5] Hope and Fear were two further stations on the Way, both concerned with the future, since Hope looks forward to what is desired, while Fear dreads what is hated. An old Ṣūfī, al-Rūdhabārī (*ob.* A.D. 933), compared Hope and Fear to the two wings of a bird flying straight on its course; if one wing fails, its flight falters, and if both fail, it must die.[6] Abū 'Amrū al-Dimashqī said of Fear, "He fears (rightly) who fears his self

[1] al-Kalābādhī, *op. cit.*, fol. 25*a*.
[2] al-Sarrāj, *op. cit.*, p. 44.
[3] *Ibid.*, p. 43.
[4] *Risāla*, p. 106.
[5] al-Kalābādhī, "Ma'ānī al-Akhbār," fol. 50*b*.
[6] *Risāla*, p. 82.

more than his enemy."[1] Among the sayings of a very early Ṣūfī, al-Fuḍayl b. 'Iyāḍ, was the statement that "He who knows God by way of love without Fear perishes through pleasure and ease. He who knows Him by Fear only is cut off from Him by slavish avoidance, but he who knows Him by both means together, loves Him and is near to Him and knows Him."[2] But the true Fear of God, to the Ṣūfī, is the fear of grieving Him and of doing that which may be a cause of separation from Him.

Other stations on the Path are those of Poverty (*faqr*), Renunciation (*zuhd*) and Dependence, or Trust in God (*tawakkul*), in which the Ṣūfīs were following in the steps of the Christian ascetics and mystics who had preceded them. Isaac of Nineveh had written, "The man whose soul is night and day given to the works of God, and who therefore neglects to prepare dress and food, and to fix and prepare a place for his shelter and the like, that such a man trusts in God that He will prepare in due season all he needs, and that He will care for him . . . this is really true trust and a trust of wisdom,"[3] and this is almost identical with what Abū Ya'qūb al-Sūsī says of the people of *tawakkul*, who are the elect of God, chosen by Him, who put their trust in Him, and are contented with Him, and so they find rest from the troubles of this world and the next.[4] Sahl al-Tustarī had said, "Real dependence is to lie passive in the hands of God," a view in accordance with the quietistic tendencies of these early Ṣūfīs, whom al-Shiblī describes as "little children in the bosom of God," as acquiescent and as contented as babes at the breast.

Another station still higher on the ascent was that of Satisfaction (*riḍā*), which meant that man, on his side, was completely acquiescent in all that God ordained for him, and God, on His part, was completely satisfied with His servant's attitude towards Him. "Human satisfaction," says al-Hujwīrī, "is equanimity under the decrees of Fate, whether it withholds or whether it gives, and steadfastness of the

[1] al-Kalābādhī, "Kitāb al-Ta'arruf," fol. 26*b*.
[2] al-Munāwī, *op. cit.*, fol. 71*a*.
[3] *Op. cit.*, p. 67.
[4] *Qūt al-Qulūb*, ii. 3.

soul in regarding passing events, whether they are a manifestation of the Divine Majesty or of the Divine Beauty. It is all the same (to the true servant) whether he remains in want or receives bounteously, he remains equally satisfied thereby, and whether he be consumed in the fire of wrath of the Divine Majesty, or whether he be illuminated by the light of mercy of the Divine Beauty, it is all one to him because both are the manifestations of God, and whatever comes from Him is altogether good."[1] So Ibn 'Aṭā, a Ṣūfī who died in A.D. 922, says of this station, " Satisfaction is the contemplation by the heart of the eternal Will of God for His servant, for His Will for him is best."[2] This, of course, is a doctrine of pure Quietism.

The Remembrance of Death (*dhikr al-mawt*) was one of the later stages on the Way. Ḥārith b. Asad al-Muḥāsibī was asked about this station, whether it was that of the adept gnostic or of the beginner on the Way, and he said, " The Remembrance of Death is in the first place a station of the beginner, and in the end a station of the adept." He was asked to explain, and said, " It is so, for it belongs to the novice, in that this remembrance is the first thing which takes possession of his heart, and therefore he abandons sin from fear of (eternal) punishment, and as the remembrance of death rises up in his heart, the lusts within him are destroyed. As for the adept, his remembrance of Death is the love of it, and the choice of it rather than life in this world of affliction, from which his heart turns away in longing for God and the meeting with Him, in hope which expects to look upon His face and abide in nearness to Him, when his heart is overcome by the beauty of his conception of his Lord, as it has been said, ' The yearning of the righteous for God lasts long, but God yearns still more to meet with them.' "[3] al-Qushayrī relates how when al-Junayd was told that Abū Sa'īd al-Kharrāz (*ob.* A.D. 899) was in a state of the greatest rapture at his death, he said, " No wonder, for his soul has taken its flight full of longing to see its Lord."[4] So

[1] *Op. cit.*, p. 220.
[2] al-Kalābādhī, " Kitāb al-Ta'arruf," fol. 27*b*.
[3] Abū Nu'aym, " Ḥilyat al-Awliyā," fol. 236*a*.
[4] *Risāla*, p. 161.

also the Christian ascetic Pachomius used to admonish his monks, saying, "Let us work with all our souls, keeping death always before our eyes." We find also great emphasis laid on the remembrance of death in the Syriac-speaking Church. Ephraim the Syrian in his "Evening Prayer" writes:

> "O Lord, may I remember the day of my death,
> And feel remorse; and let trembling seize me,
> For the evils which have been done by me;
> For I know that I am about to be judged
> By a great Judge, in Thy presence.
>
> O Lord, I have thought upon my end,
> And trembling and remorse have seized me
> Lest I should be condemned for my wickedness;
> If the angels are moved with fear
> And the ranks of the spirits tremble,
> I should earnestly pray to Thee.
> Save me and have mercy upon me."[1]

The final stages of the Ṣūfī Way were Love and Gnosis, leading to the Vision of God, and the ultimate Goal of the quest, Union with the Divine, towards which the mystic had been ever ascending on the upward Path. But these stages, representing the Unitive Life, belong rather to a more developed stage of Ṣūfism, when the Ṣūfīs had evolved a theosophic doctrine of their own, and were concerning themselves with the nature of the Goal rather than with the early stages of the Way, and when they had passed beyond these early ideals, which were represented by asceticism and quietism.[2]

We will now consider in more detail the lives and teaching of certain representatives of early Ṣūfism, who were conspicuous for their adherence to these ideals. One of the earliest of these ascetics, claimed by the Ṣūfīs as one of themselves, yet much more of an ascetic than a mystic, was Ḥasan al-Baṣrī, who was born in A.D. 643, and died in A.D. 728, and

[1] *Repentance of Nineveh* (tr. H. Burgess).

[2] For a more detailed account of the Ṣūfī Way, see my *Rābiʿa the Mystic and her Fellow-saints in Islām,* chaps. vi. to x.

was well known, not only for the austerity of his life, but for his sermons preached at Baṣra, by which his ascetical teachings were made known to the people of his generation. Abū Ḥayyān Tawḥīdī said of him, " Ḥasan was not only among the shining stars in learning, asceticism, abstinence and virtue, and devotion to God, but also pre-eminent in jurisprudence and rhetoric, in knowledge of Divine things and in fraternal admonition ; his sermons touched all hearts and his methods disturbed the minds of his listeners."[1] His life was characterised not merely by scrupulous piety and abstention from all actions which might not be approved by the religious law, but by an extreme asceticism and the renunciation of this world and all its concerns. 'Aṭṭār tells us that he lived in such seclusion that he had no expectations from any creature, and that he was never seen to laugh.[2] He won great respect from his contemporaries and was regarded as the " Helper " (*ghawth*) of his epoch, and some of the Guild fraternities of later days made him their religious leader (*pīr*) and reckoned him as one of their founders. His immediate disciples included the orthodox Muslims, the Mu'tazilites, and the Ṣūfī mystics.

The main theme of his teaching and preaching was a call to repentance because of the wrath that was to come, and he urged his hearers to despise this transitory life and all that belonged to this world which perishes. This insistence on asceticism was based on the motive of fear, which was very real to Ḥasan himself. We are told that when Ḥasan heard of the man who would be saved in the end, after a thousand years in Hell, he fell to weeping and said, " Would that I might be like that man !"[3] When asked about his own state, he said it was that of a man who had embarked upon the sea, whose vessel had been broken up, and he remained upon a plank, so parlous was his state.[4] When asked what mode of conduct was most beneficial in this world and able to bring one nearest to God in the next, he replied, " The study of the religious law, for it turns the hearts of those

[1] Yāqūt, *Mu'jām al-Udabā*, vi. 69-70.
[2] *Tadhkirat al-Awliyā*, i. 27.
[3] *Qūt al-Qulūb*, i. 101.
[4] 'Aṭṭār, *Tadhkirat al-Awliyā*, i. 40.

who study it towards God; asceticism in this world, for it brings man near to the Lord of the two worlds; and the knowledge which is possessed by perfect faith, of what God has in store for him."[1] On the subject of self-discipline Ḥasan says, "Restrain these carnal souls of yours, for they seek ever to assert themselves, and mortify them, for if you give way to them, they will bring you into great evil—and exhort them with the remembrance of God, for they are swift to become defiled."[2] The root of religion, he said, was abstinence (*wara'*), and when asked what it was that corrupted abstinence, he answered "Desire" (*ṭama'*).[3] To his fellow-ascetic, Sa'īd Jubayr, Ḥasan said, "Three things you ought not to do. Set not your feet upon the carpet of kings (*i.e.*, have no dealings with them); sit not alone with any virgin, even though it were Rābi'a (the famous woman Ṣūfī already mentioned): and lend not your ear to others."[4] His exhortations to his hearers to despise the things that were temporal for the things that were eternal were many and constantly repeated. "Sell this present world of yours," he advised, "for the next world, and you shall gain both in entirety, and do not sell the next world for this world, for so shall you lose the two together."[5] To the same effect was his statement, "That is a wise man who regards this world as nothing, and so regarding it seeks the other world, instead of setting at nought the other world and seeking this. Whosoever knows God regards Him as a friend, and whoso knows this world regards Him as an enemy."[6] Again he wrote to a friend, 'Amr b. 'Abd al-'Azīz, "Act towards this world as if it were not, and towards the world to come as if it would never cease to be."[7] He exhorts all the sons of Adam, when they see others doing good, to vie with them in so doing, and if they see others doing evil, not to emulate these, for the sojourn in this world is brief and the abiding over yonder is long. He bids men beware, for this world will depart with all its pleasures, but the deeds done here will cling about the necks of the children of Adam.[8]

[1] al-Sarrāj, *Kitāb al-Luma'*, p. 142.
[2] al-Jāḥiz, *al-Bayān*, i. 162.
[3] 'Aṭṭār, *op. cit.*, i. 27.
[4] *Ibid.*, p. 31.
[5] al-Jāḥiz, *op. cit.*, iii. 68.
[6] 'Aṭṭār, *op. cit.*, i. 40.
[7] al-Jāḥiz, *op. cit.*, iii. 71.
[8] *Ibid.*, iii. 68.

He points men to the Way which leads towards salvation from sin, and the attainment of bliss hereafter. " He who is content, who needs nothing, and who has sought solitude apart from mankind will find peace, and he who has trodden the lusts of the flesh under his feet will become free, and he who has shaken himself free of envy will win friendship, and he who has patience for a little while will find provision for Eternity."[1] Blessed are those to whom even in this life God grants a vision of the future in order that they may guide their steps aright. " There are servants of God," he says, " who already see the people of Paradise dwelling there eternally, and the people of Hell tormented in the fire ; their hearts are tranquil, and their joys are secure ; their needs are light, and their souls are chaste. They endure their days in patience, knowing that the time is short and their rest will be long. They spend the night attentive, standing upright, while the tears flow down their cheeks, and they beseech their Lord, saying, 'O Lord, our Lord.' In the daytime they appear as wise, learned, devout, experienced. He who regards them, considers them as weaklings, but these are not weaklings, or if they are affected with any affliction, it is that of people who are deeply afflicted by the thought of the future life."[2] This might well be the description of a community of Christian monks. Ḥasan emphasises the need for meditation (*fikra*) in the life of the believer. " Meditation," he says, " is a mirror which reveals to you your virtues and your vices."[3]

In all these sayings Ḥasan lays his chief emphasis upon asceticism and the Purgative life, but occasionally he gives teaching of a more definitely mystical type, as when he says of the relation between God and man, " When My servant becomes altogether occupied with Me, then I make his happiness and his delight consist in the remembrance of Me, and when I have made his happiness and his delight consist in that remembrance, he desires Me and I desire him, and when he desires Me and I desire him, I raise the veils between Me and him, and I become manifest before his eyes.

[1] 'Aṭṭār, *op. cit.*, i. 37.
[2] Abū Nu'aym, " Ḥilya " (*Recueil*, p. 3).
[3] 'Aṭṭār, *op. cit.*, i. 37.

Such men do not forget Me when others forget. Their word is the word of the Prophets; they are the true heroes, those whom I will remember, when I desire to bring punishment and affliction upon the people of the earth, and I will avert it from them."[1] Here is a forecast of the later Ṣūfī teaching upon the Divine Vision, and Ḥasan speaks elsewhere of that Vision as revealed to the blessed in the Hereafter, where he says, "When the inhabitants of Paradise first open their eyes there, they remain in ecstasy for seven hundred thousand years, because the Lord Most High reveals Himself to them in all His Glory. When they look upon His glory they are overcome by His Majesty, and when they behold His Beauty they are overwhelmed by His Unity."[2] To Ḥasan, while he was deeply conscious of the transcendence and the majesty of God and His wrath against sinners, there was a way of access to Him. Man by purification, by complete renunciation of this world, by utter submission of his human will to the Divine Will, might receive grace to realise that mystical state of "satisfaction" in which man could find the fulfilment of all his needs, and his chief joy, in God, and God could find satisfaction in the complete acquiescence of His servant in His will, and man's search for God would result in God coming forth to seek and to find Him.

Another of these early Ṣūfīs, of a very different type from Ḥasan of Baṣra, though no less of an ascetic, was Ibrāhīm b. Adham b. Manṣūr Abū Ishāq, of Balkh, who died in A.D. 777. He was of royal birth, his father being one of the kings of Khurāsān, and it is related that Adham the father made the pilgrimage to Mecca with his wife, and while there she gave birth to Ibrāhīm. His father carried the infant round the Ka'ba and begged of the multitudes assembled there that they would implore God's blessing on the child, and the effect of these prayers, offered up by the devout in such a sacred spot, was manifested many years later.[3] Ibrāhīm himself gives an account of his conversion. While out hunting, having started a fox, he was pursuing it when he heard a heavenly voice, rousing him from his heedlessness, and

[1] Abū Nu'aym, *op. cit.* (*Recueil*, p. 3).
[2] 'Aṭṭār, *op. cit.*, i. 37.
[3] Ibn Khallikān, ii. 13 (note).

recalling him from the pleasures of this world, saying, "O Ibrāhīm, did I create thee for this?" He was much afraid and fell down from his horse.[1] This occurred three times, and then a voice spoke to him from just in front of his saddle, "Verily thou wast not created for this, and not in this wilt thou die." Ibrāhīm then dismounted and coming across one of his father's shepherds, he took the man's woollen garment and put it on, and paid the man for it with his mare, and with nothing left in his possession set his face towards Mecca.[2] Another legend of his conversion relates that one of his disciples asked him what had induced him, being a king's son, to abandon this transient world, and to seek that which abides for ever. He told the questioner how he had been seated in the palace diwan, with his courtiers around him, when on looking out of the window he saw a beggar outside, eating dry bread, which he soaked in water and seasoned with coarse salt. Having satisfied his hunger thus, he prayed and went to sleep. Ibrāhīm watched the beggar and then sent to fetch him when he awoke. The servant told the beggar that the lord of the palace wished to speak to him. "In the Name of God," he replied, "there is no lordship and no strength save those of God, but I will come." Ibrāhīm asked him whether his hunger was satisfied by the piece of bread. "It was," replied the old man. Had he slept afterwards without any anxiety or sorrow? Yes, he had rested thoroughly. Ibrāhīm pondered over this and over his own dissatisfaction with life, and wondered what he could do to secure contentment like the beggar. That same night he discarded his royal garb and put on haircloth, and left his palace and betook himself to a life of poverty and wandering, like the beggar.[3]

[1] *Cf.* the legend of St. Hubert. On Good Friday he went forth to the chase, and as he was pursuing a stag, it turned, and he saw a crucifix surrounded with light between its antlers, and heard a voice saying, "Hubert, unless thou turnest to the Lord and leadest a holy life, thou shalt quickly go down into Hell." He dismounted and gave himself up from that time to the service of God.

[2] al-Sulamī, "Ṭabaqāt al-Ṣūfiyya," fols. *3b*, *4a*.

[3] *Cf.* Goldziher, J.R.A.S., 1904, pp. 132 *ff.* It is to be noted that certain features of the story of Ibrāhīm b. Adham bear a strong resemblance to that of Prince Gautama, the Buddha.

After his conversion, while he was still in the desert, on the way to Mecca, a man who had apparently neither cruse of water nor provisions joined him, and when evening came he prayed the sunset prayer. Provisions were miraculously forthcoming and Ibrāhīm ate and drank and continued for some days in the company of this stranger, who, he tells us, taught him the " Most Exalted Name " of God. Then the man vanished and Ibrāhīm was left alone in the desert, and being overtaken with fear, he called upon God by that Name. Immediately someone appeared at his side, who said to him, " Ask and it shall be given thee." This speech made Ibrāhīm even more afraid, but the stranger bade him take courage and said, " I am thy brother Khiḍr,[1] and it was my brother Dawūd (David) who taught thee the Most Exalted Name of God." The prophet admonished him to call upon God to strengthen his weakness and comfort his loneliness and refresh his sense of strangeness, at all times. Then al-Khiḍr departed and left Ibrāhīm to go on his way.[2] At Mecca he consorted with Sufyān al-Thawrī and al-Fuḍayl b. 'Iyāḍ, two noted Ṣūfīs.

After his visit to Mecca he went to Syria, and there lived the life of a Ṣūfī, eating only what food he had earned by the labours of his hands, gardening, reaping, grinding wheat, and so on. He lived a life of the greatest asceticism, and al-Hujwīrī tells us that though Ibrāhīm fasted from the beginning of Ramaḍān to the end, yet even when it fell in the month of July, with the days at their hottest and longest, he worked every day harvesting, and gave his wages to the dervishes. He also spent the whole night, until daybreak, in prayer; he was closely watched, but those who were watching saw that he neither ate nor slept.[3] Jāmī, commenting on Ibrāhīm's life of self-sacrificing labour, says, " The Ṣūfī does not fail to serve, but Ṣūfism is not service. The Ṣūfīs do not neglect service, indeed they go beyond

[1] Otherwise al-Khaḍir (the Green), a prophet and a saint, who presides over the well of immortality, who is regarded as God's *khalīfa* on the sea and His *wakīl* on land. He is the spiritual director par excellence, and several of the great Ṣūfī saints traced their initiation to him.

[2] al-Sulamī, *op. cit.*, fol. 4*b*.

[3] *Kashf al-Maḥjūb*, p. 418.

others in that respect, but they do not reckon it as of any account, in that they seek no object or reward or recompense and their stock in trade is something different, it consists in what is inward, not what is outward. They neglect the outward as deceptive, and in the inward, live in another world." A fellow-Ṣūfī, Abū al-Qāsim Naṣrabādhī, said that in love and knowledge and fellowship Ibrāhīm b. Adham exceeded anything accomplished by man or jinn.[1] al-Hujwīrī says of him, " He was unique in his Path and preeminent among his contemporaries," while al-Junayd of Baghdād declared that Ibrāhīm was the " key " of the Ṣūfī doctrine.

It is related that Ibrāhīm b. Adham, after he had become a Ṣūfī and a wanderer, once came upon a young man whom he recognised as his son, and for a time his natural feelings almost overcame him, but he kept them under control and, according to the legend, repeated these lines :

" O God ! for love of Thee I forsook mankind,
I made my children orphans, that I might look on Thee ;
And if Thou madest it a condition of Thy love to hew
me in pieces,
Yet would I turn to none for help beside Thee."

So saying, he took leave of his son, and as he went on his way expressed only the wish that God would cleanse his son from all sin and help him to fulfil His commandments.[2]

Ibrāhīm is said to have told this story, which reminds us of similar stories told of the Christian hermits in the Egyptian desert. " When I was in the desert, an old man came up and said to me, ' O Ibrāhīm, do you know what place this is, in which you are journeying without any provision for the way ?' I knew that he was Satan. Now I had with me four silver dāniqs, the price of a basket which I had sold in Kūfa, and at once I took them out of my pocket and threw them away, making a vow that I would perform a prayer of four hundred *raka's* (prostrations) for every mile that I travelled. I remained four years in the desert and God continued to give me my daily bread when I needed it, without

[1] *Nafaḥāt al-Uns*, p. 46. [2] *Cf.* Goldziher, *J.R.A.S.*, p. 134.

any effort on my part, and during that time Khiḍr consorted with me. . . . Then my heart became altogether empty of all save God."[1]

Twice in his life he said that he had attained his desire. Once on board ship where no one knew him. He was meanly dressed, his hair unkempt, and his appearance such that all present made a jest of him, especially a buffoon who used to come and pull his hair or tear it out and to mock at him. At that time, said Ibrāhīm, he felt completely satisfied. On another occasion he arrived at a village in pouring rain, with his patched robe soaked through and his body chilled by the bitter cold. He went to a mosque, but was refused admittance, and at three others he failed to find shelter. Then in despair he entered a bath-house, and sat close to the stove, the smoke from which blackened both his face and his clothes. Then, too, he felt entirely satisfied.[2]

Ibrāhīm appears to have spent the rest of his life in Syria; one account of his death says that it took place while he was taking part in a naval expedition against the Greeks; his grave was reputed to be at Sūqīn, a fortress in Rūm.[3]

Most of Ibrāhīm's sayings and teaching have an ascetical tendency, as might be expected from one who had found salvation by fleeing from the world and becoming an outcast. He said of Poverty that it was a treasure which God kept in heaven and bestowed only on those whom He loved. To a man whom he saw circumambulating the Ka'ba, Ibrāhīm said, "Know that you will not attain the degree of the righteous until you have passed certain stages: first, you must lock the door of pleasure, and open the door of hardship; second, you must lock the door of power and open the door of weakness; third, you must lock the door of wealth and open that of poverty; and finally, you must lock the door of hope and open the door of the preparation for death."[4] He constantly taught his disciples to despise and flee from this world; "A man is free when he gives up this world," he said, "even before he has left it"; and again, "Shun the world as you shun a beast of prey." He asked a certain man if he desired to become one of God's saints, and when he

[1] al-Hujwīrī, *Kashf al-Maḥjūb*, p. 130.
[2] *Ibid.*, pp. 76, 77.
[3] Yāqūt, iii. 196.
[4] al-Sulamī, *op. cit.*, fol. 6*b*.

answered, "Yes," Ibrāhīm said to him, "Covet nothing in this world or the next, and devote thyself entirely to God and turn thy face to Him, having no desire for this world or the life to come. To covet this world is to turn away from God, for the sake of that which is transitory, and to covet the next world is to turn away from God for the sake of that which is everlasting; that which is transitory passes away and its renunciation also perishes, but the renunciation of that which is everlasting is also imperishable."[1]

There is not much of a definitely mystical nature in Ibrāhīm b. Adham's teaching, but he teaches a whole-hearted devotion to God and the rooting out of the heart of regard for anything save Him. "Take God as thy companion," he said, "and leave mankind alone."[2] He had some idea of the mystic gnosis, which to the later Ṣūfīs was a stage granted at the end of the Path. He tells how a certain shaykh of Alexandria was asked what was the nature of Patience, and the old man answered, "The lowest of the stages of Patience is that the servant should train himself to endure the struggles of his carnal soul. Then God will make a light to shine upon the heart, which will show the distinction between the true and the false, and the corrupt and the dubious." And Ibrāhīm, as he listened, said, "This is an attribute of the friends (*awliyā*, commonly used to designate the saints) of the Lord of the two worlds."[3] Ibrāhīm is thoroughly representative of the early Ṣūfīs in his asceticism and quietism and in the stress which he lays in his teaching upon the absolute renunciation of the world and the entire suppression of ordinary human feeling. But the aim of this renunciation and self-mortification was the aim of all the mystics; it was endured in order the better to attain to a knowledge of the only Reality, God.

Prominent among these early Ṣūfī ascetics was 'Abd al-Wāḥid b. Zayd (*ob.* 793), renowned for his austerity as much as for the sanctity of his life, a theologian and a preacher, and an advocate of solitude for those who sought the way to God. He himself observed a vow of chastity for forty years, and was the founder of a monastic community which

[1] al-Hujwīrī, *op. cit.*, p. 274. [2] al-Sulamī, *op. cit.*, *loc. cit.*
[3] *Ibid.*, fol. 4*b*.

he established at 'Abbadān, near Baṣra. There is a story told of how a number of these early Ṣūfī monks deserted 'Abd al-Wāḥid, because he bade them practise self-discipline and give themselves to devout worship, and eat only what was lawful, and renounce the world. 'Abd al-Wāḥid met one of these renegades after a time and inquired after his welfare and that of his companions. The man replied, "O teacher, every night we enter Paradise and eat of its fruits." 'Abd al-Wāḥid asked the man to take him with them that night, and they took him into the desert. When night fell, a company appeared, clad in green robes, and there appeared gardens full of fruit-trees. 'Abd al-Wāḥid looked at the feet of those who were clothed in green robes, and behold, they had cloven hoofs, and he knew that they were the emissaries of Satan. When they wished to part company, he said to the quondam monks, "Whither are you going? When Idrīs the Prophet[1] had entered Paradise, he never left it again." When the morning dawned, they found themselves on the dung-heaps. So their eyes were opened to the error of their ways, and they followed 'Abd al-Wāḥid and returned to their communal life with him.[2]

The background of 'Abd al-Wāḥid's sermons was eschatological; like others of the early Ṣūfīs, he laid stress on the motive of the fear of judgment hereafter, and he appealed to the emotions of his hearers more than to their reason. He sought to make them afraid rather than to convince them of any special doctrine. He said on one occasion, "That man has never truly feared who imagines that he will not enter the fire of Hell, nor is the fear sincere, of him who imagines that he will enter Hell and come out of it again"—*i.e.*, real fear is dread of entering Hell and then of remaining there for ever.[3] In one of his sermons he makes this appeal to the impenitent and the indifferent: "O my brothers, will ye not weep from desire for God, to Whom belong glory and majesty? Can it be that he who weeps from desire for his Lord shall be denied the Vision of Him? O brothers, will ye not weep from fear of Hell-fire? Shall not he who weeps

[1] Identified by Muslim writers with the Biblical Enoch.
[2] al-Sarrāj, *op. cit.*, p. 429.
[3] Abū Ṭālib, *op. cit.*, i. 101.

from fear of Hell-fire be saved therefrom by God? O brothers, will ye not weep from fear of the burning thirst (which shall afflict you) on the Day of Resurrection?[1] Surely. Weep then for the cool refreshing water, while ye are yet in this world, that it may be poured out to you in Paradise, in the company of the best of fellow-guests, and the companions of the Prophets and the faithful and the righteous. How glorious a company are they!"[2]

'Abd al-Wāḥid was once asked who were the true Ṣūfīs, and he answered, "Those who apply their whole minds to their (spiritual) concerns, and are diligent therein with their whole hearts, turning aside from the evil of their carnal selves, and cleaving unto their Lord—such are the Ṣūfīs."[3] He knew that the Way to God meant the treading of a hard and lonely road, and there are verses attributed to him in which he says:

"The ways are various, the way to the Truth is but one;
And those who travel on the way of Truth must go on their road alone.
They are not known, nor is their purpose manifest, for they go quietly on their way, stage by stage.
The rest of mankind are heedless of what is desired of them;
And long sleep keeps them from following the Way of the Truth."[4]

In 'Abd al-Wāḥid, then, we find an ascetic who followed the Christian monks in believing that the Ṣūfīs, if they were to follow the Path to God in very truth, must keep themselves entirely apart from the world, and in holding that this could best be done in a monastic community composed entirely of those who had this high aim before them.

One of the best-known among these early Ṣūfīs of the ascetic school was Rābi'a al-'Adawiyya, the woman saint and mystic of Baṣra, who was born about A.D. 717 and died

[1] *Cf.* the Christian ascetic Abbā John, "Let us weep that our eyes may overflow with tears before we come to the place where the tears of our eyes will burn our bodies."

[2] *Recueil*, p. 5.

[3] al-Sarrāj, *op. cit.*, p. 25.

[4] Abū Talib, *op. cit.*, i. 153.

in A.D. 801. Although, as we shall see, she is to be included among the earliest mystics of Islām, for her teaching in parts is definitely mystical, she was also pre-eminent as an ascetic. Her biographer writes of her as "that one set apart in the seclusion of holiness, that woman veiled with the veil of religious sincerity, that one on fire with love and longing, enamoured with the desire to approach her Lord and be consumed in His glory, that woman who lost herself in union with the Divine, that one accepted by men as a second spotless Mary—Rābi'a al-'Adawiyya."[1]

She eschewed marriage, though legend states that she received many offers from the men Ṣūfīs who were her friends, and sometimes her disciples. To one of them she said, "The contract of marriage is for those who have a phenomenal existence (*i.e.*, who are concerned with the affairs of this material world). But in my case, there is no such existence, for I have ceased to exist and have passed out of Self. I exist in God and am altogether His. I live in the shadow of His command. The marriage contract must be asked for from Him, not from me."[2] We are reminded here of the admonition of the monk Aphraates to the Christian "Daughters of the Covenant," to say to those who would seek them in marriage, "To a royal Husband am I betrothed, and to Him do I minister; and if I leave His ministry, my Betrothed will be wroth with me and will write me a letter of divorce and will dismiss me from His house."[3]

Rābi'a lived a life of great poverty; one of her friends told how he went into her house in her old age, and found there only a reed-mat and a screen and an earthenware jug, with a bed of felt, which served also as her prayer-carpet.[4] Her renunciation of the world was complete. Some of her acquaintances suggested to her one day that they should ask her kinsmen to procure a servant to do the work of her house for her, but she said, "I should be ashamed to ask for the things of this world from Him to Whom the world belongs, and how should I ask for them from those to whom

[1] 'Aṭṭār, *op. cit.*, i. 59.
[2] *Ibid.*, i. 66.
[3] See above, p. 45.
[4] Ibn al-Jawzī, "Ta'rīkh al-Muntaẓam," fol. 132.

it does not belong?"[1] On another occasion a wealthy merchant brought a purse of gold to the door of her cell and a friend came in and told her of it. Rābi'a said to him, " Shall not He Who provides for those who revile Him, provide for those who love Him? He does not refuse to sustain one who speaks unworthily of Him, how then should He refuse to sustain one whose soul is overflowing with love to Him? Ever since I have known Him, I have turned my back upon mankind. How should I take the wealth of someone of whom I do not know whether he acquired it lawfully or not? "[2] One of her companions said of her that Rābi'a used to pray all night, and when the day began to dawn she would allow herself a brief interval of light sleep in her place of prayer until the dawn tinged the sky with gold. Then she used to spring up in fear from her sleep and say, " O soul, how long wilt thou sleep and how often wilt thou wake? Soon wilt thou sleep a sleep from which thou shalt not wake again until the trumpet-call of the Day of Resurrection."[3]

Much of Rābi'a's teaching was on the same ascetical lines as her life and practice. Repentance, the first step on the Ṣūfī Way, was to her mind a gift from God. She said once to someone who asked if God would accept the penitent sinner, " How can anyone repent unless his Lord gives him repentance and accepts him?"; and on another occasion she said, " Seeking forgiveness (merely) with the tongue is the sin of lying. If I seek repentance of myself, I shall have need of repentance again."[4] While Rābi'a taught that the sinner must fear the punishment of his sins, and that fear might lead him into the right way, her teaching on Hope and Fear was of a more spiritual type than that of the ascetics with whom we have already dealt. There is a story told of how a number of the Ṣūfīs saw that Rābi'a had taken a torch in one hand and water in the other and was hastening on her way with them. They asked her the meaning of her action, and she said, " I am going to light a fire in Paradise and to pour water on to Hell, so that both veils (*i.e.*, hindrances to

[1] al-Jāḥiẓ, *al-Bayān wa'l-Tabyīn*, iii. 66.
[2] 'Aṭṭār, *op. cit.*, i. 70.
[3] Ibn Khallikān, *Wafayāt*, i. 34, No. 230.
[4] 'Aṭṭār, *op. cit.*, i. 67.

the vision of God Himself) may vanish altogether from before the pilgrims and their purpose may be sure, and the servants of God may see Him, without any object of hope or any motive of fear. What if the hope of Paradise and the fear of Hell did not exist? Not one would worship his Lord or obey Him."[1] Yet though she realised that Fear and Hope were the common motives of service to God, Rāb'ia herself held up a higher ideal to those who sought to be saints. "He is a bad servant," she said to a number of shaykhs who were discussing the question with her, "who worships God from fear and terror or from the desire of reward—though there are many of these." When asked if she herself had no desire for Paradise, she rejoined, "The Neighbour first, and then the house. Is it not enough for me that I am given leave to worship Him? Even if Heaven and Hell were not, does it not behove us to obey Him? He is worthy of worship without any (self-interested) motive."[2] Rābi'a raised the teaching of the Ṣūfī doctrine to a high spiritual level, and, as we shall see in a later chapter, she was as much of a mystic as an ascetic, one of the first in Islām to whom the title of mystic can justifiably be given.

One of the most outstanding of these early Ṣūfīs was Abū 'Abdallah al-Ḥārith b. Asad al-Muḥāsibī, who was born at Baṣra about A.D. 781, taught in Baghdād, and died at Kūfa in A.D. 857. He was a man of great learning, one of the most learned of the shaykhs of his day in knowledge of phenomenal things and of general laws, and also in practical knowledge, so writes al-Sulamī. He has been called by a modern writer on Ṣūfism[3] "the true master of primitive Islamic

[1] Aflākī, "Manāqib al-'Ārifīn," fol. 114*a*. *Cf.* a similar incident related in de Joinville's *Histoire de St. Louis*, telling how Brother Yves saw an old woman in the streets of Damascus, carrying in her right hand a brazier of fire and in her left a vessel of water. Asked what she was going to do, she said that she was going to set Paradise alight and pour water on to Hell, in order that none should do good for the sake of gaining Paradise or from fear of Hell, but only out of love to God, Who is worth more than all else, and is the Giver of all good (Ed. de Wailly), p. 158.

[2] 'Aṭṭār, *op. cit.*, p. 69. So also a contemporary of Rābi'a, Wuhayb b. al-Ward (*ob.* A.D. 770), had said, "Paradise is to glorify God and to know Him."

[3] Prof. L. Massignon.

mysticism," but he has his place among the ascetics also, and a good deal of his teaching is concerned with asceticism and quietism, which he also practised assiduously throughout his life. We are told that for four years he never leant against a wall either by night or by day, and never rested except on his two knees. When asked why he wearied himself thus, he replied, " I should be ashamed in the presence of the King not to deport myself as a slave."[1] Like other Ṣūfīs, he was scrupulous in avoiding what was unlawful, and we are told that al-Muḥāsibī never put his hand to any food that was suspicious.

His name of al-Muḥāsibī was given to him as an " examiner " of conscience, and the chief emphasis of his teaching was laid upon the need for inner purification. " He who does not cleanse his soul by self-discipline," he said, " will not have opened to him the way to the mystic Path."[2] Like others among these early Ṣūfīs, he was orthodox in his ideas as to the line of conduct to be observed by the seeker after salvation. In his " Waṣāyā " (Book of Precepts) he tells how he himself found the way of salvation through the careful observance of the canonical law. He writes: " I exerted myself in the search for what I had not found for myself of Divine knowledge, from the people in whom I had found indications of devoted piety, of abstinence and of preference for the next world rather than this. I found that their directions and their maxims were in agreement with the advice of the imāms of the Way of Salvation; that they were agreed to give good counsel to the community, not giving to any freedom to sin, yet not despairing of the Divine mercy because of any defection; recommending patience in misfortune and adversities, and acquiescence in the Divine Will and gratitude for favours received. They seek to make God loved by His servants, in reminding them of His favours and His benefits, calling upon the faithful to repent before God. Such persons are wise in knowledge of the Majesty of God and in the fullness of His Power . . . learned in His Book and in His Law, well acquainted with the true faith, knowing well what ought to be loved and what hated, scrupulous in the matter of heresies and sen-

[1] Jāmī, *Nafaḥāt al-Uns*, p. 66. [2] *Ibid.*

sual desires, wise in their knowledge of the other life and of what is to be feared at the Resurrection from the dead, of God's liberality in recompense and His severity in punishment. God has made them to grieve continually with a special concern, by means of which He keeps them from preoccupation with the pleasures of this world. Desirous of following their rule of life, and having learned much from their gifts, I saw that no further proof was needed for one who had grasped the argument. I realised that to adopt this manner of life and to act in accordance with its sanctions was incumbent on me. I bound myself to it in my conscience and I concentrated on it with my inner vision; I made it the foundation of my faith and I based my acts upon it."[1] These principles, based on the observance of the religious law, al-Muḥāsibī carried out in his own life and in his teaching. "From knowledge (of the sacred law)," he said, "comes godly fear, and from asceticism, peace of mind, and from gnosis, repentance." Again he said, "The man who purifies his inner life by self-examination and complete sincerity, God will adorn his outward life in striving, and in obedience to the Sunna."[2] He urges the seeker after salvation to repentance and to continual, godly fear. The qualities to be sought after are patient endurance of injury, slowness to wrath, a frank and open face, and good words. The true resignation of the servant to his Lord's will consists in remaining steadfast when misfortunes occur, without being moved by them either outwardly or inwardly.[3] Of patience, he says, "Everything has its essential property and that of man is reason, and the essential property of reason is Patience." When asked about the nature of Hope he said, "It is the desire for the grace of God and His mercy, and sincerity in fair thoughts of Him at the approach of death."[4]

"Satisfaction," he said, "is the acquiescence of the heart in what comes to pass by the Divine decree."[5] Here we see his tendency to quietism, and his otherworldliness is shown in his statement that "the oppressor has need of repentance, though men praise him, and the oppressed is safe,

[1] "Waṣāyā," fols. 2*b*, 3*b*.
[2] al-Sulamī, *op. cit.*, fol. 12*a*.
[3] *Ibid.*, fol. 12*a*.
[4] *Ibid.*
[5] al-Kalābādhī, "Kitāb al-Ta'arruf," fol. 28*a*.

though men blame him ; so also the contented man is rich, though he be hungry, and the covetous man is poor, though he own the whole world."[1] All his teaching was directed towards the subjugation of the carnal self, since in the desires of self he recognised the root of all sin. "The true service of God," he says, "means ensuring that your self has no power, and knowing that neither injury nor benefit has any power over your self."[2] We have reason to know that Muḥāsibī was most certainly acquainted with the New Testament—*e.g.*, he bases certain of his ascetical teaching on the Parable of the Sower, holding that the Divine word can bear fruit only in ground prepared by self-renunciation.[3]

In this way al-Muḥāsibī pointed his disciples to the Purgative life as the first stage on the mystic Way, and he gave them the hope that after they had trodden that stage and learned its lessons, and purified the soul from the desires of self and the claims of the senses, and had freed it from the attachments of this world, they might attain to the stage of the Illuminative life, and thence might pass to the ultimate goal, the Unitive life in God.

An Egyptian representative of these early Ṣūfīs is to be found in Abū al-Fayḍ, called also Thawbān, b. Ibrāhīm Dhū al-Nūn (He of the Fish) al-Miṣrī, who was born at Ikhmīm in Upper Egypt about A.D. 796. His father appears to have been a Nubian, and Dhū al-Nūn is said to have been a freedman. Sa'dūn of Cairo is mentioned as his teacher and spiritual director.[4] He travelled to Mecca and Damascus and went to visit the ascetics of Mount Lukkām, south of Antioch. He met with hostility from the Mu'tazilites because he upheld the orthodox view that the Qur'ān was uncreated, and was condemned also for his public teaching of mysticism. Towards the end of his life he was arrested, sent to Baghdād and imprisoned there, being allowed, however, to receive the visits of Ṣūfī friends. Being released by the order of the Caliph, he returned to Egypt and died at Gīza in A.D. 857.

It is related that at his funeral the birds of the air gathered together above the bier and made a shade for it,[5] and after

[1] al-Sulamī, *ibid.*, fol. 12*b*.
[2] Jāmī, *op. cit.*, p. 66.
[3] "Ri'āya," fols. 4*b*, 11*b*.
[4] al-Sarrāj, *Maṣāri'*, p. 130.
[5] al-Hujwīrī, *Kashf*, p. 125.

his burial there appeared an inscription on his grave which ran, " This is the beloved of God, who died from his love to God, slain by God," and whenever that inscription was erased, it reappeared again.[1] We are told that on the night after his death seventy persons saw the Prophet in a dream, and he said, " I have come to meet Dhū al-Nūn, the friend of God."[2]

Dhū al-Nūn was reckoned as a *Quṭb* or Axis in the Ṣūfī hierarchy, this being the title given to the spiritual head of all the saints, and he was also counted as one of the " hidden Saints " (*'Ayārān*), and 'Aṭṭār describes him as " That celibate among the people of blame (*malāmat*, *i.e.*, those who concealed their devotions, and neither boasted of their good works nor hid what was bad),[3] that candle of those assembled at the Resurrection, that demonstration of spiritual rank and detachment, that Sultan of spiritual knowledge and the doctrine of the Unity, that demonstration of poverty—Dhū al-Nūn, one of the keys of the Path, and a traveller on the Way of affliction and blame, possessed of great insight into the Divine mysteries and doctrine of the Unity, who practised perfect observance (of the religious law) and complete self-discipline, and was blessed with the power to work miracles."[4] Dhū al-Nūn says of himself and his travels in search of the Way to salvation, " On my first journey, I found a knowledge acceptable to both the elect and the crowd, and on the second, knowledge acceptable to the elect, but not to the crowd, and on the third knowledge acceptable to neither the elect nor the crowd, and I remained an outcast and alone. The first knowledge was repentance, which both the elect and the crowd accept, and the second was trust in God and fellowship with Him and love, which the elect accept, and the third was the knowledge of reality, which is beyond the power of human learning and reason, so they reject it."[5]

[1] Jāmī, *op. cit.*, p. 36. [2] al-Hujwīrī, *op. cit.*, p. 125.

[3] The same tendency had been found among the early Christian fathers who sought to be despised and blamed. Isaac of Nineveh says, " To expose oneself to disdain indiscriminately is to be freed from all things, to disregard life and to love men " (*Mystical Treatises*, pp. 97, 239).

[4] 'Aṭṭār, *op. cit.*, i. 114. [5] Jāmī, *op. cit.*, p. 36.

It was on his travels, too, that Dhū al-Nūn learnt to become a master in asceticism and self-discipline. He once saw an ascetic who had hanged his body on a tree, and was telling it that unless it submitted to all observances required by the religious law, it would be left there to die of hunger, and when Dhū al-Nūn inquired as to what crime the body had committed, the man said that it desired to have intercourse with worldly things, and from worldly intercourse all manner of evil would follow. Again Dhū al-Nūn passed by a man who had cut off one of his feet. A woman had passed by his cell, after whom his body yearned, and he had put one foot outside his cell when he heard a voice saying, " Art thou not ashamed after serving God and obeying Him, to serve Satan now ? " So he cut off the foot which had sought to lead him into temptation.[1]

Dhū al-Nūn had many disciples during his lifetime, and he never ceased to teach them the duty of repentance, self-mortification, renunciation and otherworldliness. " Ordinary men," he said, " repent of their sins, but the elect of God repent of their heedlessness."[2] He was asked who was the best of friends and he replied, " That one who will visit you when sick, and who will recall you to repentance when you sin."[3] He also distinguished between the repentance of return (*tawbat al-ināba*), inspired by fear of Divine punishment, and the repentance of shame (*tawbat al-istiḥyā'*) inspired by shame at the Divine mercy.[4] The self, that is, the carnal soul, was to Dhū al-Nūn the chief obstacle to spiritual progress. He was asked which of the veils (between the soul and God) was the chief concealment, and the greatest hindrance to clear vision of the Truth, and he replied, " The vision of the carnal self and its promptings."[5] On another occasion he said, " Have no intercourse with God except that of perfect acquiescence (in His will), nor with mankind except that of perfect sincerity, nor with the carnal self except that of opposition, nor with Satan except that of

[1] 'Aṭṭār, *op. cit.*, i. 115. *Cf. above*, p. 166.
[2] al-Hujwīrī, *op. cit.*, pp. 384, 385.
[3] al-Sarrāj, *Kitāb al-Luma'*, p. 176.
[4] al-Hujwīrī, *ibid.*
[5] al-Sulamī, *op. cit.*, fol. 6*b*.

enmity and warfare."[1] As we have seen above, he welcomed affliction as a means of self-discipline; to a friend who was ill and wrote to Dhū al-Nūn asking for his prayers that he might recover and be relieved of his suffering, Dhū al-Nūn replied, " You ask me to pray to God for you, that He would remove grace from you. Know, O my brother, that the Ṣūfīs desire fellowship with sickness and misfortune, (they) keep company with anxiety and weakness, for such things in their life lead to healing. He who does not reckon affliction as a grace is not one of the wise, and he who has not entrusted himself to the All-Compassionate, has confided his affairs to people who cannot be trusted. Therefore, my brother, may God make you ashamed and keep you from complaining, and so farewell."[2] al-Miṣrī's teaching on Patience was in accordance with this view of affliction as a gift sent by God. " Patience," he says, " means acquiescence in the face of the repression and obstruction caused by trials, and it means the outward appearance of wealth combined with the obligations imposed by poverty in all spheres of life."[3]

We have another instance of Dhū al-Nūn's feeling that the soul gained more from adversity than from prosperity, in the reply which he sent to a man who wrote to him, " May God favour thee with His proximity." Dhū-al-Nūn wrote in answer, " May God keep thee far from His proximity, for if He favours thee by drawing nigh, it is His decree for thee, and if He withdraws far from thee, it is also His decree, and His decree is not accomplished until it leaves thee heart-broken in longing for Him."[4] Humility was essential for the soul that would seek to draw nigh unto its Lord. " God gives His servant no source of strength more powerful for

[1] al-Sarrāj, *op. cit.*, p. 177.

[2] *Ibid.*, p. 235.

[3] al-Munāwī, " Kawākib," fol. 110*a*.

[4] al-Sarrāj, *op. cit.*, p. 235. *Cf.* the Christian mystic Francis Thompson:

" All which I took from thee I did but take,
Not for thy harms,
But just that thou might'st seek it in My arms."

The Hound of Heaven.

him than when He leads him to humiliate himself."[1] Again he says, " Let him who desires humility look towards the Majesty of God Most High, and verily his soul will melt away and be purified, for in regarding the power of God, the power of the self departs, and the human soul becomes completely subdued by the awe which God inspires."[2] Dhū al-Nūn says to the novice, " Let him who seeks to follow the Path come to the wise with his ignorance, to the ascetics with his desires, and to the people of knowledge—the gnostics, with silence." The true gnostic becomes more humble every day, for every day he is drawing nearer to his Lord.[3]

When the knowledge of God is established in the heart, godly fear is established there also. " The lover," says Dhū al-Nūn, " does not pour out the cup of love until fear has made his heart ready."[4] Fear he considers to be the guardian of actions, *i.e.*, it restrains man from doing evil, while Hope is the intercessor for the afflicted, that is, it leads them to look for relief from their present troubles.[5] Yet Dhū al-Nūn, like Rābi'a, takes a higher view of Fear than that involved in the dread of material consequences, the fear of judgment to come, for he says, " The fear of Hell-fire is to the fear of separation from God like a drop which has fallen into the bottomless sea. Every believer in God Most High fears Him, but his fear is in proportion to his proximity to Him."[6]

Like all the Ṣūfīs, Dhū al-Nūn teaches that service to God must be an undivided allegiance. The seeker must be prepared to cut himself off from all ties and attachments that would hinder him in his quest for the Divine. Sincerity in the search for righteousness, says Dhū al-Nūn, " is the sword of God on earth, which cuts whatsoever it touches."[7] By it all unworthy motives are cleared away, all bonds severed between the aspiring soul and this downward-dragging world with its attractions and its snares. When asked what love to God really meant, Dhū al-Nūn said, " It

[1] Jāmī, *op. cit.*, p. 37.
[2] al-Sulamī, *op. cit.*, fol. 7*a*.
[3] *Ibid.*, fol. 8*b*.
[4] Abū Ṭālib, *op. cit.*, i. 225.
[5] al-Sulamī, *op. cit.*, fol. 8*a*.
[6] Abū Ṭālib, *op. cit.*, i. 225.
[7] al-Sulamī, *op. cit.*, fol. 8*a*. *Cf.* Heb. iv. 12.

is to love what God loves, and to hate what He hates, and to do nought but good deeds, and to cast out everything which distracts you from God, and not to shrink from His rebuke, for His rebuke is mingled with sympathy towards the believers, and with harshness towards the infidels, and it is to follow the Prophet in matters of faith." So it comes about that when the Ṣūfī speaks, his speech concerns what is true, and when he is silent, his actions speak for him, for he shows that he has cut off all (creaturely) attachments—*i.e.*, his sincerity appears in both his speech and his conduct.[1] Yet Dhū al-Nūn, stern ascetic though he was, realised that the love of God, however all-absorbing, must not exclude love for man, for love to mankind is the foundation of righteousness, and he who loves his fellow-men is holding fast to the chief corner-stone of sincerity. At the same time, like all the mystics, he is an advocate of solitude for the one who seeks to know the inner mysteries of fellowship with God. He says on this subject, "I have seen nothing more conducive to righteousness than solitude, for he who is alone sees nought but God, and if he sees nought but God, nothing moves him but the Will of God." Again he says, "Fellowship with God comes from purity of heart towards Him, and being alone with God is the cutting off of everything else but God."[2]

Dhū al-Nūn's teaching on the Way to be followed and the end to which it leads the faithful traveller therein is summed up in an account he gives of the true servants of God. "There are servants of God who have planted the trees of (their) sins before their eyes, and have watered them with the tears of contrition, so that they have brought forth the fruits of repentance and sorrow. These are they who have become distraught without madness, and foolish without weakness, for they indeed are the eloquent in speech, the orators, those wise in the knowledge of God and of His prophet. For they have drunk of the cup of purity and acquired patience through their long affliction. Then were their hearts filled with longing for the Kingdom of Heaven, and in their meditations they have thought upon its mansions hidden by the veils of the Divine Majesty, and they

[1] al-Sulamī, *op. cit.*, fol. 6*b*. [2] *Ibid.*, *op. cit.*, fol. 7*a*.

sought shelter under the porticoes of repentance, and they studied the record of their sins, and their souls were filled with grief, until they attained to the highest degree of asceticism by means of chastity. Thus have they sweetened the bitterness of the renunciation of this world, and softened the roughness of their couch, to such an extent that they even conquered the desire for salvation and the Way which leads to peace.

"Their spirits have wandered through the highest heavens, in order that at last they may pause in the Gardens of the Blessed, and plunge into the river of life. They have sealed up the channels of affliction and have crossed the bridges of desire; they have halted at the point where earthly knowledge passes away and have drunk from the river of true wisdom, and they have embarked upon the vessel of the Divine Bounty, and have set sail with the wind of salvation upon the sea of peace, until at last they have reached the gardens of repose, and the abode of Glory and Grace."[1]

[1] *Recueil*, p. 17.

CHAPTER IX

THE MYSTICAL DOCTRINES OF EARLY ṢŪFISM

WHILE the earliest Ṣūfīs, for the most part, were content with the practice of asceticism and a doctrine of quietism, a tendency towards a definitely mystical doctrine soon became apparent in the teaching of the chief Ṣūfīs. As in most systems of Mysticism, this tendency showed itself in the development of philosophic conceptions concerning the nature of the Godhead, the relation of the human soul to God, the possibility of an ascent from the human to the Divine and the means whereby it could be achieved, and finally the characteristics of that Unitive state when it had been attained.

In their conception of the nature of the Godhead, the earliest Ṣūfī mystics, as might be expected, adhere closely to the language of the Qur'ān and to the orthodox belief. God is Self-Existent from eternity, Infinite, having no relation to space or time, in His Essence and in His attributes unchangeable. He is Living, All-Wise, Forgiving, Merciful, Willing, All-powerful, Hearing and Seeing all things, Speaking, Abiding. He is Omniscient; nothing that can be known is outside of His knowledge, for it pierces through to that which is hidden and comprehends that which is made manifest. All that exists is dependent on His will; what He wills, that He does, and what He wills is that which He has known aforetime, and no creature has any knowledge of His hidden mysteries. His decrees are absolute, and it is for His servants to submit themselves thereto in complete resignation to His Will. He alone has the power of predestination, both of good and evil, and He is the only One Who is worthy to inspire either hope or fear. To Him judgment belongs and His judgment is all-Wise.[1] He is the Creator of mankind, and the universe was brought into existence out of non-existence by His act. "All that we behold and perceive

[1] al-Hujwīrī, *op. cit.*, pp. 13, 358, 16.

by our senses bears irrefutable witness to the existence of God and His power and His knowledge and the rest of His attributes, whether these things be manifested or hidden, the stone and the clod, the plants and the trees and living creatures, the heaven and the earth and the stars, the dry land and the ocean, fire and air and substance and accident, and indeed we ourselves witness to Him, but, just as the bat, through the weakness of its sight, cannot bear the full light of the sun in the daytime, but can see only when the light is veiled by the darkness, so the human mind is too weak to behold the glory of God in its fullness."[1]

To Him belong Beauty, Majesty and Perfection, and it is sometimes by one and sometimes by another that His adoring worshippers come to know Him and to love Him. "For he whose evidence in gnosis is the Beauty of God longs continually for the vision of Him, and he whose evidence is the Majesty of God is always abhorring his own attributes, and his heart is filled with awe. Now longing is the result of love and the abhorring of human attributes likewise, since the unveiling of human attributes is of the essence of love. Now faith and gnosis are love, and the sign of love is obedience."[2] God, to the Ṣūfī, is not only the Supreme Beauty, but He is also Light. Abū Ṭālib gives us a prayer (which he states was taught by Gabriel to the Prophet, but which is much more probably of Ṣūfī origin), in which the Deity is addressed in these terms: "O Light of the heavens and the earth, O Beauty of the heavens and the earth, O Thou Who hast laid the foundations of the heavens and the earth, and Who art their Creator, Thou Lord of Majesty and Glory, Thou Who dost bring succour to those who cry unto Thee, Thou Goal of the desire of those who seek, Thou Consolation of those who grieve, Thou Who dost give rest to the afflicted, and dost answer the cry of those who call upon Thee."[3] This idea of God as the Supreme Beauty and as Light can, of, course, be traced back to Hellenism. "For man strives to know the dignity of the intellect and its light and its splendour, and to know the value of that thing which is above the intellect, that is,

[1] al-Ghazālī, *Iḥyā*, iv. 275. [2] al-Hujwīrī, p. 370.
[3] *Qūt al-Qulūb*, i. 8.

the Light of lights and the Supreme Beauty and consummate Splendour."[1]

From the conception of God as the Only Agent and Sole Cause of all existence, the Ṣūfīs passed to the idea of God as the only real existence, the Sole Reality; they maintained that to conceive of any other real existence beside Him would be polytheism, and that this conception of Him was involved in the confession of His Unity. He was not only One, Unique and peerless, but the One and All, and All in All. So the Unity of God became Universal Unity, and His universal manifestation Universal Existence. An early Ṣūfī teacher, Sahl Tustarī, says, "His Unicity, in its origin, meant that He was, and there was nothing else, and He dwelt in solitude, apart. He knew and He wished and He ordained and predestined and directed. Actions are attributed to His servants, but the beginning is from Him and the end rests with Him. All things exist in the knowledge of God and by His decree."[2] Such a doctrine of God as the Only and Ultimate Reality inevitably led to the pantheism which is so characteristic of the later Ṣūfīs. al-Hujwīrī tells us that God can be known only by God, and all that is not God by the Light of God, and in a fine passage he describes the universe as being in truth full of the Presence of God, Who is hidden from mortal eyes because of their imperfection. "Know," he says, "that I have found this universe to be the shrine of the Divine mysteries: to created things has God entrusted Himself, and within that which exists has He hid Himself. Substances and accidents, elements, bodies, forces and properties, are all the veils of these Mysteries. In the doctrine of the Unity (of God) the existence of all these would be polytheism, but God Most High has ordained that this universe, by its own being, should be veiled from His Unity. Therefore the spirits of men are absorbed in their own phenomenal existence, so that their minds fail to perceive the Divine mysteries and their spirits but dimly apprehend the wonderful nearness of God. Man is engrossed with himself and heedless of aught else, and so he fails to recognise the Unity behind all things and is blind to the Beauty of Oneness, and will not taste the joy offered to him

[1] *Uthūlūjīya Ariṣṭāṭālīs*, p. 44.

[2] *Recueil*, p. 41.

by the One, and is turned aside by the vanities of this world from the Vision of the Truth and allows the animal soul to predominate, though it is the most potent of all the veils between man and God."[1]

With regard to the Ṣūfī conception of the relation of the soul to God, we have to note that the Ṣūfīs made a distinction between the lower animal soul, the carnal self (*nafs*), the seat of all evil, and the higher, the spirit (*rūḥ*), the source of good. The higher was distinguished by intelligence, and the lower by passion, and here we find a strong resemblance to the Platonic conception of the two steeds of Reason and Passion, pulling the soul in opposite directions. The higher soul, the Ṣūfīs believed, had existed before the creation of the body to which it was assigned; it consisted of heart (*qalb* or *dil*), of spirit (*rūḥ* or *jān*), and of conscience (*sirr*), which was the inmost part, that which later mystics called the " ground " or " spark " of the soul. Of this latter all-Sarrāj says that it is that part in which the evil suggestions of the self are not felt, it is the secret shrine of God Himself, wherein He knows man and man can know Him.[2]

Of the pre-existence of the higher soul the Ṣūfī 'Amr b. 'Uthmān al-Makkī (*ob.* A.D. 909) wrote: " God created the hearts seven thousand years before the bodies and kept them in the station of proximity to Himself, and He created the spirits seven thousand years before the hearts and kept them in the garden of intimate fellowship with Himself, and the consciences, the innermost part, He created seven thousand years before the spirits and kept them in the degree of union (*waṣl*). Then He imprisoned the conscience in the spirit, and the spirit in the heart, and the heart in the body. Then He tested them . . . and sent Prophets . . . and each began to seek its own station. The body occupied itself with prayer, the heart was joined with love, the spirit arrived at proximity, and the inmost part found rest in union with Him."[3]

The Ṣūfīs therefore held that the soul, previous to its existence in a body in this world, had dwelt in the presence of God, and had been one with Him. The saying that " He who knows himself best knows his Lord best " points to

[1] *Op. cit.*, p. 9. [2] *Kitāb al-Luma'*, p. 231.
[3] al-Hujwīrī, *op. cit.*, pp. 399, 400.

the belief in a " Divine spark " within the soul of man, and we have already seen that orthodox Islām regarded man as made in the image and likeness of God.[1] al-Ghazālī writes that the heart was created pure in its origin, but that purity has become defiled by foul deeds, and that fair countenance disfigured by the darkness of sin.[2] The cause of impurity and defilement is the downward drag of the lower soul, with its propensity to what is evil and creaturely. Abū Ṭālib says, " The carnal self is by nature prone to action (*i.e.*, taking its own evil way), and it has been commanded to be still (that is, to be acquiescent in the will of God), so He afflicts it in order that it may feel the need of its Lord and be cleansed from its own tendencies and desires."[3] The believer's spirit, that is, the higher soul, calls him to Paradise, of which it is a type in this world, while his lower soul calls him to Hell, of which it, too, is a type in this world. The lower soul must therefore be mastered by the higher, for this latter is the shrine of the Divine mysteries.[4] The soul of man, then, is akin to the Divine, and therefore the mystic can set about that transformative process which shall purge away the dross and leave only what is pure and godlike. " Purity of heart," says Abū Ṭālib, " exalts (the mystic) stage by stage in contemplation of the Essence, until there is no remembrance within the soul save that of God."[5]

This process of purification, and elimination of evil from the soul, is what the Ṣūfīs called the Way, the ascent which led at last to the reunion of the soul with God. There are three stages of the Way, according to al-Hujwīrī. The first is that of the " stations " (*maqāmāt*), which indicate the degree of progress attained by the seeker in the Path of God ; the obligations of each station must be fulfilled and the virtues pertaining to it acquired, before he passes on to the next. The last of the stations of this stage are Satisfaction and Love. This stage means earnest striving and effort on the part of the traveller, though at the same time he cannot hope to make progress without the help and guidance of God. It represents the Purgative Life in which the mystic

[1] See above, p. 144.
[2] *Iḥyā*, iv. 11.
[3] *Qūt al-Qulūb*, i. 84.
[4] al-Hujwīrī, *op. cit.*, p. 250.
[5] *Qūt al-Qulūb*, i. 80.

becomes stripped of self, and acquires those qualities which enable him to persevere to the end of the Quest. As we have seen in the last chapter, it was with this first stage of the Path that the early ascetic Ṣūfīs concerned themselves. The second stage may follow the first, or it may be experienced at the same time, since it is different in kind. This is the stage of " states " (*aḥwāl*) which are the mystic states of ecstasy bestowed upon the seeker's soul, as signs of favour and grace to encourage him on his path. They are the gift of God alone, and in no way depend upon the mystic's own striving. This stage corresponds to the Illuminative Life. The third and last stage is that of " achievement " (*tamkīn*), and this is the end of the Path, the goal of the Quest, the attainment of the Unitive Life. The mystic now dwells in the abode of perfection and has found rest within the very shrine of Deity. Now has the lover of God become like the sun shining in a cloudless sky, for he is dead unto his own attributes and abiding in those of his Beloved. In the light of Love and Union he sees the glory of God and while still in this world penetrates into the mysteries of the world to come.[1]

It is Love, then, an all-absorbing love for God, which leads the mystic onward and upward, and finally leads to union with the Divine. " It is impossible for the servant, when he sees the grace of God, not to love Him, and when he has loved, he will feel fellowship (*uns*), because awe of the beloved is estrangement and fellowship is oneness."[2] Some of the finest and most beautiful of the mystical teaching which has come down to us from the Ṣūfīs is devoted to this theme of Love. " Among the signs of Love," says Abū Ṭālib, " is the desire to meet with the Beloved face to face, to see Him unveiled within the abode of Peace and the place of proximity ; that desire means a longing for death, which is the key to meeting, and the door of entry to manifestation."[3] Asma al-Ramliyya, a woman zealous in devotion,

[1] *Op. cit.*, pp. 484 *ff.*, pp. 37, 38. [2] *Ibid.*, p. 490.

[3] *Qūt al-Qulūb*, ii. 51. So also Isaac of Nineveh writes : " Love annihilates fear (of death). It not only fears not, but it even longs after, departure. Love is the dissolver of temporary life. He that has reached the love of God does not desire to stay here any more " (*Mystical Treatises*, p. 288).

relates that she had asked a fellow-Ṣūfī, Bayḍa bint al-Mufaḍḍal, what was the sign by which the lover of God could be known, and Bayḍa replied, " O my sister, the lover of the Lord conceals himself, but though he strives to hide himself, he is not hidden." Asma said, " Describe him to me in his character, his food and drink, his sleep and waking hours, and his actions." She replied, " Truly you have asked much of me, but I will describe him as far as I can. If you have seen a lover of God, you have seen a very wonderful thing, of one in grief, not settling in the earth, but like a wild bird, whose delight in solitude has kept him from rest, while he yearns in remembrance of the Beloved, and his food is love in hunger, and his drink is love in thirst, and his sleep is the thought of union, and his waking hours mean no neglect. There is no tranquillity for him, and he finds no solace in patience. . . . The passage of time does not change him, nor does he grow weary of the length of his service to God, as (other) servants grow weary, until at last, through love and long service, he attains to the degree of all-absorbing love (*shawq*), then his tranquillity returns, and his fire dies down, and its sparks are quenched, and his grief decreases, and he becomes one with the Object of his longing."[1]

We read how one of these lovers of God was asked, " Whence have you come ?" He said, " From the Beloved." They asked, " Where are you going ?" and he answered, " Near to the Beloved." They said, " And what do you desire ?" He replied, " To meet with the Beloved." He was asked, " What is your food ?" and he said, " The remembrance of the Beloved." They said, " What is your drink ?" He replied, " Longing for the Beloved." They asked him, "Wherewith are you clothed ?" He said, " With the veil of the Beloved." They said, " Wherefore is your countenance pale ?" and he replied, " Because of separation from the Beloved." Impatiently they asked him, " How long will you say 'the Beloved, the Beloved'?" and he answered them, " Until I see the Face of the Beloved."[2] The only love which is

[1] " Ḥilyat al-Awliyā," fol. 212*a*.

[2] M. b. Ḥ. Imād al-Dīn, *Ḥayāt al-Qulūb* (margin) *Qūt al-Qulūb*, ii. 176. *Cf.* Raymond Lull, " Where art thou, O lover ? Whither goest thou ? Whence camest thou ? And where hast thou thy treasure ?"

worthy of God is "pure love," which is free from any interested motive, and depends on nothing in the way of reward or object. The love of the sincere and the gnostics, says al-Sarrāj, arises from their vision, and their knowledge of the eternal and causeless Love of God, and therefore they love Him without a cause.[1] al-Ghazālī distinguishes between three kinds of love : the first is self-love, pure and simple, which leads a man to self-preservation and to give only that he may receive. The second is love of others because of the benefits they bestow, as the doctor is loved because he brings the gift of healing, and the teacher because he has the power to bestow knowledge, and this kind, as al-Ghazālī notes, also comes back to self-love. But the third kind of love is love of a thing for its own sake, not for any benefit received from it apart from itself, for the thing itself is the essence of its enjoyment, it is its own reward, and this alone is true and perfect love which can be relied upon to last. Such is the love of Beauty and all fair things, for all Beauty is loved by him who has eyes to perceive Beauty, and that belongs to the essence of Beauty, for the perception of Beauty contains the essence of delight, and the delight is loved for its own sake, not for anything apart from it. It is an error to suppose that the love of beautiful forms cannot be conceived except for the sake of fulfilling the sensual desires, for the satisfaction of such desires is a different type of delight. Beautiful forms are loved for their own sakes, and the very perception of Beauty is itself delightful, and it cannot be denied that it should be loved for its own sake. So also green things and running water are loved, not for the sake of drinking the water and eating the green things, or for anything obtained from them, except simply the sight of them. So it is with the stars of heaven, and the flowers and the birds with their fair colours and beautiful forms and perfectly proportioned shapes ; the sight of them without any desire for them causes keen delight and all pleasure is loved. "None can deny," al-Ghazālī concludes, "that

"I am in my Beloved ; I go to my Beloved ; I come from my Beloved ; and in my remembrance, honour, service, love, and understanding of Him is my treasure" (*The Tree of Love*, pp. 103, 104).

[1] *Kitāb al-Luma'*, p. 59.

where Beauty exists, it is natural to love it, and if it is certain that God is beautiful, there can be no doubt that He will be loved by the one to whom His Beauty and His Majesty are revealed. The greater the beauty, the greater the love, and since complete and perfect Beauty is found only in God, He alone can be worthy of true love." Such love will become a passion for God, by cutting off all dependence on this world and excluding from the heart love for any save God.[1]

Such is the love which the true Ṣūfī gives to his Beloved, of which Yaḥyā b. Mu'ādh al-Rāzī said: " True love does not decrease because of injury suffered, nor increase because of benefits and favours received, for these are motives for love, and motives in the existence of the thing itself are of no account. The lover takes pleasure in affliction which comes from the Beloved, and benefit and injury, to the true lover, are all one, since Love remains."[2] The lover has no will of his own, that he should desire anything, whether good or ill, for he who loves God, desires only what He desires, and he whom God loves, desires naught but God Himself.[3] Those who need neither gifts nor happiness, nor trials, but are satisfied with being chosen by the Beloved, who look from the gift to the Giver, are His lovers, " whose existence is an illusion in satisfaction as in affliction, for their hearts dwell only in His Presence and their secret abode is to be found only in the garden of intimate fellowship with Him . . . their hearts have escaped from created things and from the fetters of 'stages' and 'stations.' Their soul has passed from all that has been brought into existence, and has attached itself to God."[4] Pure love, then, has no place for personal volition: the Ṣūfī al-Shiblī (*ob.* A.D. 945) said: " Love is a fire in the heart, consuming all

[1] Iḥyā, iv. 255-258, 271. This finds a singular confirmation in a modern philosophic writer, Leibnitz, who says: " Since true Pure Love consists in a state of soul which makes one find pleasure in the perfections and the felicity of the object loved, this love cannot but give us the greatest pleasure of which we are capable, when God is the Object of it. And, though this love be disinterested, it constitutes, even by itself, our greatest good and deepest interest" (Leibnitz [Ed. Gebhardt], vi. 605, 606).

[2] al-Hujwīrī, *op. cit.*, p. 404.

[3] *Ibid.*, p. 198.

[4] *Ibid.*, p. 221.

save the Will of the Beloved,"[1] and Jāmī, writing much later, but dealing with the earliest Ṣūfīs, says, "The Ṣūfī has no individual will; his will is obliterated in the Will of God, nay, indeed, his will is the very Will of God."[2] So he who desires to know anything or to speak of any save God, is not single-minded in his love, for the true lover does not desire to think of his service, but only of Him Whom he serves.[3] "True Love," said Abū 'Abdallah al-Qurashī (*ob.* A.D. 941), "means to give all that thou hast to Him Whom thou lovest, so that nothing remains to thee of thine own."[4] And this meant not only the sacrifice of personal possessions, which might be a cause of separation between the lover and his Beloved, and the giving up of the personal will, but a complete self-surrender. Only the lover who is emptied of self can hope to be the dwelling-place of the Divine.[5] "Since the Beloved is subsistent, the lover must be annihilated, for the jealousy of the Beloved requires that the subsistence of the lover be negated, so that His own dominion be made absolute. The annihilation of the lover's attributes can only be accomplished by the establishment of the Essence of the Beloved, and the lover cannot remain in his own attributes, for in that case he would have no need of the Beauty of the Beloved, but since he knows that he lives by the Beauty of the Beloved, he seeks of necessity to negate his own attributes, since by retaining them he is veiled from the Beloved.

[1] al-Qushayrī, *op. cit.*, p. 189.

[2] *Nafaḥāt al-Uns*, p. 11.

[3] Abū Nu'aym, *op. cit.*, fol. 214*b*.

[4] al-Qushayrī, *op. cit.*, p. 189.

[5] *Cf.* the English mystic poet, T. E. Brown:

"If thou couldst empty all thyself of Self,
Like to a shell dishabited,
Then might He find thee on the ocean shelf
And say: 'This is not dead,'
And fill thee with Himself instead.

"But thou art all replete with very thou
And hast such shrewd activity,
That when He comes He says: 'This is enow
Unto itself—'twere better let it be,
It is so small and full, there is no room for Me.'"

So out of love to his Friend, he becomes an enemy to himself."[1]

Love, then, to such lovers, becomes as the wine of life, a draught which never fails and never satisfies, and yet leads to the highest bliss. "I have drunk of Love, cup upon cup, and the draught was not exhausted, nor was I satisfied," says one Ṣūfī.[2] It is related that Yaḥyā b. Mu'ādh wrote to Abū Yazīd Bisṭāmī, "What would you say of one who, from one drop of the ocean of Love, becomes intoxicated?" and Bāyazīd wrote in reply: "What would you say of one who, if all the oceans in the world were composed of the wine of Love, would drink them all, and yet cry aloud because of his consuming thirst?"[3] So also al-Shiblī said: "Verily love to the All-Merciful has intoxicated me; hast thou seen any lover who was not drunken with Love?"[4] and al-Qushayrī writes with reference to this effect of Love, "Intoxication is disappearance in a mighty ecstasy. The beginning of it is tasting, then drinking, then satisfaction of thirst."[5]

Such love, which has become an all-consuming passion, leads to the mystic ecstasy, which is like a flame rising up in the heart. "Love," said one of the Ṣūfīs, "is of two natures, the love which is tranquil—and this is found among both the elect and the crowd—and the love which is rapture, which is found only among the elect, and that is by the direct road (*i.e.*, that which leads straight to God); therein is found no vision of the self or the creaturely, nor any vision of motives or states, but the lover is absorbed in the Vision of God and what is from Him." Of such a nature is the love which makes the lover blind and deaf, so that he is blind to all save the Beloved, nor does he hear the claims of any save Him.[6]

[1] al-Hujwīrī, *op. cit.*, p. 402.
[2] al-Qushayrī, *op. cit.*, p. 51.
[3] al-Hujwīrī, *op. cit.*, p. 233.
[4] Iḥyā, iv. 300. *Cf.* the Christian Evagrius: "If anyone is accomplished in the love of God, he is a drunken man. He is constantly captivated by the love of his Lord, so that he does not see this world, but his thoughts abide continually in heaven."
[5] *Op. cit.*, p. 50.
[6] Kalābādhī, "Kitāb al-Ta'arruf," fol. 30*b*.

By Pure Love, then, the mystic is guided from one station to another until he comes to the end of the first stage of the Way, when the mirror of the soul has become as pure from self as flame from smoke, and is fitted to reflect the Light of God, by which it is illuminated in the second stage, that of ecstasy; and now the mystic enters upon that third stage, of attainment, which is indeed the end of his journey. There he receives that mystic knowledge of the Divine, the gnosis (*ma'rifa*), which will enable him to see God face to face, and in seeing Him, to become one with Him. Love it is which leads to gnosis, and is bound up with it, for none loves God worthily, who does not know Him, and whoso knows Him loves Him.[1] This gnosis is an utterly different thing from the earthly knowledge (*'ilm*), which can be acquired by human effort, and from human teachers. "All that the eyes behold," says Dhū al-Nūn, "belongs to earthly knowledge, but that which the heart learns, belongs to certainty (the true knowledge)," and another of the Ṣūfīs said of it, "Ecstasy (which belongs to an earlier stage of the Way) is but transient, while gnosis does not pass away."[2] al-Nūrī was asked by what means he had come to know God, and he said: "By means of God. The intellect (*'aql*) is weak, it has no power except over what is as weak as itself. When God created the intellect, He said to it, 'Whom am I?' and it remained silent. Then He shed upon it the light of the Unity, and it said: 'Thou art God,' and it is not possible for the intellect to know God except by means of God." Gnosis, then, in its origin, is the gift of God, and a Ṣūfī writer draws a clear distinction between it

[1] al-Sarrāj, *Kitab al-Luma'*, p. 36. Evagrius Ponticus had already connected love and knowledge, "For the end of love is the knowledge of God."

[2] Kalābādhī, *op. cit.*, fols. 28*a*, 31*b*. So Isaac of Nineveh had said, "When knowledge elevates itself above earthly things . . . and begins to try its impulses in things hidden from eyesight . . . and stretches itself upwards . . . then faith swallows knowledge, gives a new birth to it, wholly spiritual. . . . Then it is able to direct its flight towards non-bodily places and to examine spiritual mysteries which are attained by the simple and the subtle intellect. Then the inner senses awake to spiritual service, as the order of things which will be in the state of immortality and incorruptibility" (*Mystical Treatises*, p. 250).

and faith. Gnosis is fire and faith light, gnosis is ecstasy and faith a giving; the difference between the believer and the gnostic is that the believer sees by the light of God, and the gnostic sees by means of God Himself; the heart of the believer finds rest in worship, but the gnostic finds rest only in God.[1] Again we are told that God makes His servant to know Him through Himself, by a knowledge unrelated to any faculty, in which the existence of man is seen to be transient, so that egoism in concern for this existence to the gnostic is treachery, therefore his remembrance of God is without forgetfulness, and his service without shortcoming, for his gnosis is a state of inspiration by God, not a matter of mere words. So, when the unveiling of the Divine glory is vouchsafed to anyone, "his existence becomes a burden to him, and all his attributes a source of reproach; he who belongs to God and to whom God belongs, has no concern with anything else. The real meaning of gnosis is to know that the Kingdom is God's. When anyone knows that all power is in the hand of God, what further concern has he with the creatures, that he should be veiled from God by himself or by them? All veils come from ignorance; when ignorance has passed away, the veils vanish and this life, by means of gnosis, becomes one with the life to come."[2] Gnosis, then, is the life of the heart in God, and the turning away of the eye of the soul from all save God. "The purpose of the gnostics," says al-Ghazālī, "is only to attain to this knowledge and possess it, for it is a consolation unknown to the souls from which it is hidden, and when it is attained, it destroys all anxieties and sensual desires and the heart becomes filled with its grace. Even if the gnostic were cast into the fire, he would not feel it, because of his absorption, and if the favours of Paradise were spread out before him, he would not turn towards them, because of the perfection of the grace that is in him and his perfect attainment, which is above all else that can be attained."[3]

This gnosis is constantly identified, by the Ṣūfīs, with light, a light which shines upon the soul and enlightens it,

[1] al-Sarrāj, *Kitab al-Luma'*, pp. 40, 41.

[2] Hujwīrī, *op. cit.*, pp. 347, 351.

[3] Iḥyā, iv. 267.

and which comes from the Light of lights, and as it is one in nature with that inaccessible, essential Light, so it shall be commingled with it once again, and the two become one, as the spark returns to the flame and is absorbed in it once more. "Verily knowledge is a light which God casts into the heart," says Abū Ṭālib, and again, "The servant does not attain to contemplation of the doctrine of the Unity, except by means of gnosis, and gnosis is the light of certainty."[1] It is the light which sheds its rays from the Face of the Essence, and the same writer gives a Ṣūfī prayer which runs, "O God, give me light in my heart and light in my tomb, and light in my hearing and light in my sight and light in my feeling and light in all my body, and light before me and light behind me and light on my right hand and light on my left, and light above me and light beneath me. O Lord, increase light within me, and give me light and illuminate me. These are the lights which the prophet asked for, verily to possess such light means to be contemplated eternally by the Light of light."[2] This gnosis is the knowledge which comes, therefore, not by hearing, but by seeing, concerning which al-Ghazali says: "Take what you see, and leave that which you only hear; when the sun rises, you have no need of Saturn,"[3] and Abū Ṭālib writes in the same strain that true gnosis lies in contemplation and it is the eye of certainty itself.

Gnosis, then, means the Vision, for when the eye of the soul is stripped of all the veils which hindered it from seeing God, then it beholds the reality of the Divine attributes by its own inner light, which goes far beyond the light which is given to perfect faith, for gnosis, as we have seen, belongs to a sphere quite other than that of faith.[4] So also Isaac of Nineveh had said: "You see God as soon as you know Him." The Prophet himself had said; "Worship God as if you saw Him," and on this saying the Ṣūfīs based their doctrine of Contemplation and the Vision of God face to face, even in this life, for those who had attained to gnosis. He who is most sincere in self-discipline, we are told, is most assured in contemplation, for there is a close relation

[1] *Qūt al-Qulūb*, i. 133, 119 (*cf. Ūthūlūjiya Arisṭāṭālīs*, p. 3).
[2] *Ibid.*, i. 6. [3] *Iḥyā*, i., 22. [4] *Qūt al-Qulūb*, i. 135, 151.

between outer mortification and inner contemplation, but when self-will is annihilated in this world, contemplation is attained, and when contemplation is assured, there is no difference between this world and the next. Muḥammad b. al-Faḍl said, on this subject of contemplation, " I wonder at those who seek the House of God (the *Ka'ba*) in this world; why do they not seek to contemplate Him in their hearts? For sometimes they find the House, and sometimes they fail to find it, and contemplation they might always find. If it is incumbent on them to visit a stone, where they may behold Him, once a year, surely there is a greater obligation to visit the heart, where He may be contemplated hundreds of times each day. For the true sanctuary is the place where contemplation is; and only that one to whom the whole world is the trysting-place where he draws near to God and a place of retreat where he finds fellowship with Him, knows what it is to be the friend of God. When the veil has been removed, the whole world is his sanctuary, but while he is still veiled, the world will remain dark to him, for the darkest of things is the dwelling-place of the Beloved, without the Beloved." There are two kinds of contemplation, one which arises from perfect certainty, and the other which arises from rapturous love, for when the lover arrives at the abode of Love, his whole being becomes absorbed in the idea of the Beloved and he sees naught else.[1] So Abū Sa'īd al-Kharrāz says: " From one who contemplates God in his heart is hidden all else, and all things are reduced to naught, and he passes away in the Presence of God's Majesty and there remains naught in his heart save God alone."[2]

Of the effect of such contemplation, we read that, " When God manifests Himself to the heart of His servant by displaying His Majesty he is filled with awe (*hayba*), and when He manifests Himself to the heart of His servant by displaying His Beauty, he feels the intimacy of fellowship (*uns*). Those who feel awe because of His Majesty are troubled, but those who feel fellowship because of His Beauty are full of joy. There is a difference between the heart which from the sight of His Majesty is consumed in the fire of love, and

[1] al-Hujwīrī, *op. cit.*, pp. 423 *ff.*
[2] al-Sarrāj, *Kitāb al-Luma'*, p. 68.

that heart which from the sight of His Beauty is illumined by the light of contemplation. The power of awe is brought to bear on the carnal soul and its desires, and causes what belongs to human nature to perish, and the power of fellowship is brought to bear on the inmost heart and gives rise to gnosis there. Therefore God, by the revelation of His Majesty, causes the carnal souls of His lovers to pass away, and by the revelation of His Beauty gives immortality to their hearts."[1]

al-Ghazālī writes of the stages of the mystic experience which leads, through contemplation, to the unveiling of the Blessed Vision. The inclination of the Ṣūfīs, he says, is towards the knowledge which is the result of inspiration not study, therefore they are not eager to study human knowledge, nor to assimilate what authors have written, but they say that the Way is the choice of contemplation, and the annihilation of blameworthy qualities and the cutting off of all ties, and concerning oneself completely with God, and when anyone attains to that, it is as if God Himself had taken possession of His servant's heart, and was responsible for illuminating him with the light of gnosis. And when God controls the affairs of the heart, mercy is bestowed upon it, and light shines within it, and the breast is enlarged, and the secret of the invisible world is revealed to that one, and the veil of heedlessness, by God's mercy, is taken away from before the heart, and the inner meaning of the Divine Truth is made perfect therein. The servant is able only to be prepared for the Divine penetration, and his concern is with the sincere will and the ardent desire, and the watching in continuous expectation for what God of His grace shall reveal to him, for to the prophets and saints is the mystery revealed, and upon their hearts the light is shed, not by learning and study and the reading of books, but by asceticism in this world, and escape from its claims, and freedom of the heart from all preoccupations, and by concerning oneself wholly with God, and when anyone belongs to God, God belongs to him. The Ṣūfīs assert that the beginning of the Way consists in cutting off all ties, so that the heart will reach the stage in which the existence or non-existence of

[1] al-Hujwīrī, *op. cit.*, pp. 490, 492.

everything will be all one. Then the mystic will go into retreat alone, and there with a heart at leisure will strive to occupy his mind with nothing but God. It is not for him to choose to attract the mercy of God, but in what he does he exposes himself to the breath of the Divine grace, and there remains only the expectation of what God will reveal of His grace. Then if the mystic is free from all distractions, the Light of God will shine upon his heart, and it will be at the first like a blinding flash of lightning. Its sojourn is but brief, but it will return, for it is the prelude of a constant communion with God.[1] al-Shiblī also, with the mystic experience in his mind, had defined Ṣūfīsm as "a burning flash of lightning,"[2] and al-Qushayrī says, "It begins with flashes of light, then rays of light, then the light shining forth in its full splendour; for the flashes are like lightning which appears only to vanish again, and the rays appear from the flashes and do not cease so speedily, but the light in its full splendour remains for a longer time, and is greater in its power and more enduring in its stay."[3] So it is with the Divine Vision.

This is the moment when God reveals Himself (*mukāshifa*), when the veil is taken away and the Divine Glory is manifested in all its splendour to the mystic, so clearly that he has no doubt of it. But the unveiling of that Divine Glory is among the "unspeakable things" which it is not permitted to describe, nor in truth is it describable. It is an experience not to be shared with any to whom God has not unveiled Himself, and were any to seek to share it with others, the world itself would dissolve into ruins, so observes al-Ghazālī. To that one to whom the Vision is revealed, the delight arising from the Beauty of the Lord means joy unspeakable. "How can he who understands only the love of sensible things, believe in the joy of looking upon the Face of God Most High? For such a one there is no Vision—and what meaning is there for him in the promise of God Most High to His worshippers and in His

[1] *Iḥyā*, iii. 16, 17.

[2] Pascal, to whom the overwhelming consciousness of God came in the flash of a single moment, described it by the one word "Fire."

[3] *Risāla*, p. 53.

statement that He gives the greatest of all graces? But he who knows God, knows that all joys (save only those of sensual desire) are included in this joy."[1]

In the moment of beholding that Vision of the Beauty Supreme, the soul passes away from itself, from all sense-impressions and from knowledge of all creaturely states. This is the annihilation of the personal self (*fanā'*), and though the self may seem to be there, it is in truth dead to all save God Himself.[2] It was of this that al-Junayd said, "God gives to the adept the sharp desire to behold His essence, then knowledge becomes vision, and vision revelation, and revelation contemplation, and contemplation existence (with and in God). Words are hushed to silence, life becomes death, explanations come to an end, signs are effaced, disputes are cleared up. Mortality (*fanā'*) is ended and immortality (*baqā'*) is made perfect. Weariness and care cease, the elements perish, and there remains what will not cease, as time that is timeless ceases not."[3]

Ya'qūb al-Nahrajūrī, the Ṣūfī, asked about the true meaning of *fanā'* and *baqā'*, said: "True *fanā'* is the vision of the relation of the worshipper to God Most Glorious, and true *baqā'* is the vision of the relation of God to all worship."[4] So also another Ṣūfī wrote, "The end of the worship of God is that he who worships should pass away in worship from worship, and be absorbed in Him Whom he worships, not to return again to the station of worship, and this is the state in which perishability perishes, *fanā al-fanā*."[5] In dying to itself, the soul has become alive in God, with Whom it is now united in a deathless union. "The meaning of union (*ittiṣāl*) is that the heart should be separated from all save God and should glorify none save Him and hearken to none save Him. It means the heart's attainment to the state in

[1] *Iḥyā*, iv. 267.

[2] Qushayrī, *op. cit.*, p. 49. *Cf.* also Kalābādhī, *op. cit.*, fol. 31*b*. So the Christian mystic St. John of the Cross wrote some five centuries later: "The soul knows well that in the instant of that Vision it will be itself absorbed and transformed into that Beauty, and be made beautiful like it."

[3] al-Munawwar, *Asrār al-Tawḥīd*, p. 378.

[4] al-Sarrāj, *Kitāb al-Luma'*, p. 213.

[5] Jāmī, *Nafaḥāt al-Uns*, p. 161.

which it is occupied by the glory of the One to the exclusion of all else."[1]

This is the end of the Path, when the mystic is rapt up into union with the Divine and the soul becomes one with God—not by annihilation, for it subsists in Him, as the drop subsists when it is merged in the ocean, and the spark when it returns to the flame, no longer as a separate entity, but by absorption and transmutation, for the part has returned to become one with the Whole. Those who have trodden the mystic Way, we read, are agreed that when a man has passed through the "stations" and the "states," and is no more subject to change or decay, and has acquired all virtuous qualities, he is no longer endowed with qualities. His presence with God is continuous, and when he has reached this stage he has passed away from this world and the next, and in the disappearance of his humanity he has become Divine (*rabbānī*). Gold and clay are all one to him, and the commands which others find most difficult to observe become easy to him. He is submerged in the sea of the Unity, lost to feeling and action, absorbed only in the Divine Reality. God has fulfilled in him that which He willed for him, that his last state should become his first state again, and that he should now be as he was before he came into existence, when the spirit, not joined as yet to the body, dwelt in the Light and Presence of God.[2]

Mortality has become immortality, the corruptible has put on incorruption. These terms, says al-Hujwīrī, "are applied by the Ṣūfīs to the degree of perfection attained by the saints who have escaped from the pain of conflict and the fetters of the 'stations,' and the vicissitudes of the 'states,' and whose search has ended in discovery. They have beheld all things visible and have heard all things audible, and have come to know all the secrets of the heart, and have realised how imperfect is all that they have discovered, and turning aside from it all, have of set purpose become annihilated to all desire, and have become without desire, and having thus passed away from mortality, they

[1] al-Kalābādhī, *op. cit.*, fol. 30*a*.
[2] al-Hujwīrī, *op cit.*, pp. 38, 363.

have attained to perfect immortality."[1] This is the Unitive Life, the transcending of the temporal and the material in union with the Abiding and the Real, the dying to the old life of the natural man, with all its limitations and desires, and the attainment of a new supernatural life, which is everlasting. Of this state of Union, one of the Ṣūfī gnostics said: "If God Most Glorious manifests His Essence to anyone, that one will find all his own essence and attributes and actions utterly absorbed in the light of God's Essence and the Divine qualities and actions and will; and he sees his essence to be the Essence of the One, and his attributes to be the attributes of God, and his actions to be God's actions, because of his complete absorption in Union with the Divine; and beyond this stage, there is no further stage of union for man. For when the eye of the soul—the spiritual vision—is rapt away to the contemplation of the Divine Beauty, the light of the understanding, whereby we distinguish between things, is extinguished in the dazzling light of the Eternal Essence, and the distinction between the temporal and the eternal, the perishable and the imperishable, is taken away, and this state is called "Union."[2]

The Quest has ended and the Path has led the seeker to the Goal. The soul, purified and perfected, has passed away from self and is abiding in God; in His Presence it dwells for evermore, contemplating the Divine beauty, penetrating the mysteries of the Divine Unity, knowing naught but the Beloved, and doing naught save in accordance with His Will. It has returned to, and become one with, the One and the All.

[1] al-Hujwīrī, pp. 312, 313. *Cf.* Evelyn Underhill: "To be a mystic is simply to participate here and now in real eternal life, in the fullest, deepest sense which is possible to man" (*Mysticism*, p. 534).

[2] Jāmī, *op. cit.*, p. 527. *Cf.* Suso, the German mystic of the fourteenth century: "This highest stage of union is an indescribable experience, in which all idea of images and forms and differences has vanished. All consciousness of self and of all things has gone and the soul is plunged into the abyss of the Godhead, and the spirit has become one with God."

CHAPTER X

SOME EARLY ṢŪFĪ MYSTICS

AMONG the early Ṣūfīs whom we have mentioned as being conspicuous for their asceticism were some who were also true mystics and responsible for definitely mystical teaching which has come down to us.

(*a*) RĀBI'A AL-'ADAWIYYA OF BAṢRA[1]

Such was Rābi'a al-'Adawiyya of Baṣra, a mystic of a fine and saintly type, of whom her biographer, the poet 'Aṭṭār, wrote, " Rābi'a was unique, because, in her relations with God and her knowledge of things Divine, she had no equal. She was deeply venerated by all the great Ṣūfīs of her time and was an unquestioned authority to her contemporaries."[2] She was one who was not content to follow the leading of others, and to accept their authority in matters of religion ; unlike most of the Ṣūfīs, she seems never even to have studied under any shaykh or spiritual director, but she sought for a direct and personal experience of God. 'Abd al-Qādir al-Jīlānī, the patron saint of Baghdād and founder of the Qādiriyya order of dervishes (*ob.* A.D. 1166), considered that true believers were of two classes, first those who sought a master to teach them the way leading to God, to act as an intermediary between them and God, and this class would not accept as evidence of the right path anything in which they could not see the footsteps of the Prophet before them ; and second, those who in seeking to tread the Path, did not look before them for the footprint of any of God's creatures, for they had removed all thought of what He had created from their hearts, and concerned themselves solely with God. It was to this second class, he said, that Rābi'a belonged.[3]

[1] See above, pp. 185 *ff*.
[2] 'Aṭṭār, *op. cit.*, i. 59.
[3] al-Munāwī, " Kawāqib," fol. 51*b*.

Rābi'a's conception of the nature of God was in the main that of an orthodox Muslim, as we might expect from her early date. He was to her the One, and to set any other beside Him was polytheism. So she could feel no reverence even for the House of God, the sacred Ka'ba. " It is the Lord of the house Whom I need," she said; " what have I to do with the house?" Her Lord was her *miḥrāb*, and towards Him she faced as her *qibla*.[1] Beside the One Reality all other things to her seemed transient and unreal, whether in this world or the next. One fair spring morning her servant said to her, " O mistress, come out to behold the works of God," but Rābi'a, occupied within in the worship of God, replied, " Come you inside that you may behold their Maker. Contemplation of the Maker has turned me aside from what He has made."[2] So also when asked if she had no desire for Paradise, she answered, " The neighbour first and then the house."[3] God, to her, was the giver of all good gifts, for He was the Sole Cause of all existent things and the Sole Agent. Rābi'a speaks of God as her Sustainer and her Life, the Bestower of all favours, the Giver of all assistance, all grace, all gifts.

Yet, with all her reverence for the infinite Greatness and Majesty of God and her sense of the infinite littleness of His creatures in comparison with Him, Rābi'a believed that there might be the closest and tenderest relation between the soul and God. She held that the spirit had come from God and must return to Him. Asked whence she had come, she said, " From that other world." When asked again, " Whither are you going?" she replied, " To that other world."[4] Rābi'a, therefore, believed that it was possible for the soul to ascend again to God, and, when made fit by purification to receive His revelation, and to look upon God unveiled in all His glory, and in that Vision to pass into

[1] 'Aṭṭār, *op. cit.*, i. 62; al-Ḥurayfīsh, *al-Rawḍ al-Fā'iq*, p. 214. The *miḥrāb* is the chief niche in a mosque, facing towards Mecca, where the Imām leads the congregation in prayer, and the *qibla* is the direction in which Mecca lies, towards which all Muslims pray.

[2] 'Aṭṭār, *op. cit.*, i. 68.

[3] al-Ghazālī, *Iḥyā*, iv. 269.

[4] 'Aṭṭār, *op. cit.*, i. 67.

union with Him. She speaks of the "eye" of her heart, that spiritual sense beyond and above reason, by which the Divine could be apprehended, to which those high mysteries could be revealed.[1]

She has much to say of the Way of purification and self-stripping by which the soul was fitted to receive the gifts which enabled it to attain to spiritual perfection, and so to become one with the Divine. Her peace, she says, she had found in solitude, and it was undoubtedly the years spent in retreat in a cell in the desert, before which she had been but a novice in the Way, which led her, through meditation and contemplation, to the joy of the mystic experience and the Unitive life. She speaks of her separation from all creatures, that is to say, that she would not allow any created thing to distract her for one moment from the service of the Creator. There is a story told of her, which illustrates her feeling that not even the most homely and necessary things in life could be allowed to separate her from her highest work, the contemplation of God. One night, after reciting the night-prayers, she fell asleep, and saw in her sleep a fair green tree, of great size and beauty, and upon it were fruits white, red and golden, such as were never seen in this earth, and they shone like stars and suns among the green leaves of the tree. Rābi'a was greatly struck by its beauty, and asked to whom it belonged. She was told that it was hers and the fruits thereon her praises of God. As she walked around it, she saw a number of golden fruits lying on the ground under the tree, and she said, "Surely it would be better that these fruits should be among the others on the tree," and she was told, "They would have been there, but that you, when you were praising God, were thinking to yourself, 'Is the dough leavened or not?' and so these fruits fell off."[2] So Rābi'a learnt to give her whole mind to her prayers and her worship of God. Like others of the early Ṣūfīs and of the early Christian mystics, she felt the downward drag of this present world and its attractions, and therefore cut herself off from its temptations. None realised more thoroughly the impossibility of serving two masters, and she gladly sacrificed the temporal and that which to her was unreal, for the

[1] al-Ḥurayfīsh, *op. cit.*, p. 213. [2] Abū Ṭālib, *op. cit.*, i. 103.

sake of the abiding and the Real. She said once : " If a man possessed the whole world he would not be wealthy thereby," and when asked the reason for such a seeming paradox, she said, " Because it perishes and passes away."[1] When her disciple, Sufyān al-Thawrī, asked her, " What should the servant do who desires proximity to his Lord ?" she replied : " He should possess nothing in this world or the next save Him."[2]

Rābi'a taught that it was necessary to add to the purification of the soul from the grosser desires of the senses and of self-indulgence, the purification of the inward faculties, so that the feelings and the will might be brought into complete harmony with the Eternal Will of God. To her friend Sufyān, who asked her what she desired, she said, " I am a servant, and what has a servant to do with desire ? If I will anything and my Lord does not will it, this would be unbelief. That should be willed which He wills, in order to be His true servant." Urged by the same visitor to pray for relief from illness which had laid her aside, she said, " O Sufyān, do you not know Who it is that wills this suffering for me ? Is it not God Who wills it ?" He agreed, and she continued, " When you know this, why do you bid me ask for what is contrary to His will ? It is not well to oppose one's Beloved."[3] To Rābi'a, prayer was not primarily a matter of intercession, it was rather a time of communion with her Lord, in which she might discover what was His will for her. To Mālik Dīnār, a fellow Ṣūfī, who suggested that he might ask wealthy friends of his to alleviate her poverty, Rābi'a said : " Is it not the same One Who gives daily bread both to me and to them ?" He said, " It is," and Rābi'a then said, " Will He forget the poor because of their poverty or remember the rich because of their riches ? Since He knows what is my state, what have I to remind Him of ? What He wills, we should also will."[4] In one of her prayers which has come down to us, she prays : " O my God, my concern and my desire in this world is that I should remember Thee, above all the things of this world, and in the next, that out of all who are in that world, I should meet with Thee alone.

[1] al-Munāwī, *op. cit.*, fol. 51*a*.
[2] Jāmī, *Nafaḥāt al-Uns.*, p. 716.
[3] 'Aṭṭār, *op. cit.*, i. 70, 71.
[4] *Ibid.*, i. 71.

This only I would say, 'Thy Will be done.'[1] So she taught the doctrine of Unification (*tawḥīd*), the merging of the personal will in the One Divine Will.

But Rābi'a, though she served her Lord with reverence and humility, was primarily a lover, and to her, God was, first of all, the Beloved and the Friend. She was one of the first among the Ṣūfīs to teach that Love was the guide of the mystic on the Path, and that only through Love could the seeker be perfected, and the soul, with the dross purged away by that all-devouring flame, be enabled to penetrate into the very shrine of the Divine Mysteries. To her Lord, Rābi'a speaks in the language of Love. "O my Joy and my Desire, my Life and my Friend. If Thou art satisfied with me, then, O Desire of my heart, my happiness is attained."[2] At night, alone upon her roof under the eastern sky, she used to pray, "O my Lord, the stars are shining and the eyes of men are closed, and kings have shut their doors, and every lover is alone with his beloved, and here am I alone with Thee."[3] This all-absorbing love filled her heart to the exclusion of all lesser affections. Asked if she loved the Lord of Glory, Rābi'a answered, "Yes," but when asked if she hated Satan, she replied that her love for God left no room for hating Satan. She said of herself, "My love to God has so possessed me that no place remains for loving or hating any save Him." She was asked, "What is Love?" and she said in reply: "Love has come from Eternity and passes into Eternity."[4] Asked by Sufyān al-Thawrī what was the essence of her faith, Rābi'a answered, "I have not served God from fear of Hell, for I should be but a wretched hireling if I did it from fear; nor from love of Paradise, for I should be an unworthy servant if I served for the sake of what was given, but I have served Him only for the love of Him and desire for Him."[5] This teaching of Rābi'a's reminds us of what the Christian mystic John Climacus wrote on this subject: "All those who have gladly renounced the world, have done so either because of their many sins or because of the Kingdom

[1] Aṭṭār, *op. cit.*, i. 73. [2] al-Ḥurayfīsh, *op. cit.*, p. 213.
[3] *Cf.* al-Ghazālī, *Iḥyā*, iv. 353.
[4] Aṭṭār, *op. cit.*, i. 67. *Cf.* above Dionysius, p. 83.
[5] Abū Ṭālib, *op. cit.*, ii. 57.

to come, or from love of God. Every turning away from the world that does not spring from one of these motives is irrational. Renunciation of the first type is called idle by the Initiated ; for they say : " Where there is no sin, there does not originate fear of torment." The like is said of the second type of renunciation. For the Initiated say : " He who turns his back to pleasures in view of remuneration, is the mill of the ass, which is always set into motion on account of the same motive. But he who turns away on account of the love of God will at once, even in the beginning, acquire warmth like fire. And when his fire is thrown on the fuel, it will gradually become strong and blazing."[1]

Rābi'a's verses on the two kinds of love to God, the self-seeking, and that which is pure from all self-interest, have become famous. They run thus :

" I have loved Thee with two loves, a selfish love and a love
that is worthy of Thee.
As for the love which is selfish, therein I occupy myself
with Thee, to the exclusion of all others.
But in the love which is worthy of Thee, Thou dost raise
the veil that I may see Thee.
Yet is the praise not mine in this or that,
But the praise is to Thee in both that and this."

And one writer adds another fragment to these verses :

" O Beloved of hearts, I have none like unto Thee,
Therefore have pity this day on the sinner who comes to
Thee.
O my Hope and my Rest and my Delight,
The heart can love none other but Thee."[2]

Rābi'a, then, taught the doctrine of Pure Love, love that sought for no reward, and that loved only for the sake of the Beloved and His glory. To such a lover she taught—and we cannot doubt that her teaching rested on her own experience—that the Beatific Vision was revealed, and God unveiled Himself in all His Beauty. She tells how she herself knew what it was to contemplate that Beauty Supreme

[1] *Cf.* A. Wensinck, *Book of the Dove*, pp. cxiv., cxv.
[2] al-Ḥurayfīsh, *op. cit.*, p. 213. *Cf.* also al-Kalābādhī, *op. cit.*, fol. 30*b*.

with the eye of the soul, made athirst for that Vision by its love. For that Vision of surpassing loveliness she was prepared to give up all lesser joys. "O my Lord," she prayed, "if I worship Thee from fear of Hell, burn me in Hell, and if I worship Thee in hope of Paradise, exclude me thence, but if I worship Thee for Thine own sake, then withhold not from me Thine Eternal Beauty." As we have seen from her verses quoted above, that prayer was granted, and to this ardent lover of His the Beloved unveiled Himself, that she might look upon Him face to face. And in that supreme moment was consummated the mystic marriage of the soul with God. She had said to an earthly suitor, "I have ceased to exist and have passed out of Self. I exist in Him and am altogether His." This temporal life for her had ceased to be, for she had entered into the eternal life with God. From the beginning of her Quest, Rābi'a had looked unfalteringly towards that supreme Goal. "My hope is for union with Thee," she prayed, "for that is the goal of my desire."[2] Once, when sick with longing, she had said, "The healing for my wound is union with the Friend; only so can I find ease."[3] Again she said: "The groaning and the yearning of the lover of God will not be satisfied until it is satisfied in the Beloved."[4] She knew what that satisfaction meant, for she was herself living the unitive life in union with her Beloved, so that she could say, "My Beloved is always with me," and there are lines of hers which show how she was ever conscious of that life of union within:

"I have made Thee the Companion of my heart,
But my body is available for those who seek its company,
And my body is friendly towards its guests,
But the Beloved of my heart is the Guest of my soul."[5]

She had trodden the mystic Way to the end, the loving soul had been made one with its Beloved, and so Rābi'a the mystic, "that one on fire with love and longing, that one

[1] 'Aṭṭār, *op. cit.*, i. 73.
[2] al-Ḥurayfīsh, *op. cit.*, p. 214.
[3] 'Aṭṭār, *op. cit.*, i. 69.
[4] Suhrawardī, *'Awārif al-Ma'ārif* (margin), *Iḥyā*, iv. 343.
[5] Ibn Khallikān, *Wafayāt*, i., No. 230.

enamoured of the desire to approach her Lord, and be consumed in His Glory," attained to the goal of her desire, and "lost herself in union with the Divine."[1]

(*b*) Ḥārith al-Muḥāsibī

Another of the early Ṣūfīs who, though he laid much emphasis in his teaching on asceticism and quietism, was a true mystic—to whose mystical writings later Ṣūfīs were much indebted, and not least among them al-Ghazālī himself—was Ḥārith b. Asad al-Muḥāsibī[2] the author of a number of mystical works, among them being the *Kitāb al-Ri'āya liḥuqūq Allah wa'l Qiyām biha* ("The Observance of the Law of God and the Abiding therein"), which has been described as the finest manual of the interior life which Islām has produced.[3] This is concerned chiefly with the Way, but others of his writings give us more definitely mystical teaching.

His ideas of the nature of God are those of the early orthodox Ṣūfīs. God is the All-Sufficing, the Merciful, the Loving (*wadūd*), the Hearing, the All-Knowing, Who is constantly acting, and distracted by nothing from His work. He knows what is hidden and what is beyond the hidden; He penetrates into the secret recesses of the heart and sees all the actions of men, and is aware of what they whisper among themselves, and of their private concerns and wishes and the evil thoughts suggested to them by Satan, and all things above them and below them.[4]

al-Muḥāsibī held that the soul of man, in its spiritual part, the higher soul, had existed before it was united with the body, and he believed that God had implanted within it something of His own Essence, which would enable it ultimately to return to union with Himself.[5] The lower soul, however, the carnal self (*nafs*), was in his view the seat of

[1] A full account of the life and teaching of Rābi'a of Baṣra is given in my *Rābi'a the Mystic and her Fellow-Saints in Islām*.

[2] See above, pp. 188 *ff*.

[3] L. Massignon.

[4] "Muḥāsibat al-Nufūs," fol. 66*b*.

[5] *Faṣl fi'l Maḥabba*, "Ḥilya," fol. 232*b*.

all evil. Therefore the first and most essential duty for the one who sought to return to God was to conquer the self. " Put your carnal self where God has put it," he writes, " and describe it as He has described it, and get the better of it, for whether it be your servant, it is from Satan, or whether it overpowers you, Satan is within it. Everything which comes from it is deceitful, and no deed of it is praiseworthy, or tends to the Truth. When you hope to be quit of it, it will strengthen itself, and if you neglect to examine (*muḥāsibat*) it, you will fall under its control, and if you weaken in your struggles against it, you will be overwhelmed, and if you follow it in its desires, you will go down into Hell. The truth is not in it, nor any tendency to good. It is the source of affliction and the origin of all evil. None knows it save its Creator. It is incumbent upon you to examine the self continually, and to seek to know it and to oppose it, and to fight against it in all to which it summons you."[1] For each one, therefore, who would tread the upward way, knowledge of four kinds is most important : first, knowledge of God, that is, the knowledge of His Unity and His power, which will lead a man to conversion, when he turns his back on all that belongs to the self and the world, and sets his face towards God ; second, knowledge of the enemy of God (Satan), for this will prepare a man for pitfalls on the upward Way ; third, knowledge of the Self, so prone to evil, which will lead to its conquest ; and fourth, knowledge of the work of God, which will enable a man, by His grace, to go forward and upward on the right Path.[2] " Knowledge," says al-Muḥāsibī, " is the place of perfection, and ignorance the place of search, and knowledge at the outer entrance is better than ignorance at the door. Knowledge brings a man to the degree of perfection, but ignorance does not allow him to pass through (even) the door. Knowledge, in truth, is greater than action, because it is possible to know God by means of knowledge, and none can find Him merely by action. If it were possible without knowledge to find the way to Him, the Christians and monks in their austerities would behold Him face to face, and sinful believers (Muslims) would fail of that sight. Ignorance is an attribute of

[1] " Muḥāsibat al-Nufūs," fol. 68*b*.
[2] *Ibid.*, fol. 67*a*.

the slave, but knowledge is an attribute of God Himself."[1] Self-examination, then, is essential for the process of purification, and so also is a rule of life, which represents the first stage of the Way. This will lead on to the second stage, that of Illumination, when the mystic ecstasy (*aḥwāl*) will be experienced by the soul, and this is the stage of meditation and contemplation (*murāqiba*) which is the "gate" of gnosis. "Action by the movements of the heart in the contemplation of invisible things," he says, "is better than action by the movements of the limbs."[2]

Those who faithfully follow out the rule of life which will purify them from the evil of the carnal self, and who give themselves to meditation upon their Lord, are His lovers, for love of what He ordains arises from love of Himself, and it is God Who has enabled His servants to love Him. "That is because it is He Who has made Himself known to them, Who has led them to obey Him, Who has showed love towards them, though they had no claim upon Him. He deposited love for Himself as a trust in the hearts of His lovers. Then He invested their utterances with shining light, through the strength of His love in their hearts. When He had thus done, He showed them to His angels, rejoicing in them. Before creating them, He praised them, and before they praise Him, He has thanked them, because He knew aforetime in regard to them, that He would inspire them with what had been written of them, and told of them by Him. Then He brought them forth to His creation, when He had appropriated their hearts exclusively to Himself, and so He delivered the hearts of the Wise over to creation (*i.e.*, He invested the spirits of His saints with mortal bodies and brought them into existence in this world), having endowed their hearts with the precious secret which would lead them into union with the Beloved. Then, desiring that they, and mankind by means of them, should find life in Himself, He granted unto them the mystic gnosis. When they are in trouble, by the light of this gnosis, they know where to look for a remedy. Then He causes them to know how the remedy does its work, and how they can be helped

[1] al-Hujwīrī, *op. cit.*, pp. 134, 135.
[2] al-Sulamī, *op. cit.*, fol. 12*b*.

to heal their own hearts. Then He commands them to comfort those who suffer, and to intercede on their behalf, and He promises them an answer to such intercessions. He calls upon them to concentrate their minds in listening with the ear of the heart to His words, as He says to them, " O you, you who are My witnesses ! If any comes to you sick, because he has lost Me, heal him ; or a fugitive from My service, bring him back ; or heedless of My comfort and My grace, remind him of them. Verily, I shall be your best Physician, for I am gentle, and he who is gentle takes as His servants only those who are gentle."[1] God does not reveal the secret of Love to the unworthy, for He guards it jealously as that which must be given to Himself alone, since it came from Him and subsists in Him.[2]

This is the yearning love of those who are conscious that they have come from God and seek reunion with Him again. al-Muḥāsibī speaks of love to God as being " a strong yearning," which is the heart's remembrance in contemplation of the One yearned for, and its expectation of the state of reunion.[3] " Love to God," he says, " is the kindling of the heart with joy, because of the proximity of its Beloved, for when the heart is alight with joy, it finds delight in solitude, in the remembrance of its Beloved, for in solitude love rises up triumphant. Fear, too, is necessary to the heart, but it does not rise up until all desire for disobedience has died away from the heart, and the foundations of desire have been overthrown by the strength of fear. Then fellowship with God finds a place in the heart, for the sign of fellowship with God is intolerance of all save Him. Then when solitude gives rise to the prayer of inward converse with God (*munājāt*), the sweetness of that inward converse pervades the whole mind, so that it is no longer concerned with this world and what is therein."[4]

With Love, Muḥāsibī associates Satisfaction, the final

[1] Here, as elsewhere in al-Muḥāsibī's teaching, there is a re-echo of the Gospel. We have here the conception of the Good Physician, and a reminder of Christ's words, " Learn of Me, for I am meek and lowly in heart and ye shall find rest unto your souls " (*Matt.* xi. 29).

[2] " Ḥilya," fol. 232*b*.

[3] *Ibid.*, fol. 232*a*.

[4] *Ibid.*, fols. 232*b*, 233*a*.

station on the Path before the seeker is granted the mystic " states " of Illumination. There is the satisfaction of God with His servant, and the satisfaction of the servant in God. al-Hujwīrī, giving us al-Muḥāsibī's teaching on Satisfaction, writes, " The Divine Satisfaction is shown in God's willingness to bestow rewards and grace and favour upon His servant, and human satisfaction is shown in carrying out God's command and accepting His decrees. The Divine satisfaction precedes the human, since until man has the assistance of God Most Glorious, he does not accept His decrees, nor carry out His command. Therefore human satisfaction is linked up with the Divine satisfaction, and depends upon it. Human satisfaction, in short, is tranquillity of heart in regard to Fate, whether it be unfavourable or propitious, and equanimity of soul in regarding events, whether the Majesty of God or His Beauty be manifested therein. It is all one to the true servant whether he be checked by hindrances or prospered by favour, whether he be consumed in the fire of the wrath and the Majesty of God or illuminated by the light of His Mercy and His Beauty, since both alike witness to God, and whatever comes from Him is good. When the servant sees God's choice and chooses it for himself, he is delivered from all anxieties, for satisfaction means deliverance. There are four classes of those who are satisfied with God. First, those who are satisfied with His gift, which is gnosis ; second, those who are satisfied with happiness, that is, this present world ; third, those who are satisfied with affliction, which includes trials of all kinds. Lastly, there are those who are satisfied with being chosen, which is love. He who looks away from the Giver to the gift accepts it in his soul, and when he has accepted it, anxiety and grief vanish from his heart. He who looks away from the gift to the Giver loses the gift, and by his own efforts treads the way of satisfaction. He who is satisfied with this world will come to destruction and loss—it is not worth while for the friend of God to set his heart upon it or that any care for it should enter his mind. Happiness is happiness only when it leads to the Giver of Happiness, and that kind of happiness which veils a man from Him is an affliction. The one who is satisfied with affliction from God is satisfied because in the affliction he sees the One Who sends it, and is enabled to endure his trouble by the contemplation of its Author, and he does not reckon it as pain, in the joy of contemplating the Beloved. Finally, those who are satisfied with being chosen by the Beloved are His lovers, whose existence is unreal whether in His satisfaction or His wrath, since their hearts dwell ever in His Presence, and the secret resort of their souls is in the garden of fellowship with Him—their hearts are detached from the creatures and from the fetters of the stations, and the states, and their souls have escaped from all existences and have attached themselves to God." Thus Satisfaction is the last of the stations; it begins with striving and effort on the part of the self, but in the end it means escape from striving, it has become a mystic state, in which the soul finds perfect peace in God.[1]

So, when Love has found its perfect satisfaction in the Beloved, the mystic is led onwards and upwards towards "the pure Vision of the Divine Essence which alone gives perfect joy," and to the reunion to which his soul had been eternally predestined.

In al-Muḥāsibī we find a true mystic, seeking first and foremost the purification of the inner self, and next the development of the life of the soul in love and knowledge until at last it shall be fit to look upon the Divine Beauty and to live the life of perfect fellowship with God.

(*c*) Dhū al-Nūn al-Miṣrī

Another of the Ṣūfīs distinguished, as we have noted, for his asceticism, who was also a great mystical teacher, is Dhū al-Nūn al-Miṣrī. Like Clement of Alexandria before him, he represented the Way of salvation to be the attainment of gnosis, and the adept Ṣūfī he calls the gnostic. We have only fragments of his writings, but these show plainly that he was a thinker who went beyond his predecessors in his development of the theosophical and mystical doctrines of Ṣūfism. Certain of his biographers have gone so far as to claim him as the chief author of Ṣūfism.[2]

[1] al-Hujwīrī, *op. cit.*, pp. 219 *ff.*
[2] *Cf.* Jāmī, *Nafaḥāt al-Uns*, p. 36.

His doctrine of God is set forth most plainly in his prayers, which show that he conceived of God as Creator, the All-Sufficient Cause of all existing things, the One Agent, Incomprehensible and infinitely above His creatures, and yet having a personal relation to them, in that He is the All-Merciful, Who will forgive their sins, and Who can be known in some measure, through His outward manifestation of Himself, and through the gift of gnosis to His elect, by which they are enabled to draw nigh to God and to enter into fellowship with Him. In one of his prayers Dhū al-Nūn says: "O Lord, Thou art the most intimate of intimates with Thy friends, in supplying the needs of those who depend upon Thee (*al-mutawakkilūn*), and in manifesting Thyself to them, for their thoughts are concerned with their inmost selves. O God, my inmost being is unveiled in Thy sight and I am distressed before Thee, (but) when sin has led me astray, the remembrance of Thee has brought me back to Thy fellowship, knowing that the control of all affairs is in Thy hand and that they originate from Thy decrees. O my God, Who is more merciful than Thyself, to all my shortcomings, for Thou hast created me weak? And Who is more forgiving than Thou, for Thy knowledge of me was from aforetime? Thy command to me is all-embracing; I have resisted Thee only by Thy permission, and Thou hast reproached me therewith. I have disobeyed Thee, and Thou wast aware of it and hast proved me in the wrong. I ask Thee for the mercy that I need, and the acceptance of my plea—for I am poor towards Thee, and Thou art bountiful towards me—that Thou wilt forgive me my sins, both of deed and thought."[1] Here the emphasis is laid on the Omnipotence and the Omniscience of God and the insufficience of the creature, and yet God is the Helper and man may be among His friends. In another prayer, he prays: "O God, the power is Thine, and all excellence is Thine, and it is Thou Who dost help all Thy creatures with Thy strength and Thy power, and thou art the Doer of what Thou hast willed. Neither weakness nor ignorance are hindrances to Thee; Thou art not subject to change nor limited by past and future, for both past and future were created and

[1] al-Sarrāj, *Kitāb al-Luma'*, p. 258.

brought into existence by Thee. Are they not among the things which Thou hast created? Thine existence has been manifested by proofs all around us, nor is anything created without Thee, for Thou art Exalted above all, and art the All-Comprehensive. All that is perceived by the senses is of Thy creation and all that limits them (*i.e.*, form and space), for it is Thy workmanship. Thou art He Who cannot be apprehended in the phenomenal world. No place can do without Thee, and none save Thyself knows Thee, except by his acknowledgment of Thy Unity, and none of Thy creation is ignorant of Thee, except him who is wanting in gnosis. Nothing can divert Thee from any of Thy purposes, nor is there any limit to Thy Power, nor is any place devoid of Thy Presence, nor does any affair distract Thee from any other affair."[1]

In his teaching on the relation of the soul to God, Dhū al-Nūn, like others of these early Ṣūfīs, shows that while he held that the lower soul was the seat of the animal passions and the desires of self, and consequently the greatest hindrance to be overcome by the seeker after the things of God, he believed that the higher soul had dwelt with God in a state of pre-existence, and by means of self-discipline, which would liberate it from the trammels of the carnal self, it might be enabled to return to that stage of primeval purity, and so to become the dwelling-place of the Most High. We are told how he learnt these truths from the mouth of one who might least have been expected to be a teacher of Ṣūfī doctrine, a negro slave-girl whom he met on his travels, of whom he says: "Her heart was rent asunder by her love of the All-Compassionate. And I said to her, 'Peace be upon you, O my sister,' and she said, 'And upon you be peace, O Dhū al-Nūn.' I said, 'Whence did you know me?' and she replied, 'O foolish one, verily God created the spirits a thousand years before the bodies, and placed them round His Throne. Those who recognised one another became on terms of fellowship, and those between whom there was no recognition, had no intercourse with one another, and my spirit knew your spirit in that place.' I said to her, 'Truly I see that you are wise. Teach me

[1] al-Sarrāj, *Kitāb al-Luma'*, p. 257.

something of what God Most High has taught you.' Then she said, 'O Abū al-Fayḍ, sift your members (*i.e.*, the instruments of righteousness and unrighteousness,[1]) as in a sieve, until there passes away all that is not God, and the heart shall be purified and contain naught save God Most Glorious. Then He will set you at His door, and give unto you a new friendship with Himself and will invest you with His treasures, because of your obedience to Him.'"[2] Dhū al-Nūn himself said, "Blessed is he who is purified and has closed the door (to sin). Blessed is he who hastens towards eternity. Blessed is he who obeys God all the day of his life."[3]

The Way, then, to Dhū al-Nūn, was first of all a process of purification in order that the soul might be set free from all the fetters of the carnal self, and all the ties which bound it to this world, or to anything, or anyone, save God Himself. Neither in fear nor in hope was He to be worshipped and loved by those who had attained to the true knowledge of Him. "God has servants," says Dhū al-Nūn, "who, after they have given up their sins out of fear of His punishment, have abandoned sin for ever out of shame at His clemency."[4] Prayer, too, must be free from the motive of the fear of misfortunes or hope of benefits; it must be the "loving converse of the soul with God," which seeks only to be in His Presence and to look upon Him, that pure prayer which is wordless. "Every intercessor," he says, "is veiled by his intercessions from contemplation of the Truth, for the Truth is present to the people of Truth, since God Himself is the Truth and His Word is Truth, and there is no need for any to make intercession when God Himself is present with him and manifested to him. If He were absent, then should intercession be made to Him."[5] Mental prayer, therefore, is the form which prayer should take for the friend of God. Meditation (*fikra*), he says, is the key to worship, that which

[1] *Cf.* St. Paul, Rom. vi. 13.

[2] Taqī al-Dīn al-Ḥisnī, *Siyar al-Ṣāliḥāt*, fol. 45.

[3] Abū Nu'aym, *op. cit.*, fol. 203*a*. The word used here to imply blessing is *ṭūbā*, used also for the Beatitudes in the Gospel.

[4] al-Sulamī, *op. cit.*, fol. 7*b*.

[5] *Ibid.*, fols. 7*b*, 8*a*.

unlocks the door and gives entrance into the Presence of the King.

It was Love which enabled the mystic to attain to gnosis and to fellowship with God, Love pure and undefiled. Dhū al-Nūn was asked what was Pure Love, free from all defilement, and he replied, "The Pure Love of God, in which is no defilement, is the thrusting out from the heart and the members of all lesser affections, until no such affection remains in them, and all shall be in God and to God, and that one (who acts thus) is the true lover of God."[1] Such an absorbing love means that to the lover who is possessed by it, death seems slow in coming, because of his longing for his Lord, and his desire to meet with Him, and to gaze upon Him.[2] True love for God is always disinterested, for such love is not increased by what benefits it nor decreased by what neglects it. Dhū al-Nūn is perhaps the first to use the imagery of the wine of love, and the cup poured out for the lover to drink therefrom, an image which was so frequently used by the mystic poets who came after him, especially those of Persia. He speaks of the cup of love poured out by the lover, and again he says: "Drink the wine of His love for thee, so that He may intoxicate thee with thy love for Him."[3] When asked to define the intimate fellowship (*uns*), which is the result of love, he said: "It is the joy of the lover in his Beloved."[4] The first step in fellowship is to meet with the Friend, and after that meeting the thought of Him will be always present.[5] The lowest stage of intimate fellowship, al-Miṣrī says elsewhere, means that if the lover is cast into Hell-fire, that will not separate him from the One with Whom he is in fellowship.[6] This fellowship with God, he tells us, is a radiant light, and fellowship with any save Him is a deadly poison.[7] In this connection, when asked what was the mark of fellowship with God, he said, "If you see that He separates you from His creatures, then He is giving

[1] al-Sarrāj, *Kitāb al-Luma'*, p. 59.
[2] al-Munāwī, *op. cit.*, fol. 110*a*.
[3] *Cf.* L. Massignon, *Essai*, p. 186.
[4] al-Kalābādhī, "Kitāb al-Ta'rruf," fol. 29*b*.
[5] al-Sulamī, *op. cit.*, fol. 8*a*.
[6] al-Kalābādhī, *op. cit.*, *loc. cit.*
[7] al-Munāwī, *op. cit.*, fol. 110*a*.

you fellowship with Himself, and if you see that He is giving you fellowship with His creatures, then know that He is separating you from Himself."[1]

We have already seen how Dhū al-Nūn speaks of a knowledge attained only by the elect, which is the knowledge of Reality, the mystic gnosis of the saints of God, " those who behold God in their hearts, so that He reveals unto them what He reveals to no others in the two worlds."[2] Dhū al-Nūn's teaching on gnosis is at the very centre of his mystical doctrine, and he has much to say of it which constitutes a new development in Ṣūfism. The signs of the true gnostic, he says, are three. The light of his gnosis does not extinguish the light of his devotion, nor does he accept inwardly any doctrines which the sacred law does not allow to him outwardly, nor does the greatness of God's grace towards him induce him to violate the secrets of God's mysteries,[3] as a later Ṣūfī, al-Ḥallāj (*ob.* A.D. 922) revealed his secret knowledge and suffered a cruel death, because he made known that which should have remained hidden. Dhū al-Nūn associates gnosis, like love, with ecstasy. " The true gnosis," he says, " means amazed bewilderment, and of this there are two kinds, the common kind, which is the bewilderment of heresy and wandering, and the special kind, which is the bewilderment of discovery ; the first gets broken and is joined up again ; the second is neither broken nor joined."[4]

To the gnostic is granted the Beatific Vision. " I have read in the Law," al-Miṣrī writes, " that the righteous who believe and are treading the Way of God, and who hold fast to obedience, look upon the Face of the Almighty, for the goal of him who hopes, the true lover, is to look upon the Face of God, and He bestows upon them when they meet with Him, no greater grace than the Vision of His countenance."[5] These are the blessed, to whose company all mystics seek to belong, and in one of the prayers left by Dhū al-Nūn he prays : " O God, range us among those whose spirits have taken their flight to the Kingdom ; for whom the veils

[1] Abū Nu'aym, *op. cit.*, fol. 202*a*.
[2] 'Aṭṭār, *op. cit.*, i. 127.
[3] al-Sarrāj, *Kitāb al-Luma'*, p. 39.
[4] Jāmī, *Nafaḥāt al-Uns*, p. 37.
[5] Abū Nu'aym, *op. cit.*, fol. 233*a*.

of Thy Majesty are lifted; who are submerged in the flood of certainty; whom the whirlwind of love has drawn, by the degrees of proximity of Glory, to the brink of right intention, and they have left behind them their sins, and have taken with them only their acts of obedience, and that is thanks to Thy grace, O Thou Most Merciful."[1]

When God has illuminated the heart with the pure radiance of gnosis, the gnostic can enter into the Unitive life and henceforth lives in, and through, God. Of this state of union, Dhū al-Nūn tells us: "The gnostics see without knowledge and without sight, without information received and without contemplation, without description, without veiling and without veil. They are not themselves and they exist not through themselves, but in so far as they exist at all, they exist in God. Their movements are caused by God, and their words are the words of God, which are uttered by their tongues, and their sight is the sight of God which has entered into their eyes. So God Most High has said, 'When I love a servant, I, the Lord, am his ear, so that he hears by Me; I am his eye, so that he sees by Me; and I am his tongue, so that he speaks by Me; and I am his hand, so that he takes by Me.'"[2]

Dhū al-Nūn, then, we may regard as a practical mystic, one who through self-discipline and self-purification had come to enlightenment by means of gnosis, and had known the mystic experience of union. He is the first to teach a classification of the mystic states, and to develop the doctrine of the mystic gnosis, as he is the first to describe in detail the journey of the soul on its upward way to the goal, and to give us also a Ṣūfī's conception of the nature of the Unitive life.

(*d*) Abū Yazīd al-Bisṭāmī

An early mystical teacher who had a far-reaching influence upon the development of the Ṣūfī doctrine, especially in the direction of pantheism, was Abū Yazīd Ṭayfūr b. 'Isā b. Suruṣhān, commonly called Bāyazīd Bisṭāmī. His grandfather appears to have been a Zoroastrian who became a

[1] Yāfi'i, *Nashr*, ii. 335.

[2] 'Aṭṭār, *op. cit.*, i. 127.

Muslim. al-Sulamī tells us that there were three brothers, Ādam, Ṭayfūr, and 'Alī, who were all ascetics, devout men who had experience of the mystic states, who belonged to Bisṭām in Persia.[1] Little is known of Bāyazīd's life, but he states that he studied under Abū 'Ali al-Sindī, and from him learnt the mystical doctrine of the Unity and the nature of Reality.[2] He appears to have known the leading Ṣūfīs of his time, including Yaḥya b. Mu'ādh Rāzī, and Aḥmad b. Ḥarb,[3] and there is evidence that he made himself acquainted with the mystical literature available in his day. Most of his life was spent in his native place, Bisṭām, and he died there in A.D. 875. We are told that after his death he was seen in a dream by someone who inquired as to his state and Bāyazīd replied, " They said to me ' O Shaykh, what have you brought ?' and I answered, ' When a poor man comes to the threshold of a King, he is not asked, " What have you brought ?" but " What do you desire ?" ' "[4]

He was a solitary ascetic whose one desire, with which he occupied himself to the exclusion of everything else, was to attain to a direct experience of God, an immediate apprehension of the Divine Essence. When he was asked, " Where is thy native land ?" he replied, " Under the Throne of God ; that is, beyond my powers of conception, and the farthest limit of my sight, and that is where my soul finds its rest, and the secret place where my work is accomplished, as God Most High said to Moses, ' Thou art a stranger here, for I am thy native land.' "[5]

God, to Abū Yazīd, was not only One, He was the Only One, the Sole Reality. Nothing could have reality apart from Him, and therefore the quest of the mystic was to abandon the unreal and to seek the Real, and even the desire to seek originated with God. Bāyazīd said of himself, " At the beginning I was mistaken in four respects. I concerned myself to remember God, to know Him, to love Him, and to seek Him, and when I had come to the end, I saw that He had remembered me before I remembered Him, that His knowledge of me had preceded my knowledge of Him, His

[1] *Op. cit.*, fol. 14*a*.
[2] al-Sārraj, *op. cit.*, p. 177.
[3] Jāmī, *op. cit.*, p. 63. *Cf.* also *Iḥyā*, iv. 160, 187.
[4] *Ibid.*
[5] *Ibid.*

love towards me had existed before my love to Him, and He had sought me before I sought Him."[1]

This conception of God as loving and seeking His own before they loved or sought for Him goes considerably beyond the ideas of the earliest Ṣūfīs, yet at the same time Abū Yazīd realised that the upward way must be trodden on the human level to begin with. The soul, hampered by its association with not-Being, the Unreal, must be purified before it could attain to the goal of its aspirations, and must tread the Way of renunciation and asceticism, and pass through the accepted stages of the Ṣūfī Path. Abū Yazīd said of himself that he had attained to gnosis only by means of a hungry stomach and a naked body.[2] He also says of his own period of self-discipline: "For twelve years I was the forger of my Self, and for five years I was the mirror of my heart, and for a year I was observing what passed between them, and it appeared that I was girded about outwardly with the belt of infidelity, and I was occupied for twelve years in severing that belt. Then I looked and behold within me also was a belt of infidelity, and it took me five years to cut that away. I looked about to see how I could cut it, and that was revealed to me, for I regarded the creatures and saw that they were as dead to me, and I said over them four prayers (by way) of burial."[3] So he was enabled to bring both his outward and his inward life into conformity with the One Will of God.

Humility, which meant a true vision of the insignificance of the self, and of the infinite greatness of God, was the first essential for the seeker. One day, Bāyazīd says that he heard a Voice, which said to him, "O Bāyazīd, Our treasure-house is brimful of acts of adoration and devotion offered by men: do thou bring Us something which is not in Our treasury." " 'What then shall I bring, O Lord?' I said; and the Voice answered me, 'Bring me sorrow of heart, humility, and contrition.' "[4] We are told also how one night, after reciting the evening prayer, Bāyazīd remained standing till the morning, shedding tears. When morning came, his servant

[1] al-Sulamī, *op. cit.*, fol. 15*a*. [2] *Ibid.*, fol. 15*b*.
[3] al-Qushayrī, *Risāla*, p. 63.
[4] 'Aṭṭār, *op. cit.*, Uyghur version, pp. 216, 217.

asked what had happened to him during the night, and he answered, "I thought I had arrived at the very throne of God, and I said to it, 'O Throne, they tell us that God rests upon thee.' 'O Bāyazīd,' replied the Throne, 'we are told here that He dwells in a humble heart.'"[1] This teaching is the more interesting because Abū Yazīd was frequently accused by his enemies of presumption in his attitude towards the Most High. He said on another occasion that the one loved by God was known by three qualities: his liberality was like the sea, his kindness like the sun, his humility like the earth, because it allows itself to be trampled on by everyone.[2] His personal humility showed itself in amazement that his Lord should love even himself. "It is no wonder that I love Thee, since I am a poor slave," he said, "but the wonder is that Thou dost love me, seeing that Thou art a mighty King."[3] Yet, to Abū Yazīd, asceticism of any kind represented only a very early stage of the Way. "The gnostic," he says, "is concerned with what he hopes, the ascetic with what he eats. Blessed is he who is concerned with one thing only, and whose heart is not distracted by what his eyes behold and his ears hear."[4] So the seeker must strive to pass away from all that is creaturely, for all that belongs to the sphere of the unreal. Abū Yazīd said once: "When I had arrived at the station of Proximity (to God), a Voice said to me, 'Ask whatsoever thou dost desire.' I answered, 'Thou art the Object of my desire,' and it was said to me, 'O Bāyazīd, if there remains in thee one atom of thine own desire, that is impossible. Only lose thyself and so shalt thou find Me.'"[5]

Love, as we have seen, was the all-impelling motive which led the seeker to embark on the Quest, and that love was an all-absorbing passion. "When from enmity to the world I fled to the Lord, His love so took possession of me that I became an enemy to myself," he says.[6] Again he says, "I sought my heart one night and I could not find it (for it was

[1] 'Aṭṭār, *op. cit.,* i. 157. [2] *Ibid.,* i. 164.
[3] Abū Nu'aym, *op. cit.*, fol. 218*b*.
[4] al-Sulamī, *op. cit.*, fol. 15*b*, *Cf.* also Abū Nu'aym, *op. cit.,* fol. 219*b*.
[5] 'Aṭṭār, *op. cit.,* i. 158. [6] *Ibid.,* i. 161.

lost in love to God), and when dawn came I heard One saying, 'O Abū Yazīd, why seekest thou aught save Me? What concern hast thou with thy heart?'"[1] This love must be without interested motive. "Paradise is of no worth to those who love," he says, "for those who love are veiled by their love," that is, they look at nothing beyond it.[2] So also he says: "The true lovers of God, whether they sleep or wake, they seek and are sought, and they are not occupied with their own seeking and loving, but are enraptured in contemplation of the Beloved. It is a crime in the lover to regard his love and an outrage in love to look at one's own seeking while one is face to face with the Sought."[3]

Love leads the mystic to gnosis, that knowledge which is the direct gift of God. "The gnostic," said Bāyazīd, "is not the one who commits to memory from the Qur'ān and if he forgets what he has learnt, relapses into ignorance. He only is the gnostic who takes his knowledge from his Lord at any time, without committing it to memory or studying, and this knowledge lasts for a lifetime. He does not forget his knowledge, but remembers it for all time, needing no book; he is the true spiritual gnostic."[4] It was only to those fitted to receive it and make use of it that God granted this most precious gift. Bisṭāmī tells us that God looks upon the hearts of His saints, and those who are not fitted to receive this great gift, He occupies with worship. In one of his own prayers Abū Yazīd asked it for himself, saying, "O Lord, give me understanding concerning Thyself, for I cannot understand Thee except by means of Thee," and again he says: "I have known God by means of God, and what is other than God by the Light of God."[5]

To the gnostic God revealed Himself unveiled, and Bisṭāmī has left us a wonderful description of what that meant to him, in his "Miʿrāj" (Ascent to Heaven). He writes: "While I was asleep, it seemed to me that I ascended to the Heavens in quest of God, seeking union with God Most

[1] ʿAṭṭār, *op. cit.*, i. 161.
[2] Abū Nuʿaym, *op. cit.*, fol. 219*a*.
[3] R. A. Nicholson, *The Mystics of Islām*, p. 115.
[4] Abū Ṭālib, *Qūt al-Qulūb*, i. 121.
[5] al-Sulamī, *op. cit.*, fol. 15*a*.

Glorious, so that I might abide with Him for ever, and I was tested by a trial—God displayed before me gifts of all kinds, and offered me dominion over the whole heaven, and yet I turned aside my eyes from this, because I knew that He was testing me thereby, and I did not turn towards it out of reverence for the holiness of my Lord, and I said in regard to it all: 'O my Beloved, my desire is other than that which is offered to me.' Then I ascended to the Second Heaven and saw winged angels who fly a hundred thousand times each day to the earth to look upon the saints of God, and their faces shone like the sun. When I had reached the Seventh Heaven one called unto me, 'O Abū Yazīd, stop, stop, for you have arrived at the goal,' but I paid no attention to his speech and I pursued my Quest. And when God Most High realised the sincerity of my desire to seek Him He turned me into a bird, and I went on flying, past kingdom after kingdom, and screen after screen, and plain after plain, and seas after seas, and veils after veils, until, behold, the angel of the Footstool of God met me with a Pillar of Light and said to me, 'Take it,' and I took it, and lo, the heavens and all that were therein sought refuge in the shadow of my gnosis, and sought light in the light of my longing, yet all the angels seemed but as a gnat compared with my all-absorbing concern with the search for God. So I continued to fly, until I reached the Footstool of God, and lo, I was met by angels, whose eyes were as the number of the stars of heaven, and from each eye shone forth light, and those lights became lamps, and I heard sounding forth from each lamp, 'Glory to God,' and 'There is no God but God.' Then I went on flying until I arrived at a sea of light, with waves beating against one another, and beside it the light of the sun would seem dark, and upon the sea were ships of light, compared with which the light of those waters appeared to be darkness. I continued to cross seas upon seas, until I reached the greatest of seas, upon which stands the Throne of the All-Merciful, and I went on swimming therein, until I beheld, looking from the Empyrean to the earth beneath, the Cherubim and those who bore up the Throne and all whom God has created both in heaven and in earth, as less than a mustard-seed (floating) between the Heavens and the earth, in comparison with the flight of my spirit in its quest for God. And when God Most Glorious perceived the sincerity of my desire to seek Him, He called to me and said: 'O My chosen one, approach unto Me, and ascend to the heights of My glory, and the plains of My splendour and sit upon the carpet of My holiness, so that thou mayst see the working of My grace in My appointed time. Thou art My chosen and My beloved and My elect among the creatures.' And I began to melt away at that, as lead melts (in the heat of the fire). Then He gave me to drink from the Fountain of grace in the cup of Fellowship, and transformed me into a state beyond description, and brought me near unto Him, and so near did He bring me that I became nearer unto Him than the spirit to the body. And I continued thus until I became even as the souls of men had been, in that state before existence was, and God abode in solitude apart, without created existence or space or direction or mode of being, may His Glory be exalted and His Names sanctified!"[1]

So Abū Yazīd attained to his heart's desire, the goal of the mystic's quest, and it was he who developed the doctrine of *fanā'*, the passing away of the personal self, and that of *baqā'*, the abiding henceforth in God. In that state the seeker became one with the Sought, and Bisāmī speaks of deification in the plainest terms. "I have shed my Ego (my Self), as a serpent sheds its skin," he says; "then I regarded my essence, and I was, myself, He."[2] He says elsewhere: "I went from God to God, until they cried from me in me, saying, 'O thou I!'—*i.e.*, I reached the station of annihilation in God."[3] This was what Abū Yazīd had sought after all his life; he tells how when God had set him in His Presence, he had said: "Adorn me with Thy Unicity, and clothe me with Thy Personality (*ananīya*), and exalt me to Thy Oneness, so that when Thy creatures behold me, they will say, 'We have seen Thee,' and Thou wilt be there and I shall not be there."[4] The self had passed away and the

[1] *il-Qaṣd ila Allah*, chap. ix. *Islamica*, 1926, vol. ii., fasc. 3, pp. 404-408 (ed. R. A. Nicholson). *Cf.* Rev. iv. 6-8.

[2] Bīrūnī, *Hind*, i. 43.

[3] 'Aṭṭār, *op. cit.*, i. 160.

[4] al-Sarrāj, *op. cit.*, p. 382.

mystic was living the Unitive life in God. "For thirty years," said Bisṭāmī, "God Most High was my mirror, now I am my own mirror—*i.e.*, that which I was I am no more, for 'I' and 'God' represent polytheism, denying His Unity. Since I am no more, God Most High is His own mirror. Behold, now I say that God is the mirror of myself, for with my tongue He speaks, and I have vanished away."[1]

Abū Yazīd carries the doctrine of the Unity of God to its logical conclusion: since there is none but He, He must be the Sole Reality, nothing can exist apart from Him, He is the One in All as He is the All in All, and so, with this Persian mystic, the Ṣūfī doctrine becomes pure Pantheism. Though his life, as we know it, was outwardly uneventful, and he has left us only fragments of his writings, yet he has had an influence that can hardly be measured upon the mysticism of Islām. To him, the very recognition of a separate personal existence was a denial of the Unity of all existence. The human must therefore, ultimately, be merged in the Divine, for in essence they are the same, and the soul must return to the One, for it is, in truth, one with the One.

[1] 'Aṭṭār, *op. cit.*, i. 160.

CHAPTER XI

CONCLUSION

In reviewing the history of the rise and development of early Islamic Mysticism, while giving full consideration to the possibility of a direct Hellenic influence,[1] of which more will be said later, and of the introduction of Buddhistic ideas,[2] it would appear to have been influenced in the main by the teaching of Christian Mysticism, an influence which was exerted indirectly through orthodox Islām itself, and directly through the teaching of the Christian mystics, transmitted orally by their disciples and followers, or by means of their writings.

We have seen that in the Near and Middle East, with which alone we are concerned, Islām had its rise in an essentially Christian environment, and that the Muslims of the earliest period, in which Ṣūfism made its appearance, were in the closest contact on the social and intellectual side with their Christian neighbours, and that these relations, at the beginning of the Islamic era, were frequently of a friendly character. Further, we have noted that the Muslims, themselves more backward and less cultured than their Christian subjects, were obliged to depend upon their help and assistance in all matters for which intellectual training and a literary education were required, and not least in the matter of securing teachers to educate their own children. These teachers, we have seen, were not only Christian, but in several instances, to our knowledge, were Christian priests and monks, and it seems reasonable to suppose that their pupils would have access to the libraries possessed by these Christian teachers, which, at this time, must have included many ascetical and mystical works. We have observed, too,

[1] *Cf.* R. A. Nicholson, *Divān-i Shams-i Tabrīz*, Introd., pp. xxx. *ff.*, and *Literary History of the Arabs*, pp. 388, 389.

[2] *Cf.* M. Horten, *Indische Strömungen in der islamischen Mystik*, and I. Goldziher, *J.R.A.S.*, 1904, *The Influence of Buddhism on Islām*, pp. 125*ff.*

how even in the religious sphere the separation was not as complete as might have been supposed, that discussions on theological questions, which must have given the more educated Muslims an insight into the real nature of Christian doctrine, so often tinged with Mysticism, were frequent, and that Muslims were well acquainted with the habits of life of the Christian solitaries and monks, and with their religious services and ritual. Even more important than any of these contacts, perhaps, was the influence of Christian women married to Muslims, whose Christian upbringing and beliefs could hardly fail to have its effect upon their children at the most impressionable age, and must have rendered those children amenable in later years to the influence of a teaching and a manner of life which was not really alien to them, but a part of their natural inheritance.

We have seen how asceticism and the solitary life have usually been closely associated with the development of Mysticism, because they provided a favourable sphere for the growth of mystical ideas and the practice of the mystic Way. It was in respect of these ascetical practices, first and foremost, that we find Ṣūfism influenced by Christian practice, and marking out its own Path according to the pattern provided by the Christian monks and nuns, and by the Christian mystic writers. The renunciation of the world practised by the hermits of Scete, and the ascetics of Syria and 'Irāq, both men and women, found its counterpart, first in the attitude towards this fleeting world taught in the Qur'ān and the traditions, and then in the practice of the ascetics of the first century of Islām, and of the earliest Ṣūfīs. Contempt of the world, abhorrence of its snares and attractions, desire to escape from it and its fetters, were as characteristic of the Ṣūfī ascetics as of the Christian hermits, and to the former, also, the life of solitude, whether in a desert cell, such as that in which Rābi'a established herself, or in a convent secluded from the world, such as that which 'Abd al-Wāḥid b. Zayd founded within the second century of the Islamic era, seemed necessary, at least as a preparation, for the treading of the mystic Path.

Both Christians and Ṣūfīs practised self-mortification of various kinds, because to both the " carnal self," the lower soul, was the main source of evil and temptation, and must therefore be subdued if the higher soul, the spirit, was to be set free to pursue its upward flight to God. The Ṣūfīs, in one or two instances given, carried the Gospel precept to cut off an offending member to its literal fulfilment. By both Ṣūfī and Christian ascetics, this self-mortification was endured, in the first place, in order that, by the conquest of the body in this world, the soul might be saved from the pains of Hell and judgment in the next, but the ultimate aim of both, as Cassian said, was that the soul might " ever cleave to God and to heavenly things." Fasting, adopted by the Prophet as a means of self-discipline, and carried to an extreme by many of the Ṣūfīs, was undoubtedly admitted into Islamic religious practice in imitation of the fasting enjoined by the Christian Church, and practised so assiduously by the Christian ascetics. " Cultivate fasting to give you strength towards God," Evagrius had admonished the Christians of the fourth century A.D.; " it will expiate your faults and your sins: it will adorn the soul, it will sanctify the mind, it will expel demons, it will lead us to God."[1] The Ṣūfīs regarded it as no less effective as a means of purification and assistance to the onward progress of the soul. We have already emphasised the fact that in the stress they laid upon weeping as a mark of contrition, and in their observance of night-vigils, the Ṣūfīs were following the example of the Christian ascetics, and especially those of the Syrian Church.

The self-mortification involved in chastity and the adoption of the celibate life, which was so often regarded as the crown of the Christian " religious," while it found little acceptance in orthodox Islām, was considered by the early Ṣūfīs to be a most desirable means of attaining progress in the spiritual life. One writer goes so far as to say that Ṣūfism was founded on celibacy, and that sensual desire can, and should, be conquered by the force of a rival love, that of the love of God, which will dominate the whole body and its senses. Rābi'a lived the celibate life, and others among the Ṣūfīs adopted it as a means towards their end. But to both Christian and Ṣūfī ascetics, the true self-dis-

[1] *Rerum monachalium rationes*, x.

cipline and the real abstinence was not of the body and bodily things, but of the soul. It was not the cleansing of the body from its defilements and its desires—though this was a necessary preliminary—which was all-important, but the cleansing of the soul from its impurities and from all the desires which might lead it to seek its own will, rather than the will of God, and which might, in any respect, distract it from its pre-occupation with God Himself. Both the Christian fathers and the great Ṣūfī teachers lay stress on this.

In their teaching on prayer, the Ṣūfīs follow closely in the steps of the Christian ascetics and mystics who had preceded them. Not only in the Islamic adoption of the five stated times of prayer, which compare with the Christian Office and the regular prayer ritual, amounting to seven periods of prayer in the day,[1] of the Christian monks, but in the Ṣūfī conception of prayer, not as a matter of petition or intercession only, but of personal intercourse and communion with God, we find an ideal for which the only possible source would seem to be Christian teaching. Ṣūfism goes farther still, and teaches that this intercourse in prayer with God should be a silent waiting upon His will, a wordless adoration in His Presence. " Thou art enough for me," said the woman-mystic Rābiʿa of Baṣra, and so also St. Clement of Alexandria and St. Basil, John Cassian, and others of the Christian mystics, had taught that the strength of prayer lay in the purpose of the soul, and the closeness of its communion with God, not in the words uttered by the lips. Such prayer became merged in Recollection and Meditation, including both the concentration of the mind on that which would tend to lead it to higher things, and its absorption in the thought and in the adoration of God Himself. Remembrance of death and meditation on what it meant was constantly advocated by the Christian fathers. Evagrius urges his monks when sitting in their cells to collect the mind and remember the day of death and the dissolution of the body, and to meditate on what death and the release of the soul from the fetters of the body will mean;[2] and Pachomius and Ephraim the Syrian laid great emphasis on this

[1] *Cf.* above, p. 32.
[2] *Rerum mon. rationes*, ix.; *ad Anatolium*, xxxii.

as a subject for meditation. So also the Ṣūfīs regarded the remembrance of death, in the first place, as a station for the novice, because it turned his heart away from the transient to the abiding, but also as a station for the adept, who realised that Death was but a bridge between the lover and the Beloved, and who longed for the time when he should step across it. But Recollection and Meditation of the highest type was concerned only with the remembrance and worship of God, and this, with which the Christian ascetics and devotees occupied themselves for a great part of their time—in fact, for most of their solitary hours—became the *dhikr* of Islām and the Ṣūfīs, and the primary duty of all who sought to follow the mystic Path; and, to the Ṣūfīs, the term connoted not only the remembrance of God and the mention of His Name, but the constant sense of His Presence, and ceaseless, adoring worship directed to Him to the exclusion of all else.

When we come to examine the mystical doctrines taught by the early Ṣūfī mystics whose teaching we considered in the last two chapters, we find again a close resemblance to the teaching of the early Christian mystics, and this similarity, in some respects especially, suggests a Christian origin. The Ṣūfī teaching on the Nature of God was based, for the most part, on the Qur'ānic doctrine of God, but this, as we have seen, where it was not purely Jewish, was derived from what Muḥammad believed to be the Christian conception. The idea of God, not only as the Creator, but as the Sole Cause of all existence, and the One Agent, an idea which developed into the conception of God as the One Reality and the only Existence, is common to the Ṣūfīs and to St. Paul, as well as to succeeding Christian mystics, such as Ephraim the Syrian, St. Augustine, and St. Clement of Alexandria.[1] That the idea of God as the One Reality should lead to Pantheism was inevitable; the earliest of the Ṣūfīs tried to avoid this conclusion, but, as we have seen, with Bisṭāmī, the Ṣūfī doctrine of God became pure Pantheism, and the later Ṣūfīs were convinced Pantheists. This development is found also among the Christian mystics who preceded the Ṣūfīs. Ephraim the Syrian says that God has

[1] *Cf.* above, pp. 49, 74, 86.

clothed Himself in all forms that we may behold Him, and St. Augustine also teaches that God is wholly present everywhere, and that whatever has Reality must partake of the Divine.

To the Ṣūfī mystics, God was the Truth (*al-Ḥaqq*), and this designation, which became so commonly used among them that they were called *ahal al-Ḥaqq* (the people of the Truth—*i.e.*, of God), they might well have taken directly from the Christian Gospel, but it was also much used by the Christian mystical writers. St. Augustine, St. Gregory of Nyssa, and Ephraim all use the title in their mystical writings, and their choice of it was no doubt guided by their desire to emphasise their belief that God alone was truly Real. We have noted that the Ṣūfīs conceived of God as Light and the Source of all light for the soul, and the same conception is found in almost every one of the early Christian mystics, beginning with St. John the Evangelist. To St. Augustine, to St. Gregory of Nyssa, to Macarius of Egypt, He is the Light, made visible in darkness, enlightening the soul; and to Dionysius He is Essential Radiance and the Morning Star, illuminating unto contemplation; while Ephraim of Syria and Isaac of Nineveh speak of Him as the Sun, which can only be seen by the eye which is sun-like; and St. Clement of Alexandria calls Him the Sun of the soul, by which the eye of the soul is illuminated. To the true mystic, God is always Beauty, as He is always Love, and to the Ṣūfīs, those true lovers of God, He was the All-Beautiful as He was pre-eminently the Beloved, and for this conception, for which there was little enough basis in orthodox Islām, they could find ample precedent in the teachings of Christian Mysticism. St. Clement had taught that the Life of God was Love, since the Beautiful is of necessity beloved by those who recognise it; and He alone is the True Beauty;[1] and to St. Augustine also He had been the Supreme Beauty, recognised and loved too late. In their mystical doctrines concerning the Nature of God, therefore, the Ṣūfīs were following closely in the steps of the Christian mystics who had preceded them, and there is little or nothing in the Ṣūfī

[1] *Cf.* al-Ghazālī, pp. 205, 206 above.

conceptions in regard to the Godhead which was not already to be found in Christian mystical writings.

In their ideas regarding the nature of the soul and its relation to the Divine, we find that the early Ṣūfīs take a view which is to be found also among the Christian mystics. The most orthodox of the Ṣūfīs held that the soul, being created, could not be regarded as identical with the Creator, and this is also the view of St. Gregory of Nyssa;[1] but both Ṣūfī and Christian mystics agree that the soul is in its nature akin to the Divine, that there is a Divine spark, the *sirr* of the Ṣūfīs, which is the ground of the soul, that the soul was pre-existent before it was joined to a body in this world, and is, because of the Divinity within it, immortal. St. Augustine had assumed the pre-existence of the soul, and Isaac of Nineveh asserted that God was to be found within the soul. The Ṣūfī doctrine that the soul was created in order that God the Absolute and Unmanifested might be manifested forth, a doctrine based on the tradition, "I was a concealed Treasure and I desired that I might be known, so I created the creatures that they might know Me," had been held also by St. Gregory of Nyssa, who asserted that it was needful that the Divine Light should not remain unseen, nor the Divine Glory without witness. Even in orthodox Islām we find the idea that the chief aim of the soul's creation was that it might be a witness to God, and the most perfect witness is borne by the saint in whom the Divine is most clearly revealed. The comparison of the soul to a mirror, which may become rusty (since the Oriental mirror was most often made of polished silver), and clouded by sin and contact with this material world, is frequently found among the Ṣūfīs, as already mentioned, and it had been equally common among the Christian mystics before them. Ephraim the Syrian, Palladius, and Isaac of Nineveh all use this image, and they speak, as do the Ṣūfīs, of the need for polishing and cleansing the mirror that it may once more reflect, without flaw, the Divine Image.

It is the Divine within the soul which urges it upward and towards the Source whence it came; the believer's soul, said the Ṣūfīs, because it was the shrine of the Divine mysteries,

[1] *Cf.* above, p. 60.

led him to Paradise, and so also the Christian mystics, especially the "Holy Hierotheos," had taught that the soul, realising its original unity with the Divine, sought the Way to return to that former state of blessedness. The Ṣūfīs speak constantly of this world as a "prison," and its ties and attractions as the "fetters" of the soul, holding it down and keeping it back from escape to that sphere to which it properly belongs; and so also St. Clement of Alexandria and Isaac of Nineveh speak of the prison of this world and urge the soul to shake off its bonds and escape to the joy that awaits it with God.

The Christian mystics and the Ṣūfīs are at one in their teaching as to the means of escape and the Way of ascent. Purification of body and soul was the essential, a purgation which would burn up all the dross within the soul, and for the idea of a Way, marked by different stages enabling the soul to acquire virtues which would assist it still further on the upward way, the Ṣūfīs may well have been indebted to St. John Climacus (A.D. 523-606), who in his *Scala Paradisi* had set forth the idea of a ladder mounting from earth to heaven, an ascent leading by gradual stages to the perfection of the blessed life in God. The first stages, for him, had been conversion and repentance and renunciation of this world; godly poverty and the remembrance of death had also found a place in his journey, and the final stage attained by the soul was tranquillity and love, the satisfaction (*riḍā'*) which to the Ṣūfīs was the last stage before the attainment of Illumination and Union.[1] Among the Christian mystics who lived after St. John Climacus, notably in the *Book of the Holy Hierotheos*, and the teaching of Isaac of Nineveh, we find the same idea of a journey to be undertaken, and an ascent to be made by gradual and laborious stages.

That Love, to the mystic, is the wine of life, which brings the intoxication of ecstasy, and all blessedness to him who drinks thereof, as it is also the motive-power and the chief inspiration of all who tread the mystic Path, and that which leads to Gnosis and the final goal, is a fact accepted by Christian and Ṣūfī mystics alike, and, as we have seen, all

[1] John Climacus, *Scala Paradisi*; Migne, *P.G.*, vol. lxxxviii.

these mystical teachers give it a foremost place in their teaching. It seems possible that the symbolic use by the Ṣūfīs of the terms associated with wine, "the wine of life," and the cup, "the cup of love," poured out by the Divine Beloved for His lovers, may have been derived from a knowledge of the central Sacrament of the Christian Church, in which the Cup represented the gift of Eternal Love, bestowing Everlasting Life upon His lovers, and admitting them thereby to communion with Himself, and to a participation in Divinity, corresponding to the mystic union, and making the soul in very truth one with God.

The hindrances which hampered the soul on its upward way, and which kept it in ignorance of God and blind to the Truth, were frequently described by the Ṣūfīs as veils between the soul and God, a mystical idea found also in orthodox Islām, in the Traditions, and it was these veils which prevented the mirror from reflecting the Divine, and hindered the eye of the soul from seeing clearly the heavenly Vision, and this conception, too, was to be found in their predecessors among the Christian mystics. Palladius speaks of the impurity of this world as a dark veil preventing the soul from discerning spiritual things, and Isaac of Nineveh speaks also of the veil, which, however, is sometimes drawn aside.

The goal of the traveller, the end of the Way, is attained through illumination and the mystic gnosis (*ma'rifa*), which leads to the unveiling, of the Vision of God, to the soul (*kashf*) and, in the moment of the Vision, the passing away of the personal self (*fanā'*) and the entrance into Eternal Life in God (*baqā'*). St. Clement had already conceived of the Christian mystic who attained to spiritual perfection as the gnostic, and the Ṣūfīs used the same term (*'ārif*) for the spiritual adept. St. Clement it was also who used the name "friend of God" for the saint, in this, of course, following the Gospel, and this became the regular name for the saints (*awliyā*) among the Ṣūfīs.

To the saint who had attained to the mystic gnosis was granted the Vision of God face to face, and the state of the soul to which that beatific sight was revealed is described by the Ṣūfīs in terms strangely reminiscent of those used by

St. Augustine and others of the Christian mystics. The conception of the final state of the mystic who has passed away from self and entered into union with God, and henceforth lives in Him, is expressed in much the same terms by Ṣūfī and Christian mystics alike. The *Book of the Holy Hierotheos* is concerned mainly with the attainment of this mystic union, which the author calls "commingling," and to him, as to the Ṣūfī Bisṭāmī, it is the identification of God with the soul of the mystic. The soul has died unto itself and is alive unto God. "Mortality has perished," the Ṣūfī said, "and immortality is made perfect." This doctrine of deification had been taught long before by St. Clement of Alexandria, and Cassian had said of the souls living the unitive life, "whatever we breathe or think or speak is God," a formula which the Ṣūfīs reproduced practically word for word.[1] Dionysius of Syria had said plainly that God gave Himself for the deification of those who attained unto Him, and so also Bisṭāmī and others of the Ṣūfīs declared that the "I" had vanished and God dwelt in the soul in its place. There was no longer any place for "I" and "Thou," for the "Thou" and "I" had become one in perfect unity, and the human was now one with the Divine.

In thus emphasising the close analogy between the doctrines and the symbolism of the Ṣūfīs, and those of the Christian mystical teachers who preceded them, an analogy which might be carried much further, it is not to be forgotten that in Hellenistic thought, and especially among the Neoplatonists, there is to be found a common source for many, if not most, of the mystical conceptions to be found both in early Christianity and in Ṣūfism, and it is conceivable that the Ṣūfīs might have derived their mystical doctrines directly from Hellenistic sources. Some few of the more educated Ṣūfīs might have been able to read Greek and so might have read the Greek authors in the original, and we know that Arabic translations from the Greek were available as early as the ninth century A.D., and that this work of translation was carried on with enthusiasm by the philosophic school of al-Kindī (*ob.* A.D. 860) of Baghdād, and his successors. The earliest and probably the most influen-

[1] *Cf.* above, pp. 236, 243.

tial of these translations appears to have been the so-called *Theology of Aristotle*, which is in reality a translation of Porphyry's lost commentary on the *Enneads* of Plotinus, and is therefore a Neoplatonic treatise, and of this an Arabic translation appeared as early as A.D. 840. This might have supplied the Ṣūfīs with their monistic conception of God and the Universe, with their idea of the pre-existence of the soul in a state of perfect purity, with some of their psychology, and with their conception of God as the Light of lights (*Nūr al-anwār*). It is possible, too, as already indicated, that Ṣūfism might have been directly effected, in Persia and 'Irāq at any rate, by Buddhistic ideas.

Yet, when this has been admitted—and there have been great scholars to uphold the view that one or other of these has been the main external source of the Ṣūfī doctrine, it would seem more probable that the Ṣūfīs derived their mystical doctrines, or at least the forms in which they clothed them, in the main from Christianity. Few would deny that the asceticism of the earliest Ṣūfīs, with which the development of a definitely mystical doctrine was so closely bound up, was so derived, or that the germs of Mysticism which we find in the Qur'ān and the early Traditions, which the Ṣūfīs claimed as the basis of their own mystical teaching, might all have been derived from the Mysticism of the Christianity with which both Muḥammad and his successors were in contact. Neither he nor those who followed him immediately could have had any opportunity of studying Hellenism, nor could he have found any trace of such mysticism in Arab paganism. But it was to be found in the Christian Scriptures and in the teaching and practice of Christian monks and hermits all around him. After the time of Muḥammad, when Islām became the ruling power in the Near and Middle East, then predominantly Christian, we have seen how close was the contact between Muslims and Christians, and how Islām became permeated, not only by Christian culture, but by Christian ideals and beliefs, through conversion—often only partial—and marriage, by which a purely Muslim Arab stock became mingled with a Christian stock, which could not, in a single generation, divest itself completely of a heritage guarded through the centuries as its most cherished possession. So, while the Christian Near and Middle East was rapidly Islamised, Islām, in its turn, became, to some extent, Christianised, and this influence showed itself most plainly in the rise and development of Islamic Mysticism.

That early Christian Mysticism itself, from the time of St. John and St. Paul onwards, owed a great deal to Hellenistic and Neoplatonic conceptions and ideals, is of course obvious, and has been noted in previous chapters, and it would appear to be most probable that Islamic Mysticism, in its earliest development, derived its most obviously Neoplatonic elements through Christian Hellenism, rather than directly from any Greek source. The earliest of the Ṣūfīs can have had little contact with Hellenistic literature of any kind, while on the other hand we have evidence of their contact with Christian teachers and especially the solitaries, and it was among the latter, as we have seen, that Christian Mysticism had its rise. For these earliest Ṣūfīs, too, there were no Arabic versions of Greek philosophy available, yet among them were true mystics, teaching a pure mysticism, such as Rābi'a of Baṣra. In the case of those Ṣūfīs also, who had the education and culture to enable them to make a direct use of mystical literature, a knowledge of Greek or Syriac would be as likely to lead them to a study of Christian Mysticism as of pagan philosophy. The libraries of their Christian teachers, the monks of Damascus and Nisibis and Edessa, must have contained much of the Christian mystical literature of the Greek or Syriac-speaking Churches, and this would be at the disposal of their pupils, if they so wished.[1] In discussions, too, with their Christian friends and neighbours, it would be a Christianised form of Neoplatonism with which the Ṣūfīs would come into contact. It is significant that the first translators of Greek and Syriac works into Arabic were Christians, employed on the task by the Caliph Ma'mūn, and the first translator of the *Theology of Aristotle* was a Christian, Ibn 'Abdallah Ibn Na'īma, of Ḥoms. It is obvious that the Christian Church of both the Near and the Middle East was deeply affected, at the

[1] For evidence of the use made by early Ṣūfī writers of Christian ascetical and mystical works, *cf.* L. Massignon, *Essai*, p. 55.

time at which Ṣūfism developed its theosophic and mystical doctrines, by the teachings of St. Augustine, the Alexandrian School, the Egyptian fathers, and the pseudo-Dionysius, in the one direction, and those of the Syriac-speaking Church in the other. Of the Christian mystics, whose teaching has been outlined in the preceding pages, Ephraim the Syrian, Dionysius of Syria, the writer of the *Book of the Holy Hierotheos*, and Isaac of Nineveh seem to have had the most direct influence upon the development of Ṣūfism; but since the later Christian mystics made use of the teaching of those who had preceded them, the Ṣūfīs may also have derived a good deal indirectly from the earliest of the Christian mystics.

Yet, as our final reflection, when all this has been taken into consideration, we have to remember that, as was noted at the beginning of this study, Mysticism in its essence represents a spiritual tendency which is practically universal, and is often the most powerful and the most vital element in any religion which has life within itself. Therefore, while one type of mysticism may bear so close a resemblance to another, in its doctrines and terminology, that we say the two must be closely related and the later in point of time must surely be derived from the earlier, yet mysticism in itself can be a purely spontaneous growth, arising in response to the craving in the human soul for a direct and personal experience of the Divine, and for a doctrine of the relation between the soul and God which will satisfy that craving. Mysticism, therefore, which represents an innate tendency of the soul, may be expected to show itself as an element in all religions which have life and force within them, and in all environments, even the most unexpected; and so, while Islamic Mysticism may have derived certain of its doctrines and symbols from Christian Mysticism, or from Hellenic Mysticism, through Christian sources, yet its real origin and source must be found in the age-long desire of the human soul for God and its longing to attain to communion with Him—a desire not to be satisfied by any merely formal religion which maintains a rigid distinction between worshipper and the Worshipped, and imposes the need for intermediaries between man and God, but only by the intimate relation arising from true affinity, by a sense of the oneness between the human and the Divine involved in the Unity of all existence, by a belief in the possibility of realising that oneness even in this life—in short, by the faith of the mystic, who holds that the human soul is in very truth one in essence with the Divine, and that when the ascent has been made, by slow and, it may be, painful stages, through purification to illumination, and thence to the unitive life, the soul can, here and now, partake of Eternal Life, the life lived in unceasing communion and in unbroken union with the One Reality, God.

BIBLIOGRAPHY OF AUTHORS CONSULTED

A.—GENERAL

J. Amélineau. *Les Moines Egyptiens*. Paris, 1889.

Tor Andrae. *Der Ursprung des Islams und das Christentum*. Uppsala, 1926.

Aphraates the Monk. *Life and Works*. (Tr. A. E. Johnston.) *Nicene and Post-Nicene Fathers*. Oxford, 1898.

T. W. Arnold. *The Preaching of Islām*. (2nd Edit.) London, 1913.

St. Augustine. Works. Migne: *Patrologia Latina*. xxxii. Paris, 1841-1842.

St. Augustine. *Confessions*. (Ed. T. Gibb and W. Montgomery.) Cambridge, 1908.

St. Basil the Great. Writings. Migne: *Patrologia Græca*. xxix, xxx., xxxi., xxxii.

St. Basil the Great. *A Study in Monasticism*. W. K. Lowther Clarke. Cambridge, 1913.

St. Basil the Great. *The Ascetic Writings*. W. K. Lowther Clarke. London, 1925.

C. H. Becker. *Christianity and Islām*. (Tr. H. J. Chaytor.) London, 1909.

R. Bell. *The Origin of Islām in its Christian Environment*. London, 1926.

E. Blochet. *La Conquête des états Nestoriens de l'Asia Centrale par les Shiites*. Paris, 1926.

T. J. de Boer. *History of Philosophy in Islām*. (Tr. E. R. Jones.) London, 1903.

F. C. Burkitt. *The History of Early Eastern Christianity*. London, 1904.

F. C. Burkitt. *The Religion of the Manichees*. Cambridge, 1925.

A. J. Butler. *The Arab Conquest of Egypt*. Oxford, 1902.

C. Butler. *Western Mysticism*. London, 1922.

E. Caird. *The Evolution of Theology in the Greek Philosophers*. Glasgow, 1904.

John Cassian. Writings. (Tr. E. C. S. Gibson.) *Nicene and Post-Nicene Fathers*. Oxford, 1894.

A. P. Caussin de Percival. *Essai sur l'Histoire des Arabes avant l'Islamisme*. Paris, 1847.

St. Clement of Alexandria. Writings. Migne : *Patrologia Græca.* viii., ix.

St. Clement of Alexandria. *Seventh Book of the Stromateis.* (Ed. Hort and Mayor.) 1902.

John Climacus. Writings. Migne : *Patrologia Græca.* lxxxviii.

R. Curzon. *Visits to Monasteries in the Levant.* London, 1916.

H. Delacroix. *Études d'histoire et de psychologie du Mysticisme.* Paris, 1908.

Dionysius the Areopagite. *Ecclesiastical Hierarchy.* (Tr. J. Parker.) 1897.

Dionysius the Areopagite. *The Divine Names and Mystical Theology.* (Tr. C. E. Rolt.) London, 1920.

Ephraim the Syrian. Life and Writings. (Tr. H. Burgess and J. B. Morris.) *Nicene and Post-Nicene Fathers.* Oxford, 1898.

Ephraim the Syrian. *The Repentance of Nineveh, etc.* (Tr. H. Burgess.) London, 1853.

Ephraim the Syrian. *Select Works.* (Tr. J. B. Morris.) Oxford, 1847.

Eusebius. *Ecclesiastical History.* (Tr. Kirsopp Lake.) London, 1926.

Evagrius Ponticus. Writings. Migne : *Patrologia Græca.* xl., lxxxvi.

T. R. Glover. *Life and Letters in the Fourth Century.* Cambridge, 1901.

I. Goldziher. *Muhammedische Studien.* Halle, 1889.

I. Goldziher. *The Influence of Buddhism in Islām.* J.R.A.S., 1904.

St. Gregory of Nyssa. Life and Writings. Migne : *Patrologia Græca.* xlv., xlvi.

A. Guillaume. *The Traditions of Islām.* Oxford, 1924.

J. O. Hannay. *The Spirit and Origin of Christian Monasticism.* London, 1913.

A. Harnack. *The Mission and Expansion of Christianity.* (Tr. J. Moffatt.) 1908.

A. Harnack. *Monasticism.* (Tr. E. E. Kellett and F. H. Marseille.) London, 1901.

Walter Hilton. *The Scale of Perfection.* (Ed. E. Underhill.) London, 1923.

M. Horten. *Indische Strömungen in der Islamischen Mystik.* Heidelberg, 1927.

Ibn Khallikān. *Biographical Dictionary.* (Tr. de Slane.) Paris, 1842.

W. R. Inge. *Christian Mysticism.* London, 1899.

Isaac of Nineveh. *Mystical Treatises.* (Tr. A. Wensinck.) Amsterdam, 1923.

St. John of the Cross. *A Spiritual Canticle of the Soul.* (Tr. D. Lewis.) London, 1909.

St. John of Damascus. Writings. Migne : *Patrologia Græca.* xciv.

J. DE JOINVILLE. *Histoire de St. Louis.* (Ed. de Wailly.) Paris, 1868.

L. LABOURT. *Le Christianisme dans l'Empire Perse.* Paris, 1904.

H. LAMMENS. *L'Islam, Croyances et Institutions.* Beyrout, 1926.

G. W. LEIBNIZ. *Die Philosophischen Schriften.* (Ed. C. J. Gerhardt.) Berlin, 1885.

RAMÓN LULL. *Book of the Lover and the Beloved.* (Tr. E. Allison Peers.) London, 1923.

RAMÓN LULL. *The Tree of Love.* (Tr. E. Allison Peers.) London, 1926.

C. J. LYALL. *Translations of Ancient Arabic Poetry.* London, 1885.

ST. MACARIUS OF EGYPT. Homilies. Migne : *Patrologia Græca.* xxxiv.

ST. MACARIUS OF EGYPT. Homilies. English Translation. A. J. Mason. London, 1921.

D. B. MACDONALD. *The Religious Attitude and Life in Islām.* Chicago, 1909.

ST. MACRINA. *Life.* W. K. L. Clarke. London, 1916.

L. MASSIGNON. *Essai sur les Origines du Lexique Technique de la Mystique Musulmane.* Paris, 1922.

L. MASSIGNON. *La Passion d'al-Hallāj.* Paris, 1922.

L. MASSIGNON. *Recueil de Textes Inédits.* Paris, 1930.

A. MINGANA. *The Early Spread of Christianity in Central Asia and the Far East.* Manchester, 1925.

C. DE MONTALEMBERT. *The Monks of the West.* London, 1896.

R. A. NICHOLSON. *Selected Poems from the Diwān-i Shams-i Tabrīz.* Cambridge, 1898.

R. A. NICHOLSON. *A Literary History of the Arabs.* (2nd Edit.) Cambridge, 1930.

R. A. NICHOLSON. *The Mystics of Islām.* London, 1914.

T. NÖLDEKE. *Orientalische Skizzen.* Berlin, 1892.

W. G. PALGRAVE. *A Year's Journey through Central and Eastern Arabia.* London, 1908.

PALLADIUS. *Historia Lausiaca.* Greek Text. (Ed. C. Butler.) Cambridge, 1898, 1904.

PALLADIUS. *Historia Lausiaca.* English Translation. W. K. L. Clarke. London, 1918.

Paradise of the Fathers. (Tr. E. A. Budge.) London, 1907.

W. M. FLINDERS PETRIE. *Egypt and Israel.* London, 1923.

J. A. PICTON. *The Mystery of Matter.* London, 1873.

PLOTINUS. *Enneads.* (Tr. S. Mackenna.) London, 1917-1930.

A. POULAIN. *Des Grâces d'Oraison.* Paris, 1909.

L. PULLEN. *The Church of the Fathers.* London, 1906.

E. RÉCÉJAC. *Bases of the Mystic Knowledge.* (Tr. S. C. Upton.) London, 1899.

J. C. Robertson. *History of the Christian Church.* London, 1904.

A. Schmölders. *Essai sur les écoles philosophiques chez les Arabes.* Paris, 1842.

A. B. Sharpe. *Mysticism : Its True Nature and Value.* London, 1910.

Margaret Smith. *Rābi'a the Mystic and her Fellow-Saints in Islām.* Cambridge, 1928.

Socrates. *Historia Ecclesiastica.* Migne : *Patrologia Græca.* lxvii.

J. Tauler. *Twenty-Five Sermons.* (Tr. S. Winkworth.) London, 1906.

Theodoret. *Ecclesiastical History.* (Tr. Bohn's Library.) London, 1854.

Theologia Germanica. (Tr. S. Winkworth.) London, 1857.

St. Theresa. *Life.* (Tr. D. Lewis.) London, 1870.

Thomas of Margā. *Book of the Governors.* (Tr. E. A. Budge.) London, 1893.

R. W. Trine. *In Tune with the Infinite.* New York, 1906.

A. S. Tritton. *The Caliphs and their Non-Muslim Subjects.* London, 1930.

E. Underhill. *Mysticism.* London, 1912.

R. A. Vaughan. *Hours with the Mystics.* London, 1860.

A. Wensinck. *Book of the Dove.* Leyden, 1909.

A. Wensinck. *New Data concerning Syriac Mystical Literature.* Amsterdam, 1923.

G. P. Wetter. *Phōs.* Uppsala, 1915.

W. A. Wigram. *An Introduction to the History of the Assyrian Church.* London, 1910.

W. Wright. *Short History of Syriac Literature.* London, 1894.

B.—ARABIC, PERSIAN, AND SYRIAC AUTHORS

Abū Nu'aym. "Ḥilyat al-Awliyā." MS. Leyden.

Abū Ṣāliḥ al-Armān. *Churches and Monasteries of Egypt.* (Arabic Text.) Oxford, A.D. 1895.

Abū Ṭālib al-Makkī. *Qūt al-Qulūb.* Cairo, A.H. 1310.

S. al-Dīn Aflākī. "Manāqib al-'Ārifīn." MS. India Office, No. 1670.

W. Ahlwardt. *The Six Ancient Arabic Poets.* (Arabic Text.) Paris, 1913.

Aristotle (so-called). *Kitāb Uthūlūjiya Arisṭāṭālīs.* (Ed. F. Dieterici.) Leipzig, A.D. 1882.

Asin Palacios. *Logia et Agrapha.* Patrologia Orientalis. xiii., xix. Paris, A.D. 1926.

Assemani. *Bibliotheca Orientalis.* Rome, A.D. 1719-1728.

Farīd al-Dīn 'Aṭṭār. *Tadhkirat al-Awliyā.* (Ed. R. A. N. Nicholson.) London, A.D. 1905.

Farīd al-Dīn 'Aṭṭār. *Tadhkirat al-Awliyā.* Uyghur Version. Paris, A.D. 1889.

A. b. Yaḥyā al-Balādhurī *Kitāb al-Futūḥ al-Buldān.* Leyden, A.D. 1863-1866.

Abū Rayḥān al-Bīrūnī. *Ta'rīkh al-Hind.* (Ed. E. Sachau.) London, A.D. 1887.

al-Bukhārī. *Ṣaḥīḥ.* (Ed. L. Krehl.) Leyden, A.D. 1862.

L. Cheikko. *Shu'arā al-Naṣrāniyya.* Beyrout, A.D. 1890-91.

M. b. M. al-Ghazālī. *Iḥya 'Ulūm al-Dīn.* Cairo, A.H. 1272.

M. b. M. al-Ghazālī. *Munkidh min al-Ḍalāl.* Cairo, A.D. 1891.

The Book of the Holy Hierotheos. Syriac Text. (Ed. and Tr. F. S. Marsh.) London, A.D. 1927.

Taqī al-Dīn al-Ḥisnī. "Siyar al-Ṣāliḥāt." MS. Paris, No. 2042.

A. b. 'U. al Jullābī al-Hujwīrī. *Kashf al-Maḥjūb.* (Ed. V. A. Zhukovski.) Petrograd, A.D. 1926.

Shu'ayb b. 'Abd al-Azīz al-Ḥurayfīsh. *al-Rawḍ al-Fā'iq.* Cairo, A.H. 1279.

Ibn Baṭṭūṭa. *Tuḥfat al-Nuẓẓar.* (Ed. c. Defrémery and B. R. Sanguinetti.) Paris, A.D. 1893.

'Abd al-Raḥmān Ibn al-Jawzī. *Naqd al-'ilm wa'l-'ulamā (Talbīs Iblīs.)* Cairo, A.H. 1340.

Ibn Khaldûn. *Prolegomena.* Arabic Text. (Ed M. Quatremère.). Paris, A.D. 1858.

Ibn Khallikān. *Wafayāt al-A'yān.* Göttingen, A.D. 1835-1850.

Ibn Sa'd. *Kitāb al-Ṭabaqāt al-Kabīr.* Leyden, A.D. 1904.

M. b. Ḥasan Imād al-Dīn. *Ḥayāt al-Qulūb* (on margin of *Qūt al-Qulūb*). Cairo, A.H. 1310.

'Amr b. B. al-Jāḥiẓ. *Bayān wa'l-Tabyīn.* Cairo, A.H. 1332.

'Abd al-Raḥmān al-Jāmī. *Nafaḥāt al-Uns.* (Ed. W. N. Lees.) Calcutta, A.D. 1850.

J. al-Dīn b. 'A. al-Jawzī. "Ta'rikh al-Muntaẓam." MS. Constantinople.

John of Lycopolis. *The Spiritual State of the Soul.* Syriac Text. (Ed. A. Wensinck.) Amsterdam, A.D. 1923.

M. b. I. b. I. al-Kalābādhī. "Kitāb al-Ta'arruf." MS. Collection Prof. Nicholson.

M. b. I. b. I. al-Kalābādhī. "Ma'ānī al-Akhbār." MS. School of Oriental Studies, No. 200.

M. b. 'Abdallah al-Khaṭīb. *Mishkāt al-Maṣābīḥ.* Lucknow, A.H. 1319.

'A. b. H. Mas'ūdī. *Kitāb al-Tanbīh wa'l-Ishrāf.* (Ed. de Goeje.) Leyden, A.D. 1894. Bibl. Geog. Arab.

Ḥārith b. Asad al-Muḥāsibī. "Muḥāsibat al-Nufūs." MS. Brit. Mus., Or. 4026.

Ḥārith b. Asad al-Muḥāsibī. "Ri'āya." MS. Oxford, Hunt. 611.

Ḥārith b. Asad al-Muḥāsibī. "Waṣāyā." MS. Brit. Mus., Or. 7900.

Abū Ra'ūf al-Munāwī. "al-Kawākib al-Durriya." MS. Brit. Mus., Add. 23,369.

M. b. al-Munawwar. *Asrār al-Tawḥīd.* (Ed. V. A. Zhukovski.) Petrograd, A.D. 1899.

Abū al-Qāsim al-Qushayrī. *Risāla.* Cairo, A.D. 1867.

Abū Naṣr al-Sarrāj. *Kitāb al-Luma'.* (Ed. R. A. Nicholson.) London, A.D. 1914.

Maḥmūd Shabistarī. *Gulshan-i Rāz.* (Ed. E. H. Whinfield.) London, A.D. 1880.

al-Suhrawardī. *'Awārif al-Ma'ārif* (on margin of al-Ghazālī's *Iḥyā*). Cairo, A.H. 1272.

'A. al-Raḥmān al-Sulamī. "Ṭabaqāt al-Ṣūfiyya." MS. Brit. Mus., Add. 18,520.

Abū Ja'far M. J. al-Ṭabarī. *Annales.* (Arabic Text.) Leyden, A.D. 1879-1890.

Abū al-Maḥāsin b. Taghribardī. *al-Nujūm al-Zāhira.* Leyden, A.D. 1855-1861.

Yaqūt b. 'Abd Allah. *Kitāb Mu'jam al-Buldān.* Leipzig, A.D. 1866.

Yaqūt b. 'Abd Allah. *Mu'jam al-Udabā.* (Ed. D. S. Margoliouth.) London, A.D. 1907.

Details of the lives and the writings of many of the above will be found in my *Rābi'a the Mystic,* Survey of Sources, pp. xiii-xxv.

INDEX

I.—GENERAL

Arabic names to which the definite article al- is prefixed will be found under their initial letter. Titles of books, etc., are printed in italics.

Yaḥyā, b. Mu'ādh al-Rāzī, 206, 208, 237

II.—TECHNICAL TERMS, ETC.